Diversity Matters

Diversity Matters

The Color, Shape, and Tone of Twenty-First Century Diversity

Edited by
Emily Allen Williams

LEXINGTON BOOKS
Lanham • Boulder • New York • London

Published by Lexington Books
An imprint of The Rowman & Littlefield Publishing Group, Inc.
4501 Forbes Boulevard, Suite 200, Lanham, Maryland 20706
www.rowman.com

6 Tinworth Street, London SE11 5AL, United Kingdom

British Library Cataloguing in Publication Information Available

Library of Congress Cataloging-in-Publication Data

Names: Williams, Emily Allen, editor.
Title: Diversity matters : the color, shape, and tone of
    twenty-first-century diversity / edited by Emily Allen Williams.
Description: Lanham : Lexington Books, [2021] | Includes bibliographical
    references and index.
Identifiers: LCCN 2021017995 (print) | LCCN 2021017996 (ebook) |
    ISBN 9781793628299 (cloth) | ISBN 9781793628312 (paperback) |
    ISBN 9781793628305 (ebook)
Subjects: LCSH: Cultural pluralism—United States. | Multiculturalism—United States. |
    Social justice—United States. | United States—Race relations. | United States—Social
    conditions—21st century.
Classification: LCC HN90.M84 D585 2021 (print) | LCC HN90.M84 (ebook) |
    DDC 306.44/60973—dc23
LC record available at https://lccn.loc.gov/2021017995
LC ebook record available at https://lccn.loc.gov/2021017996

Contents

Beyond Rhetoric to Reality

Inclusion, Diversity, Equity, and Access

Emily Allen Williams

How did we get here?

Where is here?

What is "this" time in America and what are the root causes of the social injustice situations to which we bear witness? How does the experience of bearing witness define and sustain us during a period of varying degrees of acuity in our social justice footprints? While painful in some iterations, bearing witness can serve as a necessary engagement toward empowering voicings on the distribution of wealth, privileges, and opportunities; put another way, bearing witness accelerates lifting up the necessity of social justice in a society. I argue that bearing witness is healing, and Shelley Galasso Bonanno, a psychodynamic psychotherapist, concurs:

> Bearing witness is a term that, used in psychology, refers to sharing our experiences with others, most notably in the communication to others of traumatic experiences. Bearing witness is a valuable way to process an experience, to obtain empathy and support, to lighten our emotional load via sharing it with the witness, and to obtain catharsis. Most people bear witness daily, and not only in reaction to traumatic events. We bear witness to one another through our writing, through art, and by verbally simply sharing with others.[1]

While bearing witness through the essay renderings in this volume, scholar and practitioner colleagues examine both pronounced and shadowed articulations of how acts of social injustice dismantle both the foundational and high-impact diversity engagement strategies necessary for purposeful inclusion, equity, and access practices. Also, these examinations speak specifically to ways and means of sustaining and creating environments for diverse peoples within and without diverse communities to move beyond survival to thriving within domains defined by holistic approaches for pluralistic societies. The overarching questions writ large during this period of emerging and negatively recapitulating acts of social injustice are: (1) What are the varying degrees of acuity in our need to excessively rhetoricize inclusion, diversity, equity, and access (IDEA)? (2) Is rhetoric overpowering our engagement [reality] in authentic inclusion, equity, and access practices for our existent diverse populations? and (3) what impact does the current state of non-immersive virtual reality have on our ability to move beyond extensive and vapid rhetoric toward planning and implementation of high impact diversity engagement strategies?

Simply put, "this" time we are experiencing is no longer clothed in pretense. America is witnessing viscerally vivid scenes of violence manifesting in deaths, fear, property destruction, and dichotomized rhetoric that locates and polarizes people at the margins of tangible despair, illogical physical responses, and negatively infused wonderment as they literally navigate willingly, unwillingly, consciously, and unconsciously afflictions of physical, mental, and emotional scars predicated upon years of (mis)use of diverse peoples. What becomes viscerally visual are the images of a pluralistic majority (*read, diverse*) of the American population standing in affliction lines on the margins of social justice based on the actions of a still dominant but demographically shrinking white populace who stand at the head of distribution lines of affliction inequity.

At our *center*, are we experiencing a rapid reversal of civil rights and social justice in America? How can these actions of inequity be a reality in a country that at the *center* of its national discourse positively foregrounds its burgeoning diversity?

Can the *center* hold?

A poem written (1919) and published (1920) by W. B. Yeats entitled "The Second Coming," (curiously, some one hundred plus years earlier) lends illumination to our time. Written in the aftermath of World War I and the 1918–1919 flu pandemic,[2] even a cursory glimpse in the historical rear-view mirror creates contemporary pause as we navigate domestic warfare and the COVID-19 pandemic in the United States and worldwide:

Turning and turning in the widening gyre
The falcon cannot hear the falconer;
Things fall apart; the centre cannot hold;
Mere anarchy is loosed upon the world,
The blood-dimmed tide is loosed, and everywhere
The ceremony of innocence is drowned;
The best lack all conviction, while the worst
Are full of passionate intensity.

Surely some revelation is at hand;
Surely the Second Coming is at hand.
The Second Coming! Hardly are those words out
When a vast image out of Spiritus Mundi
Troubles my sight: a waste of desert sand;
A shape with lion body and the head of a man,
A gaze blank and pitiless as the sun,
Is moving its slow thighs, while all about it
Wind shadows of the indignant desert birds.
The darkness drops again but now I know
That twenty centuries of stony sleep
Were vexed to nightmare by a rocking cradle,
And what rough beast, its hour come round at last,
Slouches towards Bethlehem to be born?

I argue that America is currently experiencing a "Second Coming" (in this post-Civil Rights Era) with nomenclature—IDEA—that resembles too closely the nomenclature of the strivings of the Civil Rights Era, albeit not with these monikers. Clearly and by indisputable historical documentation, the post–Civil Rights Era is legislatively defined by the U.S. Congressional Civil Rights Act of 1964, Voting Rights Act of 1965, and Fair Housing Act of 1968. These major federal legislative acts *ended* legal segregation, *removed* illegal sanctions on voter registration and electoral practices in states with discriminatory voting practices, and *ended* discrimination in renting or buying housing.

ENDED. REMOVED. ENDED.

What has happened in this (our) post–Civil Rights Era? Were those *endings* and *removals* through federal legislation (in a 1960s America) about inclusion, equity, and access and predicated upon the need for respect and recognition of the diversity of a marginalized race of people? Is the embrace of IDEA simply a new façade for the work done during the Civil Rights Period? Was anything really removed? Did anything really end?

Is January 6, 2021, a *Wake-up Call* to the *Big Long Sleep on Social Injustice and Diversity Matters* in America?

Is "this" about race?
Is "this" about skin color?
Is "this" about ethnicity?
Is "this" about religion?
Is "this" about sexual orientation?
Is "this" about gender?

Is "this" about disabilities?

There is a large and looming responsibility for America to answer, decipher, and reframe "this," with and beyond burgeoning discourse and textual analyses of IDEA; it is time for Americans to be accountable and to match rhetoric to reality and to avoid endless engagement in discourse intent on defining only more discourse and verbosity on rhetoric versus reality.

So, does diversity matter? When, where, and how can diversity matter if it is entangled and choked by the weeds of misunderstanding that stultify the growth and expansion of inclusion, equity, and access? Diversity as a word flows so effortlessly from too many mouths and finds itself cozily ensconced in too many organizational standard operations procedures (SOPs) documents. How did we get "here" with the word diversity tossed about in almost all sectors of the work world as if it were a hot missile to catch if catch can? Has diversity become a word that signals persons to "do with whatever is available; by whatever means or in any way possible" as opposed to engaging in purposeful, planful, and intentional strategies to ensure that diversity is held by inclusion, equity, and access? In a *New York Times Magazine* article entitled "Has 'Diversity' Lost Its Meaning?," Anna Holmes contends:

> How does a word become so muddled that it loses much of its meaning? How does it go from communicating something idealistic to something cynical and suspect? If that word is "diversity," the answer is: through a combination of overuse, imprecision, inertia and self-serving intentions . . . what's so irritating about the recent ubiquity of the word "diversity": It has become both euphemism and cliché, a convenient shorthand that gestures at inclusivity and representation without actually taking them seriously.[3]

This volume contains voices that move pursuant to a declaration that diversity matters with an acute realization that those invested in inclusion, equity, and access work must not fall into the *Big Long Sleep of Social Injustice and Diversity Matters*, or we will again not only witness dreams deferred but also diversity deferred.

Let's examine this twenty-first century (re)awakening to an embrace of IDEA as if these were completely new ways and means of showing up in a world that purports to be colored and shaped by social justice. Post–Civil Rights Era, have we been sleeping as a nation or is there a demonstrable and documentable deferral of social justice? Langston Hughes' poem ("Harlem") provides voice to the consequences of deferral:[4]

Maybe it just sags
like a heavy load.
Or does it explode?

Dry up. Fester. Run. Stink. Crust. Sugar over. Sags. Explode.
Explode . . .

On January 6, 2021, America witnessed a debacle, which became an unscripted documentary/exposé of what I will argue is the problem of the twenty-first century—the problem of diversity and social justice and the question of whether there exists a majority population committed to the consistent creation and implementation of strategies for inclusion, equity, and access in the distribution of wealth, privileges, and opportunities for diverse populations.[5]

On what will undoubtedly become one of the most infamous days in modern American political history and matters of social justice, the entire world had a window seat toward a view of the state of inclusion, equity, and access under the umbrella of diversity.[6] As the entire world gained—at will—viewing access into the nation's capital of a frenzied mob carrying out the wish of the forty-fifth president of the United States, just days before the inauguration of the forty-sixth president of the United States, words from *The Price of the Ticket* by James Baldwin, novelist, poet, and civil rights humanitarian, echoed in my ears: "From my point of view, no label, no slogan, no party, no skin color, and indeed no religion is more important than the human being."[7]

The disdain for difference on that day, which many witnessed in a non-immersive "type" of virtual reality (television), begs the question asked at the beginning of this introduction: What impact does the current state of non-immersive virtual reality have on our ability to move beyond extensive and vapid rhetoric toward planning, implementation, and consistent fieldwork informed by high-impact diversity engagement strategies? Does the impact of non-immersive virtual reality desensitize and create the "it's not me" syndrome? Non-immersive virtual reality is explained as:

> a type of virtual reality technology that provides users with a computer-generated environment without a feeling of being immersed in the virtual world. The main characteristic of a non-immersive VR system is that users can keep control over physical surroundings while being aware of what's going on around them: sounds, visuals, and haptics.[8]

While I am loosely using television here to parallel the non-immersive virtual reality of that day, giving viewers a window-seat in real-time on the storming of the U.S. Capitol on January 6, 2021, the point here is that those watching the debacle on television still had primary control over their "physical surroundings." What emerges as dichotomous is how those looking in/viewing virtually, perhaps, maintained control while those in the physical environment/U.S. Capitol clearly lost control. Both parties, nevertheless, watched a display—one in a non-immersive mode as viewers and another in real-time mode as actors; the view was centered on the actors who sought to decimate the capacity for difference to exist per election results sanctioned by federal legislation. Those of us who maintained control over our "physical surroundings" were yet provided entry into the enactment of disdain for IDEA displayed high on banners replete with hate language and ball caps emblazoned with the message to "Make America Great Again." Question: Were virtual viewers desensitized by the violence that seemed so distant and surreal that was yet so close and real?

The Confederate Flag also was widely visible throughout the crowd of thousands during the armed siege of the U.S. Capitol. The Confederate Flag, a Civil War relic, maintains its centrality of expression among white supremacists and Southerners who claim it as part of their heritage. While it is argued that the Confederate Flag was never the official flag of the Confederacy, the battle flag has been mythologized since the late 1800s and held a disturbingly prominent presence[9] at the January 6, 2021, siege of the U.S. Capitol. Author Ta-Nehesi Coates in his article, "What This Cruel War Was Over," contends, "The Confederate flag is directly tied to the Confederate cause, and the Confederate cause was white supremacy. This claim is not the result of revisionism. It does not require reading between the lines. It is the plain meaning of the words of those who bore the Confederate flag across history. These words must never be forgotten."[10]

INCLUSION. DIVERSITY. EQUITY. ACCESS.

On January 6, 2021, the world witnessed a massive display by thousands of a public dismantling of care, concern, and practice of the work of the four words—Inclusion, Diversity, Equity, and Access (IDEA)—that slip effortlessly from many mouths in twenty-first-century America. In a matter of minutes after the January 6, 2021, inflammatory speech by the forty-fifth President of the United States, there was no more hiding behind rhetoric, no more grotesque masks, no more frosted windowpanes, no more heavy drapes of deception; humans looked squarely in the face of the thousands of people who rejected difference toward the outcome of more dreams and diversity deferred.

Yet, on that very same afternoon, the signal was strong as to the work that must be done to walk out of a false enclave of survival encapsulated too largely by—IDEA—and not pervasively by the deeds.

"This" is America's Challenge.

"This" is America's Work.

The velvety words Inclusion, Diversity, Equity, and Access must meet the gritty yet tangible deeds called work. To begin to effect real change, there must be foundational fieldwork work held by extended and extensive service to make demonstrable, ongoing, and evolving change. There is no end to the work of IDEA; it is about constant service. Many years ago, Representative Shirley Chisholm, the first African American and the first woman to run for the Democratic Party's nomination for President of the United States so eloquently said, "Service is the rent we pay for the privilege of living on this earth."[11]

Is America ready?

Is America ready, willing, and able to confront the root causes of the scars, bruises, traumas, and deaths of Black bodies in the now overwhelming discussions of IDEA? Will the clothing of social justice finally be extracted from the closets of exclusion and tailored to fit contemporary bodies in creating open spaces of inclusion—neighborhoods/communities, school systems, institutions of higher education, corporations, governments, political parties, and beyond?

ARE WE READY? COLLECTIVELY READY?

In this volume, the writers have engaged in a process that I embrace as "tilling the ground" for yield. "Tilling is simply turning over and breaking up the soil. Exactly how deep you till and how fine you break up the soil depends on your reason for tilling."[12]

I see the work and the strivings of these contributing writers as dedicated and focused in working on the soil (the soul) of America in their communities and beyond. They examine how our communities and the world have been "turned over and broken up," long before and since the Civil Rights Movement (1960s); they delve deeply into the reasons for the turning/tilling/breaking; and they interrogate ways and means of erecting systems and practices for increasing and evolving understandings of not only the rhetoric of IDEA but also the reality and intensity of the work that forms the ever-cyclical life stream of IDEA.

I am proud to be in the work of IDEA with my colleagues.

NOTES

1. Shelley Galasso Bonanno, "The Power and Strength of Bearing Witness," *Meaningful You: Voices of Contemporary Psychoanalysis*, December 3, 2013, https://www.psychologytoday.com/us/blog/meaningful-you/201312/the-power-and-strength-bearing-witness.

2. The 1918 influenza pandemic was also known as the Spanish Flu. The pandemic lasted roughly from February 1918 to April 1920. Having a worldwide impact, it infected upward of 500 million people with a death toll between 20 and 50

million people. Before our present-day, COVID-19 pandemic, it was seen as one of the deadliest pandemics in world history.

3. Anna Holmes, "Has 'Diversity' Lost Its Meaning?," *The New York Times Magazine*, October 27, 2015, https://www.nytimes.com/2015/11/01/magazine/has-di versity-lost-its-meaning.html.

4. Langston Hughes, "Harlem" from The Collected Works of Langston Hughes (2002).

5. Paying respect to and utilizing the argumentative structure of renowned sociologist, activist, and historian, Dr. W. E. B. Du Bois, it is fitting to cite a passage from his 1903 speech, "The Present Outlook for the Dark Races of Mankind": "Indeed a survey of the civilized world at the end of the nineteenth century but confirms the proposition with which I started—the world problem of the twentieth century is the Problem of the Color line—the question of the relation of the advanced races of men who happen to be white to the greater majority of the underdeveloped or half-developed nations of mankind who happen to be yellow, brown, or black."

6. Shelly Tan, Youjin Shin, and Danielle Rindler, "How One of America's Ugliest Days Unraveled Inside and Outside the Capitol," *The Washington Post*, January 9, 2017, https://www.washingtonpost.com/nation/interactive/2021/capitol-in surrection-visual-timeline/.

7. https://www.huffpost.com/entry/11-james-baldwin-quotes-on-race-that-re sonate-now-more-than-ever_n_58936929e4b06f344e40664c, January 24, 2021.

8. *CyberPulse: Tech Guides, Reviews, and News*, February 7, 2021, https://cy berpulse.info/what-is-non-immersive-virtual-reality-definition-examples/.

9. At least, the sight of the Confederate Flag is and was [that day] disturbing for proponents of social justice.

10. Ta-Nehesi Coates, "What This Cruel War Was Over," *The Atlantic*, June 22, 2015, https://www.theatlantic.com/politics/archive/2015/06/what-this-cruel-war-was -over/396482/.

11. https://www.goodreads.com/author/quotes/142616.Shirley_Chisholm, January 24, 2021.

12. https://homeguides.sfgate.com/tilling-soil-mean-43382.html,   January 24, 2021.

Part I

INTERROGATIONS OF BLACKNESS, WHITENESS, RACISM, AND BEYOND

HISTORICAL AND TWENTY-FIRST CENTURY CONSIDERATIONS

Chapter 1

Black Lives Matter

Dismantling Racism and Rewriting History in the Confederate Monuments

Nancy Wellington Bookhart

The streets were occupied for several months in the aftermath of the death of George Floyd,[1] as colorless people arguably performed the largest protest in U.S. history[2] and globally, overtaking neighborhoods, provinces, town squares, downtown, uptown, inner cities, metropolises, urban, rural, suburbs, regions, territories, states, zones, zip codes, Canada, Europe, Oceania, Asia, Africa, asseverating in their native tongue that Black Lives Matter (BLM). Monuments of despotism were dismantled. Others were defaced in acts of dissensus orchestrated against the hegemonic order that has perpetuated coded injunctions in the devaluation of Black lives. Many called these protests violent and destructive. I call these acts of dissensus war. Jean-Paul Sartre's Preface to *The Wretched of the Earth* quotes Frantz Fanon on violence as stating, "he shows perfectly clearly that this irrepressible violence is neither a storm in a teacup nor the reemergence of savage instincts nor even a consequence of resentment: it is man reconstructing himself . . . no indulgence can erase the marks of violence: violence alone can eliminate them."[3] And in another place, Sartre states, "For it is not first of all their violence, it is ours."[4] This clarion call was resounded with polyphonic utterances[5] of singularity avouching that Black lives are human lives, and they bear significance.

The historicizing of BLM is beyond the scope of this project. This chapter will instead interrogate the specificity of BLM's impact in the dismantling and defacing of the Confederate monuments in the reach for equity and inclusion. This solidarity of unity toward the more excellent end of humanity displayed from the U.S. Capitol to the shores of foreign soils is a triumph that evokes Martin Luther King, Jr. when stating that "injustice

Figure 1.1   Washington D.C. USA/ August 28, 2020: March on Washington 2020. Huge crowd of protesters march up to the Lincoln Memorial for Black Lives Matter. *Source*: Shutterstock.com. Julian Leshay.

Figure 1.2   London / UK, 06/13/2020: Black Lives Matter protest during coronavirus pandemic lockdown. BLM protesters heading to Trafalgar Square and shouting. *Source*: Shutterstock.com. Sandor Szmutko.

anywhere is a threat to justice everywhere."[6] Justice is not color-coded but is the true essence of humanity. Let me be transparent when I state that what we experienced in the recent Capitol insurrection is not isolated from the ongoing discourse of the Confederate monuments and the overall slogan "Make American Great Again," encrypted as *Make America White Again*. Markedly, every move toward solidarity and humanness signals a backlash that ever pushes society to the former edict of the master/slave narrative, where "the horrors of the past . . . merged with the horrors of the present."[7]

The problem we face is not new; it is an ever-persistent problem of the color line and the value of Black human life. It is the same problem that Du Bois encountered in his 1903 book *The Souls of Black Folk*. The problem for Du Bois was identified as belonging to the twentieth century, but I contend that this racial impasse has persisted even until this present hour touted as the age of colorblindness. One of the lines of racial indifference that has perseverated is locatable in the Confederate monuments. The Civil War, as well as the evocation of these monuments by the Lost Cause of the Confederacy,[8] is about having to cede an idyllic lifestyle bemoaned reel after reel in film and media to relinquish the status of the master race, to walk away from the profitable capitalistic venture of cotton, and the liberties and exercise of leisure lost in the dread of labor, having built the nation on the backs of Black slaves in free labor.

The Confederate monuments are intentional psychological terroristic plots in their nature to overturn freedom perpetually. These narratives embodied in the monuments belong to the Lost Cause of the Confederacy and Southern mythology, a closed chapter to a foregone history of defeat. But the glorification of these pseudo-heroes performs the battles time and time again and incessantly

Figure 1.3 Raleigh, NC/USA-062020: Crew removes Confederate monument from Capitol grounds following Gov. Roy Cooper's order. The statue honored the NC Confederate dead. *Source*: Shutterstock.com. Bryan Regan.

for a different outcome. The adherents of the Lost Cause are aware of defeat, but what they hope to achieve in the aftermath of the Civil War's battles is an off-the-battlefield victory of psychological torment and violence, which they believe to be advancing in these monuments. Art has long been a ploy of despotism in the performance of power.[9] When discussing colonialization in the Preface to *The Wretched of the Earth*, Sartre maintains that "psychological warfare was not born yesterday. Nor was brainwashing."[10]

I will discuss two strategies used in BLM's protests against police brutality that falls under the rubric of subjugations and oppression in all forms of racism. The dismantling and defacing of the monuments signify for BLM an attempt to disarm racism at its core. There have been attempts before these protests to have the monuments removed without sustainable resolve. According to the Southern Poverty Law Center, over fifty Confederate monuments were reinstalled or newly erected during the Civil Rights Movement. The Confederate monuments and other racist symbols, such as the Confederate flag, are antithetical stains in the fabric of democracy. These monuments do not illustrate a shared history of victory against a greater enemy but a glorification of white supremacy, white authority, white law, and white occupation against America's own. It is reasonable to surmise that state nor federal authorities had contemplated a creditable undertaking of this matter. The masses in the BLM protest would siege and dismantle Confederate

Figure 1.4   Richmond, Virginia, USA, June 2, 2020: Stonewall Jackson statue defaced with graffiti during Black Lives Matter protest. *Source*: Shutterstock.com. Mark Dozier.

monuments in acts of civil disobedience in the first order. No permission is/ was required. The toppling of the monuments by dissenters moved state and federal governments to order monuments to be removed. The governing bodies took action to dismantle the monuments for various reasons. Some in solidarity with the cause, while other reasons for dismantling were to preserve the monuments from further destruction and reinstallation.[11]

The second strategy was the defacing of the monuments: splattered paint, ink, markers, tar, scrawled across surfaces of pristine granite, marble, and limestone—desecration, a mural for public engagement in revolution. For many observers, these were acts of barbarism and incivility. I would argue that the dismantling and defacing of the Confederate monuments are the dismantling and defacing of hegemonic racist regimes and a rewrite of history. These are not symbolic acts as mute action; instead, this is a paradigmatic shift moving a nation toward repentance and reconciliation while negotiating the terms of diversity, inclusion, and equity in policy and practices. Through the lens of Jacques Rancière's theories of the distribution of the sensible and the regimes of art, the restaging of history is conceivable in this momentous promulgation for the "matter" of Black lives.

The question of the importance of Black lives is not *trending*. It is not fashionable or in vogue but is an irrefutable claim in keeping with human dignity and valuation. Black lives have always mattered since the foundation of the earth. They mattered when the Africans were taken from their villages under the secret cloak of darkness—a covert mission of greed and hypocrisy—blinded, bounded, gagged, silenced, and in chains to be delivered to a fate worse than death and death itself. Black lives mattered on the numerous slave ships—Antelope, La Amistad, Jesus of Lubeck, King David,

Figure 1.5   Screenshots from the 1939 film *Gone with the Wind;* adapted from Margaret Mitchell's 1936 novel bearing the same title. *Source: Gone with the Wind* (1939).

Nightingale, Hannibal, Hope—and countless more carrying slaves as cargo packaged for delivery as one transports coffee, rice, beans, and other objects of utility.[12] Disposable goods.

Black lives mattered in the marketplace on the multitudinous auction blocks, bodies naked, souls negotiated, sold to the highest bidders; plantation owners filled their coffers. Stripped of life and liberty, families were torn as flesh at the sinews; children ripped from mothers' arms violently, husbands and wives divorced by white decree. They mattered on the vast plantations where Black lives were rendered subhuman, dumb animals, whipped, raped, bargained, and forced to labor sunup to sundown with no relief in sight. They mattered when dogs attacked them in their fight for liberation in the Civil Rights Movement, Jim Crow legislature, marginalized, exiled from society, and signs posted, "No Blacks, No Dogs."[13] They mattered when Black bodies hung from trees, young bodies of the innocent, dangling, hanging, limp, lifeless, severed, mute, criminalized, and eviscerated in open courts of white spectators—entertained. Their crime, being born Black. They mattered in the names of Emmett Till, Reverend George Lee, Cynthia Wesley, Medgar Evers, Addie Mae Collins, Carole Robertson, Lamar Smith, Martin Luther King, Jr., Virgil Lamar Ware, Denise McNair, Malcolm X, and the countless unnamed soldiers of the constant struggle in the pursuit of freedom.

Regrettably, this was not the narrative endorsed by the Confederate monuments' audacity of continued existence in a country that abolished slavery with the Thirteenth Amendment. Presently, many agencies were involved in the removal of approximately one hundred Confederate monuments. Dozens of these were removed solely in the recent global protest of George Floyd. The Southern Poverty Law Center estimates that over fifteen hundred Confederate monuments are extant. These monuments are not sterile objects of testimony. They are not dead nor are they silent. These monuments echo the South's ideologies, the Confederacy, in its proponents' pronouncement of the Black race as subhuman and soulless, while installing the white race as the master race—supreme.

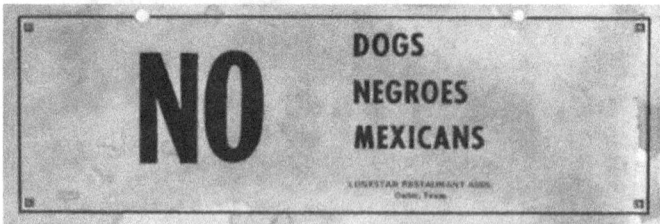

Figure 1.6   The sign, "No Dogs, No Negroes, No Mexicans," was authorized for use by the Lonestar Restaurants, 1942. *Source*: Public Domain. Library of Congress (024.00.00).

Figure 1.7 A postcard of the 1920 Duluth, Minnesota lynching of three suspects Elias Clayton, Elmer Jackson, and Isaac McGhie in the alleged rape of Irene Tusken, a white woman. *Source*: Public Domain.

The Black race as soulless is not a difficult concept to envision by American standards seeing that the treatment of the Black race as product had long been in vogue. Fanon quotes Sartre as positing, "Sartre has shown that the past, along the lines of an inauthentic mode, catches on and 'takes' en masse, and, once solidly structured, then *gives form* to the individual. It is the past transmuted into a thing of value."[14] This taking form that Sartre contends begins as formless matter, and through time and the assignment of value becomes the thing itself in the performance of race. The Black soul, argues Fanon throughout his text, is but a conjecture of white desire. He implicitly avouches that the Black man emerges on the landscape of history, in gestation, having "no culture, no civilization, and no long historical past."[15] This emergence not as a development but as a new thing is implicated in the term "gestation," not fully operational, as ahistorical.

The soul is a prominent theme that runs throughout the history of thought in the West. In his dialogues, Plato claimed the soul as the framework for all philosophical theorization from epistemology, as the seat of the intellect, to eschatology in the final judgment. So, to identify the Black race as soulless was to disavow their humanity completely. In his foreword, Kwame Anthony Appiah surmises Fanon's indictment of colonialism and the colonized in *Black Skins, White Masks* as asserting, "what is called the Black [*sic*] soul is a construction by white folk."[16]

The Black man is characterized by white representation as morally profane, psychologically inadequate, politically inept, and ontologically faulty,

Figure 1.8   Original 1909 black and white print ad for Cream of Wheat cereal with Rastus, the Cream of Wheat Chef. *Source*: Public Domain.

purported as truth through contrived forms throughout Western history. What is identified as the Black race is a characterology[17] defined under the rubric of a racist scientific agenda in the eighteen-century Enlightenment's[18] physiognomy[19] and phrenology[20] and other leading doctrines active during this period. The Confederate monuments scattered throughout the nation[21] are painful reminders of the Black man's relegation to the lot of the mule and oxen, a mere animal stripped of intellect. This unreasonable theoretic assumed authority and was validated through laws during slavery in America. These monuments represent the Hegelian fight to the death, for recognition[22] conceptually evidenced by the American Civil War, as a desire to own the Black body and soul. This privileged position of ownership by white society represents the Black race as a product, and at once posits him as "the missing link in the slow evolution from ape to man."[23]

I argue in my research that the Confederate monuments are the primal scene for the African American race. In these spectacles, the African American community experience the trauma and the monuments' audacity, which are the concretization and monumentalization of the unimaginable human atrocities involved in slavery and its profound effect on the Black race ad infinitum. Each monument in its showing and its display of righteous indignation echoes trauma through the chambers of the African American unborn for generations, in what has been coined by Dr. Joy DeGruy as post-traumatic slave syndrome and by Dr. Vivien Green Fryd as transgenerational trauma.[24] In his essay, "An Autobiographical Study," Sigmund Freud patented the term *primal scene* as part of his psychoanalytic theory of the unconscious to identify the original trauma site that subverted the normalization of subjectivity to what in neurosis is the traumatic subject. The primal scene is critical for

Figure 1.9   Film still from the 1939 film *Gone with the Wind* of Black men exiting a burning Atlanta. *Source*: Public Domain.

this discussion because the traumatic slave subjectivity replaced the African's former subjectivity.

Further, Frantz Fanon in *Black Skin, White Masks*, when discussing the Black man, stated that he is riddled with a "network of complexes."[25] Complexes here is a substitution for neurosis, psychological impairment, and so forth. The recovery of Black subjectivity is possible in the confrontation of the monuments. As much as this chapter is about the Confederate monuments, it is about the question of history and truth.[26] Heidegger asserts in his article "Being and Time" that "questioning builds a way."[27] Therefore, history must be interrogated. History has forgotten itself. Believing its own lie, it functions as truth, performing its legitimation by conferring validation on itself. How does history perform as truth in the case of the monuments? How is history, which is always already ordered, restaged to persist in the present as a new phenomenon and as emancipatory? And, how does Rancière's concepts of the distribution of the sensible and the regimes of art participate in dismantling the hegemonic order in the fragmentation and defacing of the monuments?

Through the lens of Jacques Rancière's theories of the distribution of the sensible and the regimes of art, we are aware how these monuments play out in history. These concepts do not perform in isolation but are the materialization of art's role in various historical periods. Rancière states in *The Politics of Aesthetics*:

> I call the distribution of the sensible the system of self-evident facts of sense perception that simultaneously discloses the existence of something in common and the delimitations that define the respective parts and positions within it. A distribution of the sensible therefore establishes at one and the same time something common that is shared and exclusive parts. This apportionment of parts and positions is based on a distribution of spaces, times, and forms of activity that determines the very manner in which something in common lends itself to participation and in what way various individuals have a part in this distribution.[28]

The distribution of the sensible has defined history as an agency; therefore, history is critical here in this examination. History, in many respects, as a predictor, gages human development in diverse fields of study. History measures human action in terms of psychology to that of stock market predictions. It does so to seed the future. It is primarily able to do this because history is considered concretized, reliable, and pure. But this is not the case. Instead, history has had its turn in society's construction through what Jacques Rancière argues as the distribution of the sensible and the regimes of art. Kingdoms are launched, myths are invented, and these agencies alter time and space.

Quantifiably, the distribution of the sensible is the arrangement of the world compartmentally, and the regimes of art participate in this assembly as the ethical, representative, and aesthetic regimes of art. The representative regime of art has dominated how societies make their appearance and how the world comes into visibility. In other words, what is important is made known, and what has no part in the community is obfuscated. The ethical regime is a regime established in the Platonist episteme as a regime of value judgment assigned to the community. And, in the case of art, it would be named unworthy of educating humankind in the things of wisdom, justice, virtue, and so forth. The representative regime derives from the Aristotelian domain in the autonomy of art owing to no one an assigned truth but establishing its own reality bound by an elitist art's hierarchy and efficacy, maintaining a specific world view and status quo in its showing.

In the aesthetic regime of art, history will undergo an incision that leads to the emancipation of perception through the decentered gaze, the Kantian's disinterest with interest.[29] One way in which Rancière understands the aesthetic regime is that "the aesthetic regime of the arts does not contrast the old with the new. It contrasts, more profoundly, two regimes of historicity."[30] Rancière's text *Dissensus: On Politics and Aesthetics* invokes another critical aspect of the aesthetic regime when stating, "for Rancière genuine political or artistic activities always involve forms of innovation that tear bodies from their assigned places."[31] Though Rancière is interested here in the subjugated community's liberation from their stations in life, we can imagine from this liberation occurs a dismantling that takes place in the emancipatory turn of things.

Dismantle: "To render useless for its purpose," "to pull down," "take to pieces," "destroy," "raze."[32]

In the evolution of the term, it comes as no surprise that *dismantle* is etymologically concatenated with violence. In its obsolete French form, in addition to its current definitions, it states, to "beat downe [*sic*] the walls of a fortresse [*sic*]." To beat down is a form of dismantling. Walls build formidable defenses, but they also yield under unprecedented force. The Confederate monuments are a product of the distribution of the sensible, as are many forms as an arrangement of things, not as an organic formulation, but a political one. The monuments are compositionally ideological, and in the public sphere, they dominate the political discourse that errs on the side of injustice. Rancière asserts of the distribution of the sensible that it "establishes at one and the same time something common that is shared and exclusive parts";[33] he was proposing that the object's form dictates in its visibility those belonging to the shared governance of the community and those left without due course. Their exclusivity, their non-presence, signifies their status in society. There is no arbitrariness to the historical significance in which these monuments make their declaration. What is momentous to note is that the monuments' dismantling is the second defeat of the Confederacy. Removed from public view are the conquered army, its majors, its generals, its lieutenants, its captains, its soldiers—their ranks liquidated, their pride marred, their honor blighted.

What is disassembled in these monuments are the leading figures who, in their representation, are the embodied school of thought perpetuated in this assembly. These monuments are scattered now as wind rustling through leaves, disbursed, long past their season.

Directionless, homeless, adrift.

In every corner of the nation, these tributaries steeped in racism descend from their high place, and the powerful presence of a reigning regime literally and figuratively becomes fragmented thought of an aborted mission—their throne pillaged, their speech mute, and their victory trammeled. Monument Avenue in Richmond, Virginia, has been reserved as one of the hollowed grounds replete with the Confederacy's notable soldiers. Stonewall Jackson, Jefferson Davis, Matthew Fontaine Maury, Robert E. Lee, and J. E. B. Stuart "gathered" here as their formal meeting place. These idealized statues served one purpose only, that of positing authority and dominance over the invention and postulation of the Black race in the furtherance of the Lost Cause of the Confederacy. Justifiable and unabashed, these promontories of stone were resplendent [at their pinnacle] for those who faithfully observed their legacy.

From 1900 until June 2020, this space was designated and framed for that cause. Floods of visitors took annual pilgrimages to Monument Avenue to honor and commemorate these great men of valor and virtue. These pilgrimages resembled those expeditions in *Canterbury Tales*,[34] where peoples of all ages and descent traveled great lengths to view Saint Thomas Becket's shrine at Canterbury Cathedral. Many travelers made similar pilgrimages at cathedrals all over Europe to witness and often experience transcendence while beholding the dead bones of apostles and prophets of Old Testament and New Testament biblical doctrine. The Confederate soldiers' descendants believed the monuments to be as prominent as the living bodies of the soldiers who fought and died in the Civil War for the ideology of the master/slave narrative ordained by God with Blacks as the cursed—wretched of the earth. The biblical story of Noah's sons and the new world order chronicles this invention.[35]

Year after year, for the past one hundred years or so, descendants such as the Daughters of the Confederacy, the white supremacy, and the KKK, as well as other hate groups, pause annually to pay homage. As the BLM protests in the killing of George Floyd advanced, thousands, hundreds of thousands, millions demanded that the vestiges affirming the Black race's objectification as hallowed acts and as righteous elections be excised from public shared space. As countries joined in, young and old, Black and white, Jew and gentile, every nationality and creed from all sectors and walks of life,

Figure 1.10 George Washington Custis Lee on horseback, with staff reviewing Confederate Reunion Parade in Richmond, Virginia, June 3, 1907, in front of monument to Jefferson Davis. *Source*: https://historicstruggle.wordpress.com/2017/08/18/sons-of-co nfederate-veterans-speak-out-on-confederate-monuments/. This media file is in public domain in the United States.

class, educational background, taste, and political associations, the appeal unhinged the epicenter of racism. And, as Rachel weeping for her children, and would not be comforted, so these, until freedom ring.[36]

The city of Richmond, Virginia, ordered the removal of the monuments, which meant Monument Avenue (as it had been known) became a waste-land. The enemy's camp discovered, invaded, the calvary, disarmed, their armor relinquished, their weapons dislodged, ranks and titles stripped, posts abandoned. Across America, in syncopation, decisions were made, and these heroes of Southern mythology were dismounted. Calendars were synchronized, machinery was inspected, monuments were harnessed, and then those white men who had lifted themselves above reason and virtue, democracy and truth, choosing instead a path that peddled fear in the marketplace to the masses, were debased. The pedestal that once lifted them high above the people stands alone now, empty, with no one to display, signify, and iconize. The Confederate monuments that terrorized a nation of peoples were (in the wake of Black Lives Matters demonstrations) dismantled, disassembled, and resigned, having lost their visibility and, therefore, their purpose. At Monument Avenue, Jefferson Davis's monument was removed on June 10, 2020; Stonewall Jackson followed him on July 1, 2020; then Matthew

Fontaine Maury the next day; and, finally, J. E. B. Stuart on July 7, 2020. In cities across the nation, the Walls of Jericho[37] came tumbling down.

These dismantlings were not simply symbolic acts. These were substantial shifts that ushered in change. Chief executive officers (CEOs) and corporate management called urgent meetings and reviewed outdated policy and procedures; SOP manuals were removed from dusty shelves, wiped off, and revised to include diversity policies. Fortune 500 companies, as well as small businesses that had deserted their first mission to fair and equal principles and had lost their way in the mire of capitalism and greed, regained their soul and sat down a decree of virtue. In other cities across America, the monuments toppled, and the racist ideologies were put to rest. The North Carolina State Monument in Raleigh, North, Carolina; Albert Pike Memorial in Washington, D.C. (toppled by protesters during Juneteenth);[38] Confederate soldiers' grave marker in Silver Spring, Maryland, toppled by protesters; Statue of Confederate soldiers in Frederick, Maryland, toppled by protesters; statue of Benjamin Welch Owens in Lothian, Maryland, toppled by protesters; the U.S. Confederate Veteran Memorial in Seattle, Washington, toppled by protesters; and other Confederate ghosts met their demise. Those monuments ordered removed by city, state, and federal officials are also notable: Confederate Soldiers and Sailors Monument, Birmingham, Alabama;[39] bust of Robert E. Lee, Fort Myers, Florida, removed by Sons of Confederate Veterans; Bentonville Confederate Monument, Bentonville, Arkansas, (plans for removal) by United Daughters of the Confederacy; Athens Confederate Monument, Athens, Georgia, removed by the city; Nash County Confederate Monument, Rocky Mount, North, Carolina, (City Council of Rocky Mount voted to remove the monument); John B. Castleman Monument, Louisville, Kentucky, removed to be placed at his burial site at Cave Hill Cemetery; and Jacksonville Confederate Monument, Jacksonville, Florida. What is notable is that the expanse of this listing of Confederate monuments does not signify an exhaustive naming of toppled or dismantled monuments.

The Confederate soldiers locked in stone reiterated a lost war's victories and what all those who fought in the Confederacy embraced as a divine mission, chosen and directed by God. In the dismantling of the monuments, these past concretized persons and their ideologies are lost, decentered, displaced, and invisible. Because, arguably, if a tree falls into the forest and no one is around, it does not make a sound. In comparison to the tree, it is the company of those who can recognize, who can acknowledge, who can see— those crowds of worshippers who validate existence. Now, these monuments will be placed in holding cells—waiting, watching, and anticipating the light of day. Hidden away in dark rooms and warehouses, they will be stored as one house's unusable merchandise, removed from public view or political engagement—damp, controlled, shut down, isolated, and silenced. One may argue that this is a removal of history, and I would likely agree; however, it is a removal of a dark history with no path to equity or inclusion. African Americans confronted the primal scene in the Confederate monuments. With the disposal of these monuments, there is a sense that some semblance of justice is realized, some measure of victory is meted, and the hegemonic reign of terror collapsed.

Thousands of protesters will rewrite history in the defacing of the monuments before dismantling. Defacing, simply defined, is an act of marking out, tracing over, an erasure. In other instances, to deface is an attempt to eradicate the former inscriptions, make invisible and conceive as nonexistent. There is a story told by Stephen Greenblatt in *Swerve: How the World Became Modern* in which he recalls the journey of a book hunter, Poggio, who visits a monastery in search of rare books. What was discovered by this book hunter during his time at the monastery is that some of the ancient writings were scraped off the walls by the monks. Hand rendering of manuscripts was an arduous task before the printing press emerged, which is far off during Poggio's journey. Papyrus, the surface on which the manuscripts were written had become scarce. Greenblatt relays, that "working with knives, brushes, and rags, monks often carefully washed away the old writings—Virgil, Ovid, Seneca, Lucretius—and wrote in their place the texts that they were instructed by their superiors to copy."[40] Instead of mourning of the loss of history, this type of situation can be seen as the layering of history. Curiously enough, many of the ancient writings were preserved and rediscovered beneath the new in juxtaposition. I will return to the relevance here in Rancière shortly.

Defacing indicates a marring of form, beauty, a disfigurement. In *On the Aesthetic Education of Man*, Schiller discusses in the "Sixth Letter" the necessity to create objects of beauty, forms of equilibrium to replace art that destroyed humankind.[41] Rancière in *The Politics of Aesthetics* posits the aesthetic regime as a form that at once draws a comparison of two historicities. Defacing alters the former treatise of the narratives of history. It no longer serves the hegemonic order of a certain elitist, nobility, or hierarchical station in lording over the Other. On the same site, in the same space, in the same room, in the exact ordering, both histories juxtapose the other—the slave and the master, the citizen and the marginalized, the servant and the lord, the oppressed and the subjugated—given space and voice, in what Rancière constitutes as true *politics*. Politics—not in the manner we have become accustomed to but in its original form. The current order is proposed by Rancière as policing, a censoring of communities. But, in the original place of politics, the citizen is given space and place to conjoin in governance matters. Rancière posits in *Dissensus: On Politics and Aesthetics*, "If politics is the tracing of a vanishing difference with respect to the distribution of social parts and shares, it follows that its existence is by no means necessary, but that it occurs as an always provisional accident within the history of forms of domination. It also follows that the essential object of political dispute is the very existence of politics itself."[42]

The strategy of vandalism or defacement of these monuments follows the course of action, which Rancière discusses earlier. Politics that left the people voiceless have now caused the masses to rise in the originary of politics in

Figure 1.11   Richmond, Virginia/Richmond County, June 13, 2020: 5,000-man march in Richmond protesting racism and the Confederate statues. *Source*: Shutterstock.com. Greg Rones.

political dispute. These defacements form layer upon layer of scribblings that refutes the law-and-order mandate that has ravaged Black communities in the safeguard of whites in the policing of Black communities. It is the complaints against systemic racism with laws and legislation that serve as modern-day slavery.

These writings are manifestos of grievances inscribed against governments, institutions that have intentionally colluded to marginalize and halt Black progress in educational systems, economic institutions, and unfair lending practices. The kindergarten to prison pipeline studies as the segue to mass incarceration incite angry soliloquies on power and corruption in a system constructed for moral and political loss. Affirmations of Black pride were scrawled across the enslavers' surfaces with intensity in an otherwise unfair politics of injustice and inequality, penned as annotated verses, prose, journal entries, dates, and times, writing oneself on the surface of a foregone history. The site now calls for political efficacy once denied to *all* (Blacks, included) of the citizen's place in the consensus of thought and action governing a community.

Defacement becomes a form of disfiguration that rejects previous inscriptions' in its demand for recognition. The classical pose, the composed and ordered composition, the proud soldier, the medals and honors, the suited allegiance, the mounted steed, the accouterments of the ideological creed are all disfigured, erased to establish a new perspective.

And what is this new perspective, this coming community?

Resoundingly, that Black Lives Matter.

The discreditation or defamation of one's legacy is a harsh indictment signaled in the images of defacement in the painted statues, smudged countenances. The color of blood streaming down the entire surface of the composition signals the making of these monuments as, in part, accountable for the bloodshed of Black lives lynched in the many streets of America. These defacements reveal the true nature of the monuments and the intentions of the patrons who support them. The plan's hiddenness is revealed, the cloaked pretense of the monuments as pure art and history is brought to light as a lie of history. These monuments marked out and smeared over *counts and accounts* for erasure—not of history—but racism.

While these measures appear symbolic, these strategies of dismantling and defacing are potent tools of revolution. Indeed, these dismantling and defacing strategies move the dial of acknowledgment and resolution further in the quest for justice. The dismantling and defacing of the monuments truly may be scrimmages on this elephantine battlefield of injustice. Nevertheless, any victory toward the moral end of communities of inequality is directionally expedient in a protest that was orchestrated by Black lives, demonstrated

Figure 1.12   Baltimore, Maryland/USA, June 28, 2020: A Statue of George Washington in Druid Hill Park, Baltimore was defaced with red paint over the Black Lives Matters protest. *Source*: Shutterstock.com. Shiva Photo.

by Black lives, and advanced by Black lives in this ever-challenging human project of the recognition that *Black Matters Matter*.

Black Lives Matter.

NOTES

1. George Floyd was a Black man arrested in Minneapolis, Minnesota, on charges of passing a counterfeit bill. Floyd was pinned face down on the pavement by Officer Derek Chauvin for eight minutes and forty-six seconds, which became the chant for millions protesting across the globe for human recognition and civil equity and the mantra for BLM in the continued pursuit for inclusion, human dignity, and valuation.

2. See the July 3, 2020, article in the *New York Times* by Larry Buchanan, Quoctrung Bui, and Jugal K. Patel titled, "Black Lives Matter May Be the Largest Movement in U.S. History," in which it is suggested (according to several polls) that the count of protesters a day immediately after the death of George Floyd May until June 22 was estimated at fifteen to twenty-six million protesters throughout various cities in America. This does not account for protests in other countries.

3. See Frantz Fanon's *The Wretched of the Earth*, page lv.

4. ibid, page lii.

5. For more on the conceptual turn of subjectivity as communal intersubjectivity, see Katerina Clark and Michael Holquist's *Mikhail Bakhtin*.

6. See Martin Luther King, Jr.'s "Letter from Birmingham Jail," 1963.

7. See Chris Hedges's *Wages of Rebellion*, page 24.

8. The Lost Cause of the Confederacy is a movement that upholds the mission and relevance of the South as alive through various means wherein joint agencies meet and plan commemorations, joint ventures such as the erection of monuments, and other political strategies to disseminate the lie of slavery as natural and the racist ideology of the hierarchy of races.

9. See Friedrich Schiller's *On the Aesthetic Education of Man* in which art is understood as form in the shaping of a certain type of humanity. For Schiller, this construction of humankind against the laws of nature has caused an unforgiving outcome of humankind in its sterility as touching humanness.

10. See Frantz Fanon's *The Wretched of the Earth*, page 191.

11. There are laws presently existing in many states that prohibit the dismantling of Confederate monuments. In the Southern Poverty Law Center's, 2019 report entitled, "Whose Heritage? Public Symbols of the Confederacy," the article discusses the legacy of the monuments and the protection in which they have under the law. The report further notes that states that have not previously passed laws to protect the monuments are in the process of doing so in light of the recent events.

12. For more details on the slave ship, see Marcus Rediker's, *The Slave Ship*: *A Human History* and Greg Grandin's *The Empire of Necessity: Slavery, Freedom, and Deception in the New World*.

13. The sign "No Dogs, No Negroes, No Mexicans" was authorized for use by the Lonestar Restaurant Association Sign, 1942.

14. See Frantz Fanon's *Black Skin, White Masks*, page 202.

15. ibid, page 17.

16. ibid, page xviii.

17. *Characterology* is a term commonly used to evaluate the relationship of bodily features to intellectual capacity as attributed to a race, gender, or culture, in order to determine their perceived value. This concept is primarily a racist theory that proposes that the character of these groups is determined by Nature and is unalterable. In eighteenth-century Europe, this term was used to a great extent to marginalize certain swaths of society as inferior. Those identified as subhuman included any white persons who were not Aryan or Nordic, as well as Jews and Blacks.

18. The period identified as the Enlightenment, or the Age of Reason, emerged on the European stage in the eighteenth century with doctrines considered to be the beginning of modern thought that involved the rejection of tales and superstitions and a more stringent attention given to reevaluating the course of knowledge in the further development of humankind through an interrogation of reason and a consideration of the sensible or aesthetics. The underside of this period is the racist agenda that persisted in many of the doctrines and thinkers.

19. Physiognomy is the racist pseudo-science propagated in eighteenth-century Enlightenment and founded by Johann Kasper Lavater as having the ability to judge character by facial features. This is one of the methods for promoting racist ideologies

that perpetuated the white race as the master race and the Blacks as the lower race of peoples ordained by Nature and God.

20. Phrenology is noted to be a pseudo-science for measuring the cranial to determine intellect. This method emerged during eighteenth-century Enlightenment, parallel to physiognomy and other racist inventions of history.

21. The largest standing Confederate monument is carved on a monolithic mountain in Stone Mountain, Georgia. It is not just a monument in words, it is one in deeds. The very commission of the monument was to benefit the glory and continued work of the Ku Klux Klan (KKK). The KKK gained its second life with the release of D. W. Griffith's *The Birth of a Nation* (1915). *The Birth* was based solely on the KKK's rise to power to save the South from what was illustrated as the overbearing Black man in the aftermath of the Civil War. The Black man is represented in the film as the most abominable wretched creature whose only desire is for the reversal of power and fortune, and the destruction of the white man and the ravaging of the white woman and child. It should be obvious that this is the projected gaze of the white man and his fears inverted. There was a now historical and formerly long-standing agreement that the KKK would have meetings and summits at the base of the mountain to celebrate and plan the future role of the KKK in the furtherance of the white supremacy agenda.

22. Alexandre Kojève's read of Hegel's phenomenology of the spirit is but the history of desire, maintaining that the self-conscious emerges in the "risking his life to satisfy his human Desire—that is, his Desire directed toward another Desire." This desire of the Other in Hegelian terms is understood as the recognition that should be borne out from the other and is satisfied only in the death of the other.

23. See Frantz Fanon's *Black Skin, White Masks*, page 1.

24. For further reading see Dr. Joy DeGruy's text *Post Traumatic Slave Syndrome: America's Legacy of Enduring Injury and Healing* as well as Dr. Vivien Green Fryd's essay "Bearing witness to the trauma of slavery in Kara Walker's videos: *Testimony, Eight Possible Beginnings*, and *I Was Transported*.

25. See Frantz Fanon's *Black Skin, White Masks*, page, xiv.

26. In Plato, "truth becomes . . . correctness of the ability to perceive and to declare something." Likewise, in Aristotle, there is a similar doctrine connected to understanding and declaration as an assertion in what is stated as truth or falsehood. Truth for Aquinas is that of human and divine understanding. For Descartes, too, understanding marks the major predicate for truth. For Nietzsche, truth is a type of falsification of the real, "the kind of error without which a definite kind of living species would not be able to live." Agamben offers as a "taking place," that "truth cannot be shown except by showing the false, which is not, however, cut off and cast aside somewhere else."

27. See Martin Heidegger's essay "Being and Time" in *Basic Writings*, page 373.

28. See Jacques Rancière *Politics of Aesthetics*, page 12.

29. For further examination of the theory of disinterest, see Immanuel Kant's *Critique of Judgment*, "Analytic of Aesthetic Judgement," and for an exploratory read on the decentered gaze, see Joseph Tanke's *Jacques Rancière: An Introduction—Philosophy, Politics, Aesthetics*.

30. See Jacques Rancière's *Politics of Aesthetics*, page 24.

31. See Jacques Rancière's *Dissensus: On Politics and Aesthetics*, page 1.

32. See Oxford Online Dictionary.

33. See Jacques Rancière's *Politics of Aesthetics*, page 12.

34. *The Canterbury Tales* by Geoffrey Chaucer is a collection of short stories and verse that narrates the life of the various characters on the pilgrimage, their occupation, and social status while blending satire and comedy to convey a commentary on societal values.

35. See Genesis 9:22–26, KJV, in which the story is used as a form of knowledge to perpetuate the lie of history of the racial division said to be sanctioned by God and further validated by Nature in the ordering of the master/slave narrative in perpetuity. The story speaks to the origin and hierarchy of race after the flood in the nascent womb of the new world with Noah and his sons.

36. Rachel weeping for her children is a reference found in KJV, Matthew 2:18, which can be interpreted as a symbolic mother weeping for the captivity of the Israelites who had been in bondage for many generations. The phrase *freedom ring* is referencing Martin Luther King, Jr.'s "I Have a Dream" speech delivered on August 28, 1963, in Washington, D.C., at the Lincoln Memorial in anticipation of one emancipated humanity.

37. For the story of the defeat of Jericho in the dismantling of the wall surrounding the city, see Joshua, Chapter 6, KJV.

38. Juneteenth is celebrated annually on June 19 as the official date for emancipation by many African Americans, which was first acknowledged by the state of Texas.

39. Birmingham, Alabama, is significant here for Martin Luther King, Jr.'s rebuke in his 1963 "Letter from a Birmingham Jail" in which he states, "All men are caught in an inescapable network of mutuality, tied in a single garment of destiny."

40. See Stephen Greenblatt's *Swerve: How the World Became Modern*, page 43.

41. See Friedrich Schiller's *On the Aesthetic Education of Man*, page 45.

42. See Jacques Rancière's *Dissensus: On Politics and Aesthetics*, page 35.

Chapter 2

The Black Lives Matter Movement and Anglophone African-Caribbean Impact

*Transposition of the Caribbean
Experience in the Complexities of
the African American Context*

Sharon Albert Honore

I, too, am from the Caribbean—born and raised on an American island, St. Croix, but descended from people who came from all over what the late Barbadian poet Kamau Brathwaite once called "a whole underground continent of thought and feeling and history."[1] We carry the archipelago within us, looking and listening, always, for bits of what we left behind. A bead on someone who makes a good guava tart. Figuring out the source of a Trinidadian lilt on a crowded elevator. And, then, there's the habit—a preoccupation, really—with detecting the Caribbean heritage in the people around us.

> . . .for the islanders keeping score—always reconstructing that continent of islands, if only in our minds.[2] (Fredreka Schouten, CNN, writer)

Anglophone African-Caribbean[3] people and African Americans share indisputable commonalities that stretch beyond melanin. Solidarity between the two does not require rejection of their own cultures because, unfortunately, systemic and institutionalized racism accommodates both groups. Notwithstanding the differences in culture, accent, dialect, and culinary preferences, the two groups of people, separated by oceans of water, share a history. Both groups descend from the African diaspora that incorporates "a whole underground continent of thought and feeling and history."[4] Anglophone African-Caribbean people and African Americans share a dark past, inundated with pain, anguish, and transposition. Historically, the source of these ills, white America, has sought to divide the two groups, mentally, as well as geographically. Unfortunately, law enforcement policies such as racial profiling and mistaken arrests showcase how externally undifferentiated one Black face is from another; white authority will not ask from which island or state a Black male hailed before a random stop and frisk.

The Black Lives Matter (BLM) movement[5] has proven to be a source for unification, collaboration, and cultural exchange. Arguably, BLM may serve as a common denominator and offer solutions to the problems of racial injustice, prejudice, and oppression for people of color. BLM may provide a bond to confront a common nemesis and serve as a cultural trajectory for future collaboratives. Sir Hilary Beckles, vice chancellor and professor at The University of the West Indies (UWI), president of Universities Caribbean, and chairman of the CARICOM Reparations Commission, recognizes an intertwined history between brown and Black people stateside (USA) and those in the Anglophone African-Caribbean countries. He said:

> We have always recognized our unity as one people with a common history, legacy, and cause. We fought against our enslavement together; we endured and resisted the dispossession of post-slavery plunder together; we formulated and advocated a common dream of liberty and freedom for our children together.[6]

BLM has helped to reestablish an (un)broken history of cooperation between African-Caribbeans and African Americans. This may be determined by examining leaders who used their pre-immigrant background in Black-dominated societies as a strength to demand racial equality rather than as social advantage over African Americans.

This chapter examines how the BLM movement in the United States has been significantly impacted by Anglophone African-Caribbean thought and action. Furthermore, it asserts that notwithstanding cultural disparities between mainlanders and islanders, the Anglophone African-Caribbean may bring a "woke" consciousness and resilience to the BLM movement. Indeed, Blacks in America often journey back to the Caribbean islands to reclaim their roots and to be reminded of their worth. The following statements, also made by Beckles, demonstrate the impact of the thoughts and actions of African-Caribbean people on stateside residents:

> Martin Luther King, Jr., when he felt he could not breathe came to Jamaica. When the threats to his life were constant and closing in around his neck, he took this measure to maintain his life. His visits to Jamaica's north coast filled his lungs with the "freer" air of our space. He returned to the mainland more

battle ready for the struggle to achieve the God-given right to the dignity of Black life.

Island and mainland have always been a common survival space. Borders cannot contain consciousness nor isolate the intellect. Martin was retracing the footsteps of Marcus, his mentor, the incomparable Marcus Garvey who also travelled from this north coast—his ancestral home—to Harlem, there to dedicate his life to the struggle for the dignity of Black life.[7]

This chapter also examines the theoretical and ideological frameworks of four women of Anglophone Caribbean heritage and their use of media to influence the African American landscape. Joy Reid, Guyana (broadcast media); Karine Jean-Pierre, Haiti (public relations); Nneka Jones, Trinidad (visual artist); and Fredreka Scoulten, U.S. Virgin Islands (print journalism), all use their platforms and communally affective approaches to impact the societal infrastructure of BLM radicalism.

SOCIETAL INFRASTRUCTURE OF BLM RADICALISM

A decentralized grassroots movement, BLM was cofounded as an online movement (using the hashtag #BlackLivesMatter on social media) by three Black community organizers—Patrisse Khan-Cullors, Alicia Garza, and Opal Tometi—after the acquittal of George Zimmerman on charges stemming from his fatal shooting of Trayvon Martin in February 2012.[8] The widely publicized jury trial was deemed a miscarriage of justice and led to international protests. The BLM movement expanded in 2014 after the publicized police killings of two more unarmed Black men and gathered momentum after the names of hundreds of murders came to the forefront of brown and Black men, women, and children. Some of the more famous victims associated with BLM include George Floyd, Eric Garner, Michael Brown, Sandra Bland, Philando Castile, Freddie Gray, Laquan McDonald, Tamir Rice, Walter Scott, Alton Sterling, and Breonna Taylor.[9] Large protests of these deaths in the name of BLM captured national and international attention and continue to play a prominent role in demonstrations against police brutality and racism.

Subsequently, BLM has expanded in 2020 to a global organization, Black Lives Matter Global Network Foundation, Inc., with offices in the United States, UK, and Canada. Arguably, it has changed the framework by which the conversation of race is discussed. Eight years after its inception, in response to the death of George Floyd in early summer 2020, BLM made history with demonstrations held worldwide. Carl Sudder, writer for *The American Historian,* said:

Amid a global pandemic, Black Lives Matter protests peaked on June 6, according to *The New York Times*, when nearly half a million people turned out in nearly 550 places across the United States. By July, it was estimated that about 15 million to 26 million people participated in demonstrations over the deaths of George Floyd, Breonna Taylor, and others. There have been demonstrations in all 50 states and on every continent except Antarctica.[10]

BLM continues to be led by activists in local chapters who organize their own campaigns and programs. BLM, an international movement, is dedicated to fighting racism and anti-Black violence, especially in the form of police brutality. Initially, BLM signaled condemnation of the unjust killings of Black people by police and demanded redress for the brutal and unjustified treatment of Black bodies by law enforcement in the United States. The causes, relative to societal ills, however, continue to evolve. In 2020, the official web page of BLM includes the statement, "We affirm the lives of Black queer and trans folks, disabled folks, undocumented folks, folks with records, women, and all Black lives along the gender spectrum."[11]

While the BLM movement may seem relatively new, the fight for equality and justice has its roots in slavery and prior social injustice movements. As noted by historian Christopher Lebron, "the plea and demand that 'Black Lives Matter' comes out of a much older and richer tradition arguing for the equal dignity—and not just equal rights—of Black people."[12] The ideology of BLM clearly merged and has emerged from revolutionary and intellectual leaders from various time periods in American history. Liberation for under-represented communities is ongoing and the depths of continued systemic racism are addressed in the BLM movement. The atrocities of violence perpetrated on Black people in the United States are felt among those in Anglophone African-Caribbean locations who understand that oppressive, white supremacy systems are born out of racism, cultivated through colonialism, patriarchy, and practiced through global capitalism. According to scholar and writer Angelique V. Nixon, "This is why the Movement for Black Lives Matter resonates globally."[13]

Along with other Black and brown people from the African diaspora, both populations understand that racial violence is state sanctioned through police and vigilantes who justify their actions through racist beliefs and stereotypes. Those who perpetuate violence have shared experiences with police violence, racial and economic injustice, and other forms of oppression. The juxtaposition of empathy and outrage, and a clear demand that the systems in which they live are broken and racist, and social injustice eruptions reveal commonalities, which impact how Anglophone African-Caribbean artistic thought and action impact the stateside BLM movement.

USE OF SOCIAL MEDIA PLATFORMS AND
COMMUNALLY AFFECTIVE APPROACHES

Activists with roots that extend beyond the mainland disseminate the message that, indeed, BLM. Anglophone African-Caribbean persons have been instrumental in using unique communication techniques to highlight social injustice and racism and force dialogue. The work of Anglophone African-Caribbean journalists, artists, and activists showcases imperatives of a focused and magnanimous effort to further the assertion of #BLM as more than an ethno-linguistic code.

Anglophone African-Caribbean activists Joy Reid, Karine Jean-Pierre, Nneka Jones, and Fredreka Schouten use their platforms and communally affective journalistic approaches to provoke critical thought, promote education, and increase action in the Black community. They have familial ties to the USVI, Guyana, Haiti, and Trinidad and represent disenfranchised communities such as women and LGBTQIA persons. All are activists and serve as social influencers. The voices of these Anglophone African-Caribbean women impact the societal infrastructure of BLM's radicalism and profoundly influence the African American landscape.

For example, Wesley Gibbings, a Trinidadian journalist/newspaper columnist and media trainer, has engaged in extensive journalistic work for over thirty-five years. He covers Caribbean public affairs and activism in the area of press freedom and noted:

> Do Black Lives Matter? Of course, they do. But don't all lives also matter? Yes, but that is not what we are talking about at this time. There is a sometimes lethal crisis that has existed for too long now and a focused intervention is now necessary to address it in the United States and everywhere else some of its less evident features appear, including right here. It is not that other causes are to be side-lined or denied by this. The BLM movement has everything to do with us in the Caribbean, albeit under conditions that are somewhat different from what obtains in the United States and other countries of the Americas where the millions of Afro-descendants have been the subject of systemic discrimination and violence in all its forms.[14]

JOY-ANN M. LOMENA-REID

Joy Reid is a popular broadcast personality who exemplifies how Anglophone African-Caribbean journalistic thoughts and actions might be used to challenge and qualitatively change American ideologies about race and racism, relative to peoples of the African diaspora and underrepresented populations.

Joy Reid, political commentator and host of *The ReidOut*,[15] a weekly hour-long cable program on MSNBC and former weekend host of *AM Joy*, has a large fan base of statesiders who are impacted by her words and actions. During her debut episode in July 2020, Reid drew a viewership of 2.627 million. She became the first Black woman to host a national primetime news show[16] and the first Black woman to anchor a primetime network show in the history of cable television. Her presence on social media is prominent with 356K followers on her Instagram account, 1.9 million followers on her Twitter account, and 208.26K followers on her Facebook page. Based on responses and re-tweets on her pages, statesiders are influenced by her ideological and political stances on BLM.

Reid's mother was a professor and nutritionist from Guyana; her father left for the Democratic Republic of Congo when she was a child. Speaking frankly about issues such as social reform, Reid reflects implicit and explicit awareness of her Caribbean heritage. An outspoken defender of civil rights and social justice, she frequently makes statements in support of BLM protestors and demonstrators, which directly impact stateside actions. During the social unrest in the summer of 2020, she disagreed with the charge that supporters of BLM were responsible for riots and violence following the George Floyd murder. She blamed President Donald Trump for the violence in that she said the incidents were fueled by "white nationalist mobs."[17] Furthermore, Reid stated:

> Let me repeat this for those inventing the idea of "Black Lives Matter riots." BLM doesn't "riot." They march against police violence. And note that those caught setting fires, assaulting, and shooting people are consistently of the RIGHT, not the left. So, let's stop giving in to the narrative Trump and his allies are inventing to try and help him cling to power. Autocrats always eventually get to this place: accusing the opposition of being anarchic and violent to cover up their own rot and violence.[18]

The ReidOut host continued to explain that while the BLM movement may seem relatively new, the fight for equality and justice has its roots in slavery. Reid reminded readers that, historically, social justice campaigns have continually appeared in America including the Civil Rights Movement although they might have used different names. Reid continues to affirm that when protests against police brutality and racism occurred in 2012, white America really rejected the BLM movement despite President Obama's support. With a leader (Trump) who seemed against the goals and demands of the social justice movement, Reid said the public is on the side of the Black community. She felt that was a huge, important change. Reid praised protestors in Portland who were attacked by law enforcement officials while standing in solidarity with the BLM demonstrators. She argued:

It's not just a Black people concern, this is the public realizing if they're coming for Black lives, they're eventually coming for yours. They're eventually coming for your security and peace. All of us have to be in this together. The Trump administration is so desperate to manufacture an atmosphere of left-wing violence ahead of the election and to ignore the violence being perpetrated by some of their own supporters including white nationalists.[19]

KARINE JEAN-PIERRE

With the 2021 presidential transition, Karine Jean-Pierre will be the first Black and lesbian woman to serve in the position of Principal Deputy Press Secretary as part of the Biden-Harris administration. A Democratic strategist and *NewsHour* analyst, Jean-Pierre admitted to being shocked in 2018 when the Republican president described Haiti and several African nations as "shithole countries." In an effort to address the hate and bigotry promoted by the GOP administration, she became chief public affairs officer for *MoveOn*, a progressive public policy advocacy group. She frequently uses her social media platform to highlight these issues, which align with the mission of BLM.

In an interview on PBS *NewsHour* with Judy Woodruff, Jean-Pierre shared her experiences growing up as the eldest child in a book, *Moving Forward: A Story of Hope, Hard Work, and the Promise of America*.[20] Born in Fort-de-France, Martinique to Haitian immigrant parents and raised in Queens, New York, Jean-Pierre assumed major family responsibilities at a young age and said she was expected to live up to "high expectations," which overtime became "overwhelming."[21] She confessed:

Being the oldest . . . I had to take care of my siblings while my parents were working six, seven days a week. I had to feed them. And I'm eight years older than my sister, ten years older than my brother, so I was pretty young when they were toddlers, and make sure their food was cooked, make sure diapers were changed, because they [parents] had to provide for the family. And all of that heaviness, all of that responsibility led to some dark times as well.[22]

In her much-publicized book, Jean-Pierre talks about racism, coming out as a gay women to the Caribbean community and the emotional difficulties that led to mental health issues. She also recounts her experiences with depression as she struggled with family commitments and her sexual identity. Jean-Pierre said:

There are so many things that I bring up [in the book] that you just laid out perfectly, but one of them is mental health. And one of the reasons I talk about it in the book is because there is a stigma connected to mental health. And people don't want to talk about what they go through when they are in dark times, and they don't know how to get out of it. And because of the pressures of me growing up, and just feeling like an outsider all through my growing up, my young—young days, there was a time where I attempted to take my life. I attempted suicide.[23]

Her ideological stance surrounding mental health in the Black community aligns with BLM; she agrees that the topic is taboo in the African American and Anglophone African-Caribbean communities and must become part of a larger dialogue.

Jean-Pierre lays out a blueprint for activism in her book and states that #BLM underscores the necessity to acknowledge the social ills such as mental instability, suicide, and depression that affect underrepresented populations from the African diaspora. In a tweet, Karine Jean-Pierre noted that the BLM Global Network's campaign proved that people of color are powerful voters and won't be distracted by efforts to suppress their voices.

NNEKA JONES

Nneka Jones is a twenty-three-year-old Trinidadian activist who impacts stateside persons and ideologies with her visual artwork that addresses issues of race, ethnicity, and physical and mental abuse of women and girls of color. She has received national recognition and international acclaim for her use of embroidery on canvas. Within four months of her graduation from undergraduate school, Jones was commissioned by Victor Williams, art director for *TIME* magazine to create cover art for the August 31–September 7 issue, titled *The New American Revolution.*[24] The cover features an embroidered image of the American flag with a needle stuck into the thread of one unfinished end. It is the symbolism of an unfinished story that is still unfolding, especially for people of color in the "land of the free." Jones completed the unique design in record time to meet the magazine's deadline. Although it would take sometimes up to a month to produce such a project, Jones finished in twenty-four hours. After she stenciled the outline of the black stripes onto the canvas, she hand-embroidered them with black thread. The white stripes and stars are raw canvas with black hand embroidery outlining the stars. This painstaking endeavor was visibly notable from the condition of Jones's hands and fingers, which were raw, sore, and torn.

Williams was impressed and said:

Every time she pushes the needle through the canvas, it's an act of intention that mirrors the marching, the protests, the push to form a more perfect union. It's deliberate. It's painstaking. It's long. It's hard. Each one of those stitches is a single person's story, a single person's travails. That's why we wanted to make the stitches visible.[25]

Janine Mendes-Franco conducted an interview with Jones and stated, "It's so fitting that an image created by a 'foreigner' is the symbol for TIME magazine's exploration of America's current reality: fierce nationalism in a country built by immigrants, unresolved issues around race, exploding gun violence, vast inequity."[26] The artist, Jones, was asked what she hoped to accomplish with the reassembly of the U.S. flag. She responded, "This hand-embroidered flag signifies optimism and hopes that we can all work together to build a brighter future. . . . This nation has a great impact on many other countries around the world, and so it is important that we understand the importance of equality."[27]

In a separate interview with Sara Barnes of "My Modern Met," Jones described her role as an Anglophone African-Caribbean social media influencer and said, "I consider myself an activist artist, one who uses her art to communicate with viewers and demand some kind of reaction, emotion, or conversation."[28] Jones also creates art that demonstrates an interconnectedness of women and young girls of color and their victimization of sexual abuse and trafficking. Subsequently, they are viewed as targets. In her series, *Targets Variegated*, Jones uses a round bulls-eye to emphasize the social issues of women of color being seen as sexual, physical, emotional, and verbal targets. Her unique blend of mixed media and embroidery places the image of a shooting range target in the center of the victims' faces. Her use of circular elements in the artwork showcases a bold design motif, which translates to powerful symbols. Jones stated:

I believe that Caribbean creatives and visual artists are making an effort to use symbolism, realism, patterns, and even specific color schemes that are nontraditional and that capture the raw, real truth. Art no longer serves as a pretty "cover up" but instead is the prompt for conversations surrounding race and racial injustice. In addition, some artists even feel more comfortable now exploring ideas of Black identity, beauty, pain, etc. as seen in my two series of work, "Targets Variegated" and "Layers of Identity." With these pieces, I am able to bring a Caribbean perspective that African Americans are still easily able to connect with and even those outside of the African American culture. I believe this is important to help change the perspective as people are usually drawn to new and innovative ideas that are out of the ordinary.[29]

The subjects of Jones's artwork frequently exist in a culture of silence surrounding abuse and the stigmatization of women who report abuse. The justification for abuse against women continues to perpetuate intergenerational cycles of trauma. Stigmatizing women also played a critical role in cultural attitudes toward addressing intimate partner violence, since women who seek help risk additional harm and even humiliation in their communities.[30] As the series has evolved, however, the symbols used by Jones offered an alternative meaning: Celebration of the essence of Black women who have survived despite living in a dangerous world.

Jones responded to the question about how thought and action of the Anglophone African-Caribbean artists/journalists impact the societal infrastructure of BLM radicalism and influence the African American landscape. She said:

> People view the BLM as solely a part of American culture. In reality, this issue is present almost everywhere in the world and is experienced in different ways depending on the culture of that specific region or country. As an Afro-Caribbean artist living in America, I am still affected by issues surrounding Black Lives Matter regardless of my cultural background, and so, my artwork helps to bring another voice and capture the attention of many other people in a different way. My contemporary art approach with the use of hand embroidery and mixed media paintings go above just simply having a conversation or protest. It forces you to dig deeper, see things from a different perspective and appreciate that this reality exists and there needs to be a positive change.[31]

FREDREKA SCHOUTEN

Fredreka Schouten, Anglophone African-Caribbean woman, native to the island of St. Croix, U.S. Virgin Islands, writes about the economic struggles of people of color, relative to BLM. An online article in CNN politics, "The Black Lives Matter Movement is Driving Customers to Black-owned Businesses: Owners Worry It Won't Last,"[32] presented unique perspectives of the movement—white guilt and economics in the Black community. Her story focuses on the problems faced by owners of small Black businesses during the COVID-19 pandemic juxtaposed by the social unrest underlying the racial issues in America. This situation is compounded by the economic disparity between small businesses and powerful large corporations run by wealthy entitled whites.

Schouten relates the facts behind young African American female businesswoman, Roslyn Karamoko, who struggled to keep her doors open to the public, during the COVID-19 pandemic, despite the lack of support from the government. This one situation highlights the pervasive and unequal distribution of funds that were allocated for businesses in need; Black businesses in particular were in danger of failing because many were denied funding (including the Paycheck Protection Program and the Economic Injury Disaster Loan or EIDL) designed to keep small companies afloat during the pandemic. Lending experts believed that flaws in the Paycheck Protection Program hindered small businesses owned by minorities and women from securing federal coronavirus relief.[33] "Then, came Black Lives Matter," Karamoko said, "and a rush of sales as customers raced to support Black businesses following the coast-to-coast uprising over the death of an unarmed Black man, George Floyd, under the knee of a Minneapolis police officer."[34] BLM was embraced as a national phenomenon and their message to support African American businesses resonated throughout the nation. As a result of this support, Karamoko's online business quickly tripled.

The national reckoning on race triggered by Floyd's death and COVID-19's disproportionate toll on people of color with small businesses brought fresh attention and support for Black companies and causes. Major corporate brands signaled their support for the BLM movement. Ice-cream maker Ben & Jerry called for Americans to "dismantle white supremacy." Bank of America pledged $1 billion over four years to address racial and economic inequality, Quaker Oats decided to retire its 131-year-old Aunt Jemima brand, and NASCAR banned the Confederate flag from its events and properties. On a smaller scale, social media influencers have turned over their Instagram accounts to Black business owners, and many Black-owned small restaurants and shops owned by African Americans are able to grow their business online:

> We're in the middle of a strong watershed moment, said Americus Reed, a marketing professor at the University of Pennsylvania's Wharton School. It seems like everyone is unambiguously saying, Here's where I stand. Here's where my company stands. Here's my plan to support the Black community and Black Lives Matter and social justice.[35]

In the surge of the social climate shift, and prior to the pandemic, many Americans outside of the American population became interested in the Civil Rights Movement era of the 1960s. Schouten covered another story that offered historical oversight on the Civil Rights Movement and led to the current BLM. Joanne Bland was an eleven-year-old schoolgirl in Selma, Alabama, when she marched into history, joining hundreds of activists on the Edmund Pettus Bridge for a demonstration that turned into one of the bloodiest confrontations of the Civil Rights Movement. Schouten's interview with the Alabama activist deftly described the fears of a young Black girl on the Pettus Bridge fifty-five years ago on what would be later deemed "Bloody Sunday":

Baton-wielding state troopers and horse-mounted members of the sheriff's posse, plunged into the peaceful crowd that day in March 1965, breaking bones and cracking skulls.

Bland's 14-year-old sister Linda, standing not far behind march leaders John Lewis and Hosea Williams, was struck in the face and the back of the head. "It was horrible," Bland recalls now. "There was this one lady, I don't know if the horse ran over her or if she fell, but all these years later, I can still hear the sound of her head hitting that pavement."[36]

Schouten tells a story about faith and resilience, two traits she undoubt-edly learned as an Anglophone African-Caribbean citizen in the U.S. Virgin Islands. The history recounted by Bland echoes the pain and suffering of African people of the diaspora for centuries. Bland spoke of stories she heard from her grandmother about segregation, discrimination, and racial profiling in the late 1950s during that period of American apartheid.

Blacks who wanted to register to vote were required to pay extra money labeled poll taxes and to pass literacy tests. In the state of Alabama, would-be voters were required to read aloud parts of Alabama's State Constitution and cite the exact size of Washington, D.C. as spelled out in the U.S. Constitution (10 square miles). Bland confided in news reporter Schouten that as a child, her primary concern was how to gain access to the lunch counter at Carter's Drug Store in downtown Selma:

> I wanted to sit there like those white kids and spin around on those stools and eat ice cream, she recalled. Grandmother said, Colored children can't sit at the counter, but when we get our freedom, you can do that. I became a freedom fighter the day she told me that, she said.[37]

Bland attended her first meeting of the Student Nonviolent Coordinating Committee (SNCC) at age eight. As a child, she thought the marches them-selves were fun, and the spirit of the movement was what (they) liked the most. She and her friends thought little of joining the adults headed to the bridge on that Sunday in March for what was supposed to be the first leg of a fifty-four-mile trek to the Alabama State Capitol in Montgomery to demand voting rights. The child, Bland, did not anticipate violence until she saw the police with their guns drawn. This was her introduction to a lifetime fight for social justice.

In stark comparison to this recollection, Beckles offers:

> Where there were plantation overseers there are now police officers. Through them, Black life remains prime for deletion as if on the plantation.

This Minneapolis fight was Marcus Garvey's fight; it was Martin's fight; it was Malcolm's fight; it was Marley's fight. It's a Caribbean fight and it's a global fight.[38]

USING MEDIA TO PROMOTE A
PRECOCIOUS IDEOLOGICAL STANCE

Media have become the voice of our society and subsequently reflect what and how society works. Print, electronic, and social media help inform, entertain, and educate the public. There have been enormous changes in the past two decades, which directly impact the power and authority of the African American community to exert their "voice," consequently the alliance between stateside Black media and Anglophone African-Caribbean activists is important. Disillusioned with the way the U.S. mainstream media portray marginalized communities, these individuals join with activists of color and alternative/grassroots media to serve as essential communication vehicles for significant empowerment.

It is important to consider the physical locations from the isolated islands to the crowded streets of America to understand how racism, stereotypes, and prejudices of Jim Crow America reveal a propensity to voice collective social ills that exist among people of the African diaspora.

For example, the islander who moves to America is instantly made aware of the concept of racism and racial inequality in a way that truly makes (her) a foreigner. She sees all too clearly and comprehends all too quickly that racism is the most significant challenge to the development of class consciousness in the United States.

In more than a few instances, the Anglophone African-Caribbean individual brings a precocious ideological stance to the stateside. A bond is created and commonalities are shared. Stories of injustices, discrimination, and racism are exchanged.

BLM PROMOTES A COLORFUL
AMALGAM OF TRADITIONS

Anglophone African-Caribbean people tend to align with the BLM movement and oppose perspectives taken by the status quo. Drawing on a history of social resistance, driven less by police brutality and racism and more by socioeconomic injustices, Anglophone African-Caribbean activists often use social and print media to deliver their messages. They intertwine their narratives with the history of slavery and oppression in the Caribbean and support and influence stateside protestors. This legacy of Caribbean storytelling emerged from an African oral tradition, one filled with analogies and allegories for conveying important lessons and messages and has now evolved into powerful statements of protest and prophecy.

One ripple effect of the social protests has been the denigration and defacement of symbols of Black oppression. The Caribbean, with its long history of occupation, has its own symbols of oppression to (re)consider. It is important to note that in the Caribbean, calls to rename certain places surged several months before the monument recall started in the United States. For example, King George V Park in Port of Spain, Trinidad, was renamed Nelson Mandela Park. Most regional territories have robust examples of public art that honor the slave struggle including Bussa, who led the largest slave rebellion in the history of Barbados; Cuffy, the leader of a 2,500-strong slave revolt in Guyana; and the "Redemption Song" statue in Jamaica's Emancipation Park. Throughout the Caribbean region, protests were held to remove statues that reinforced an erroneous narrative of discovery and ownership. Caribbean nations challenged the wisdom of having such statues on public display. Fictitious stories and false heroism over white discoveries incensed Anglophone African-Caribbean natives and Black Americans. Consequently, efforts by the BLM movement to embrace diversity and dismantle racism on a global and pointedly geographical scale reflect the actions taken by some Anglophone African-Caribbean people. After reportedly warning government officials through a social media post, anti-racism activists in Martinique vandalized and pulled down two statues in the spring of 2020. A statue of the controversial French figure, Josephine de Beauharnais, Napoleon's first wife, was attacked by a crowd of anti-racism demonstrators in May. Another statue of Pierre Belain d'Esnambuc, the trader who established the first French colony on Martinique in 1635, was also vandalized.[39] The protestors included young people who argued that they were insulted to be surrounded by symbols of hate and racism. Possibly impacted by actions in the Caribbean, demonstrators in the United States toppled and defaced twenty-one statues of Confederate soldiers who fought for slavery. Statues throughout southern states such as Texas, Alabama, Kentucky, South Carolina, and Mississippi were targeted.

Anglophone African-Caribbean activists have made a significant impact upon the stateside BLM movement. Activism, rebellions, unrests, protests, demonstrations, and general resistance throughout the years in the Anglophone African-Caribbean territories continue to influence the stateside BLM movement. In addition, faith and resilience exhibited by fellow members of the African diaspora in the United States impact African-Caribbean residents. A common Caribbean saying, "When the United States sneezes, the

Caribbean catches a cold," insinuates that the mainland wields a mammoth influence over the Anglophone Caribbean region. Importantly, many people with African-Caribbean heritage have played, and continue to play, active roles in the Black American socioeconomic, civil rights, and the political struggle in the United States. The far-reaching global impact of the BLM movements stridently resonates and steadfastly connects African Americans and Anglophone African-Caribbean people.

NOTES

1. Kamau Brathwaite, "Caribbean Writers and Their Art: History, the Caribbean and the Imagination (1991)," *Caribbean Writers Summer Institute Archival Video Collection*, from UMI Libraries on November 4, 2015. https://umiami.mediaspace .kaltura.com/media/Caribbean+Writers+and+Their+ArtA+History%2C+the+Car ibbean+and+the+Imagination+%281991%29/1_fxtjb11h/16168291.

2. Fredreka Schouten, "Kamala Harris' Jamaican Side and What It Means to Islanders Like Me," *CNN Politics*, August 12, 2020, https://edition.cnn.com/2020/08 /12/politics/kamala-harris-heritage/index.html.

3. Anglophone Caribbean or Anglo-Caribbean is now used in preference over the older term *British West Indies*. This includes ten independent island nations within the Commonwealth Caribbean British Overseas Territories and some mainland nations.

4. Kamau Brathwaite, *Caribbean Writers and Their Art: History*, 1991.

5. Hereafter, Black Lives Matter may be interchanged with the acronym BLM.

6. Sir Hilary Beckles, "Journey to Juneteenth: Caribbean Solidarity," *Repeating Islands*, June 19, 2020, https://repeatingislands.com/2020/06/19/sir-hilary-beckles-j ourney-to-juneteenth-caribbean-solidarity/.

7. Ibid.

8. https://blacklivesmatter.com/herstory/.

9. Hundreds more people of color have been murdered, and continue to be murdered as a result of police brutality since BLM was formed; numerous websites (https://interactive.aljazeera.com/aje/2020/know-their-names/index.html) and hashtags like #sayhername (https://www.brookings.edu/blog/how-we-rise/2 020/09/25/breonna-taylor-police-brutality-and-the-importance-of-sayhername/) are associated with BLM to keep the public informed.

10. Carl Sudder, American Historian, "Histories for Black Lives," *Organization of American Historians*, September 2020, https://www.oah.org/tah/issues/2020/history -for-black-lives/histories-for-black-lives/; Larry Buchanan, Quoctrung Bui, and Jugal K. Patel, "Black Lives Matter May Be the Largest Movement in U.S. History," *New York Times*, July 3, 2020.

11. https://blacklivesmatter.com/about/.

12. Christopher J. Lebron, *The Making of Black Lives Matter: A Brief History of An Idea* (New York: Oxford, 2017).

13. Angelique V. Nixon, "Black Lives Matter—What Does It Mean for Us in the Caribbean?" *Violence and the State, In the Diaspora*, June 25, 2020, https://intheca

ribbeandiaspora.wordpress.com/2020/06/15/black-lives-matter-what-does-it-mean-fo
r-us-in-the-caribbean/.

14. Gibbings, Wesley, "Black Lives Matter in the Caribbean Too," *Caribbean Journalism*, July 23, 2016.

15. https://www.msnbc.com/reidout.

16. Gwen Ifill, Caribbean American, hosted the PBS News Hour cable show until her death in 2016.

17. Joseph Wulfsohn, "MSNBC's Joy Reid says BLM Doesn't Riot, Blames Trump for Encouraging Violence Fueled by White Nationalist Mobs," *FOX News*, August 31, 2020, https://www.foxnews.com/media/msnbc-joy-reid-blm-doesnt-riot-blames-trump-violence-white-nationalist-mobs.

18. Ibid.

19. Alexandra Del Rosario, "Joy Reid Explains How Shift from Obama to Trump Affected White Support for Black Lives Matter," *Hollywood Reporter*, August 23, 2020, https://www.hollywoodreporter.com/news/joy-reid-white-support-black-lives-matter-obama-trump-shift-1304130.

20. Karine Jean-Pierre, *Moving Forward: A Story of Hope, Hard Work, and the Promise of America* (New York: Hanover Square Press, 2019).

21. Karine Jean-Pierre, "Karine Jean-Pierre on Her Mental Health Struggle and a Blueprint for Activism," interview by Judy Woodruff, *PBS NewsHour*, PBS, Nov 26, 2019 6:25 PM EST video, 130:650, https://www.pbs.org/newshour/show/karine-jean-pierre-on-her-mental-health-struggle-and-a-blueprint-for-activism.

22. Ibid.

23. Ibid.

24. Waxman, Olivia, "The Story Behind TIME's 'The New American Revolution' Cover," *TIME*, August 20, 2020.

25. Ibid.

26. Janine Franco-Mendes, "A Conversation with Trinidadian Nneka Jones, The Artist Who Created Compelling American Flag Image for *TIME* Magazine: Part II, GLOBAL VOICES, August 28, 2020, https://globalvoices.org/2020/08/28/nneka-jones-the-trinidadian-artist-catapulted-into-limelight-after-time-magazine-cover-talks-more-about-her-work/.

27. Ibid.

28. Ibid.

29. Nneka Jones, *Email Message to Author*, January 1, 2021.

30. Stabroek News, "Jahajee Sisters: Activism for Indo-Caribbean Feminist Futures," *In the Diaspora*, October 19, 2020, https://www.stabroeknews.com/2020/10/19/features/in-the-diaspora/jahajee-sisters-activism-for-indo-caribbean-feminist-futures/.

31. Nneka Jones, *Email Message to Author*, January 1, 2021.

32. Fredreka Schouten, "The Black Lives Matter Movement is Driving Customers to Black-owned Businesses. Owners Worry It Won't Last," *CNN Politics*, June 20, 2020.

33. Khristophe J. Brooks, "Black-Owned Businesses Headed for Disaster without Federal Aid, Poll finds," *CBS News*, October 19, 2020.

34. Fredreka Schouten, "The Black Lives Matter Movement Is Driving Customers to Black-Owned Businesses. Owners Worry It Won't Last," *CNN Politics*, June 20, 2020, https://edition.cnn.com/2020/06/20/politics/black-owned-businesses/index.html.

35. Ibid.

36. Fredreka Schouten, "She Marched in Selma as a Young Girl. Now She's Seeing History Repeat on Voting Rights," *CNN Politics*, September 25, 2020, https://edition.cnn.com/2020/09/25/politics/voting-rights-act-history-election-2020/index.html.

37. Ibid.

38. Ibid.

39. Aanchal Nigam, "Anti-Racism Activists Topple Statue of Napoleon's First Wife Josephine in Martinique," *Black Internationalist Unions*, July 31, 2020, https://abolitionjournal.org/anti-racism-activists-topple-statue-of-napoleons-first-wife-josephine-in-martinique/.

Chapter 3

The New Back-to-Africa Movement

*The Black Diaspora Seeking Opportunity
and Refuge in the Motherland*

Karl Ellis Johnson

In light of all the negative press about Africans and people of African descent from the current American president Donald Trump, people from the African Diaspora have to realize that the negative and false perceptions and stereotypes about Africans are still pervasive in America.[1] Also, they must assume that this negative and false portrayal of Africa, Africans, and African descendants must still be quite pervasive in other areas in the world, which hurts Africa and its people in terms of business, foreign relations negotiations, and sharing in world resources and political equity. Thus, Africa is subject to the above negative portrayals no matter what direction, positive or negative, America will advance to in the twenty-first century. Africans and people of the African Diaspora must become more united using practical measures such as modern technology, branding, educational collaborations, attracting vacationers, and encouraging and allowing the Diaspora to buy time-shares or even property in Africa. African nations can offer low-cost incentives such as a lottery to buy land or low(er) taxes to encourage the African Diaspora to enter into business venture partnerships with Africans on the continent.

African governments should consider removing and radically revising visa restrictions to support those from the African Diaspora with skills and positive intentions to move forward in the twenty-first century. Non-native peoples (e.g., China and their nationals) have much more access to Africa than many people from the African Diaspora who have education, skills, and resources to spend in an African nation.[2] For example, some African Diasporic Americans with financial means willingly spend thousands of dollars for a time-share in Florida and visits to Disney Land where "Stand your Ground" laws continue to kill innocent Blacks as if they are still stuck in the nightmarish Jim Crow Era. Others continue to pay for lavish trips to Paris, London, and other European destinations when it is clear (with the rise of racist nationalists' movements in Europe) that there is both fact and propaganda to support the lack of interest in the presence and business activities of Africans and African descendants. In the twenty-first century, these kinds of actions and behaviors proliferate as some European nations continue to come into Africa (stemming from the 1400s) uninvited to exploit the "Motherland."

Others in the African Diaspora who claim to have made it in America continue to gather in Black historic enclaves to feel a false sense of security in order to convince themselves that things have holistically gotten better for Blacks. The question, then, becomes why not consider sub-Saharan Africa with beautiful weather and friendlier hosts in which to spend Black money, return to American from engaging in a positive cultural experience while building up the African economies? And, importantly, why not consider how such movement could reduce "African intra-tensions among our people," and eradicate the negative myths about Africans spread through the ignorance of mental colonization and slavery. Such a movement could also provide Africans living on the continent (sub-Saharan Africa) the opportunities to build stronger relationships with those people of the African Diaspora. With these questions and despite the complexity of challenges with such contemporary movements and connectivity with Africa, I provide the following assertions for consideration that many Black peoples are currently in the beginning stages of a twenty-first century "New Back-to-Africa Movement."

To support my assertions in this chapter, I will provide evidence of this movement currently taken hold and look at the prospects of its long-term sustainability, discuss the impact of "Popular Culture" in promoting the "New Back-to-Africa Movement," and include interviews with Black Americans who went back to Africa, and then give my final reflections and summation. Thus, my main argument is that we are currently in the midst of "The New Back-to-Africa Movement" that seems more sustainable than any of those previously in the past because it has popular support from Black musical performers and film/movie and pop stars bolstered by the rise of social media and super technology.

Additionally, widely accessible cell phone technology allows even the economically poor in Africa and the Diaspora to access and utilize social media to promote this "New Back-to-Africa Movement" cost efficiently with social platforms, such as YouTube, Facebook, and Instagram, to name a few. It is important for me to note that this movement is not a fad as "The New Back-to-Africa Movement" is currently in implementation and can be further designed to sustain and defy time and space both psychologically and physically for African Diasporic peoples to create and maintain deeper connections than ever before with Africans on the continent. One important consideration is how this can happen via travel. The successful Ethiopian Airlines, which replaced the many failed independent African airlines that did not make it out of the 1980s, is a major successful, internationally reputable airline with reasonable prices and a sustainable business model that can take Africans throughout the Diaspora and back and forth to the continent for the foreseeable future.[3]

In November 2020, the African Diaspora Development Institute, a new international investment organization founded by former African Union ambassador Dr. Arikana Chihombori-Quao, made an agreement with Ghanaian president Nana Akufo-Addo to cede the Cape Coast region of Ghana to build a modern city of return for the African Diaspora nicknamed amply the Wakanda project.[4] Although fictional, the Ryan Coogler directed *Black Panther* movie (2018) changed the psychology of a twenty-first-century younger generation of how they view Africa as more modern, advanced, and livable than previously thought and advanced by the American media. Thus, I argue that "the New Back-to-Africa Movement" is a now a viable African Diasporic movement in the twenty-first century.

It is both impractical and unrealistic to call for a Marcus Garveyesque Back-to-Africa Movement. It's not the 1920s, and the political and social conditions of both Africans and the African Diaspora have changed in the twenty-first century.[5] In addition, previous Back-to-Africa Movements before Marcus Garvey were always extremely vulnerable to the realities of extreme racism and white supremacy.[6] I am arguing, at this juncture, that internet and social media have spawned the beginnings of "The New Back-to-Africa," which has educational and political consciousness elements that can improve the well-being of the whole individual and African Diaspora. The current technology along with more efficient air travel for goodwill cultural visits both to and from Africa can work out economically and bridge both space and time. As a consequence, "The New Back-to-Africa Movement" is not only a physical movement but also a shift in a mindset that has been broad enough in popular culture to argue that "the New Back-to-Africa Movement" is just as profound psychologically as it is physically/geographically.

Interestingly, as well, is that this New Back-to-Africa Movement has not been solely guided by an "educated elite" but has been led much more, instead, by popular Hip Hop/R&B and Afro-Beats musicians who have made travel and performances in Africa just as important as in America/United States. If the popular female rapper Cardi B and her husband Offset can travel to Nigeria and Ghana both to vacation and perform, it must be alright for "all African Diasporians" of various socio economic back grounds to see Africa as a realistic destination of progress and renewal.[7] Furthermore, the prior success of Akon (Senegal) and now Davido (Nigeria) who are both hip-hop artists from West Africa Heritage who helped to merge rap with "Afro-Beats" has broken open doors where their music is enjoyed worldwide, and even more so in overseas markets in the Americas.[8] In addition, no one cannot argue that the Black Panther (2018) movie has not had a profound impact on how this generation perceives Africa as more advanced than previously perceived, thus building on the New Back-to-Africa Movement.[9]

Some other trends that have opened Africa to its Diaspora have been the tangible and measurable rise of African immigration from the continent in this generation to America and other Western destinations. This has helped as a counter-narrative to the negative stereotypes against travel and people from Africa.[10] Although the negative and false perceptions and stereotypes about Africans are still present in Black American society, the fact remains that many African immigrants come from the continent with important skills and family support that has translated into their greater success in our major universities and colleges.[11] Intra-tensions among immigrant and nonimmigrant groups are indeed present, but the pervasiveness of white supremacy in the West and in America in particular has mitigated it somewhat over the past generation enough for cooperative interactions of African immigrants and Black Americans against American racism. The case of Amadou Diallo, a hardworking African immigrant from Guinea West Africa who was murdered by police in 2000, rallied the entire African American population to push back against this type of racism.[12]

The African immigration currently differs from the destinations of past African immigration being narrowly focused on northeastern cities such as New York and Philadelphia. This shift has exposed the old traditional Black American population in the South with the prospects of interacting with Africans from the continent at work, school, and as neighbors especially in Middle Class settings. Such a shift, however, cannot yet be tangibly measured on how it really facilitates the "New Back-to-Africa Movement" to take place. Interestingly, African immigrants are more likely to have a noticeable presence in Texas in the Houston and Dallas metro areas and in Georgia throughout the Atlanta metro area than in New York City. Also, the metropolitan Washington D.C./Maryland/Virginia surrounding areas have been historically considered the Upper South and large numbers of African immigrants have made it their home within this current generation.[13]

In twenty-first-century popular culture, there is, perhaps, no bigger movie star than Idris Elba whose mother is Ghanaian and father is Sierra Leonean; he has harnessed the unique chameleon-like qualities to be a favorite pop icon among Black Americans in portrayals in shows like *The Wire*, movies such as *Daddy's Little Girls*, and *Obsessed* (with Beyoncé playing his wife). At the same time, Elba's international African Diaspora following also is through the roof. It is not clear if most long-time Black Americans even identified Idris Elba as having both parents from West Africa until recent times when stereotypes of being from Africa have subsided (somewhat). Also, the less well-known case of hip-hop artist Chamillionaire (aka Hakeem Seriki, born to a Muslim Nigerian father and grew up in metro Houston, Texas Metro) came out with the popular hip-hop song "Ridin" in 2005 that fits in with the pervasive belief in African American experiences and culture of the dangers of being profiled by racist police, aka "Driving While Black," and the consequences that could befall the driver of color.[14] It is doubtful that most of his listeners could discern that he had Nigerian African heritage; he had street credibility as a hip-hop artist, viewed as a Black American with the underlying knowledge that highlighting his connection to sub-Sahara Africa was not instrumental to his career. Such a posture was arguably the case of Idris Elba early in his career. Currently a shift in popular culture now arguably supports the opposite for artists with African ancestry, as it is viewed positively to highlight one's ancestral association with Black Africa as a badge of honor. "Savage" (aka Sheyaa Bin Abraham-Joseph) openly practices the Ifa African Religion and "Sheck Wes" (Khadimou Rassoul Cheikh Fall) now wear their African Heritage on their sleeve. This profound shift in popular culture exemplars and motifs is one of the major underpinnings of "The New Back-to-Africa Movement."

The Year of Return campaign by Ghana has been central to "The New Back-to-Africa Movement" pushing it pass the boundaries of being a fad. This return has raised the attention of mainstream media outlets that have been known to treat sub-Saharan African news as marginal, relegated to low viewership with, at best, periodic weekend specials. CNN recently reported that *The Year of Return* has been so successful that it has changed the face of how we view Africa as a viable place to visit and enjoy beyond exoticism and safari.[15] More importantly, there are a rising number of sub-Saharan nations beyond South Africa, which can handle and accommodate the casual visitor from the African Diaspora with hotels, restaurants, and shopping areas to facilitate a counter-narrative against "African primitiveness and perpetual underdevelopment." This previous belief was the bulwark of white supremacists myths that had prevented such a physical movement by those in the African Diaspora in the past. The nation of Ghana is an economic model that illustrates that many African nations have been experiencing economic growth in the twentieth and twenty-first centuries while many other places in the West have experienced stagnation.[16] As important, *The Year of Ghana* campaign was featured in Black American women popular magazines such as *Essence* that now has a footprint in social media throughout the Diaspora. This news in magazines of interest and support to the Black American communities culturally signals that "The New Back-to-Africa Movement" is here to stay among the African Diaspora and is now solidly part of Black popular culture.[17] Social media and smart (cell) phone usage has allowed even the poorest Africans on the Continent and the struggling persons of color throughout the Diaspora to feel a part of this movement.

YouTube sites currently abound in showing the realities of Africa's development with examples of those who have traveled to Africa with a good experience. Black American businessman Kwame Lawson on his YouTube channel epitomized this positive outlook in his video dialogue.[18] What is also important with social media platforms like YouTube is that they track the viewership worldwide; even a relatively unknown Black American such as Kwame Lawson was able to garner 46,791 views on a physical/geographic Back-to-Africa movement. Another example prevails with a Black U.S. family who bought land in the Gambia to escape all the intractable racism in the United States; they have a popular YouTube channel titled "Black Acres of the Gambia." They offer practical ways to thrive in Africa for Black Americans within the context of a loving family experience.[19] These examples illustrate the traction that the New Back-to-Africa movement has made within the Diasporic communities. Additionally, its beginning stages of development will be difficult to halt as the available informational technology has created viable and accessible social media connectivity to Black Diasporic communities worldwide.

Adding more to the credibility of the New Back-to-Africa Movement has been the substantive number of high-profile stars that have visited Africa for the Year of Return, a culminating event with some being granted African citizenship. Ghana has led this effort for some time with the granting of 126 people from the Diaspora, citizenship in 2019, but it has not stopped there.[20] Southern (Atlanta, Georgia) hip-hop artist and movie star Ludacris recently went back to Gabon, the homeland of his wife Eudoxie Mbouguiengue, and was granted citizenship there.[21] The fact that these citizenship grants are now visible on social media and garner so much attention is a major shift. President Nana Akufo-Addo said those conferred with the citizenship join a generation of Diasporians, including civil rights activist William Edward Burghardt "W. E. B." Du Bois and American poet Maya Angelou who lived in the country.[22] Until recently, however, never has a granting of citizenship to sub-Saharan African nations garnered so much attention and admiration. Famous hip-hop artists have offered to move from America and gain citizenship as a Nigerian due to their frustrations with American bipartisan politics that have rarely addressed issues seriously and satisfactorily to Black Diasporans. Cardi B the most popular hip-hop women star on the planet mentioned in regard to Donald Trump foreign policies that she was filing for her Nigerian Citizenship.[23]

In addition, the list of stars that have come to Ghana for its Year of Return campaign is extensive. Along with Steve Harvey and Idris Elba rubbing shoulders with supermodel Naomi Campbell, TV sports presenter Mike

Hill, and author Luvvie Ajayi, many Black celebrities made their way to Ghana. Social media provided significant coverage of this event, giving it widespread attention throughout the African Diaspora and, indeed, the world. From notable names such as Bozama Saint John, Boris Kodjoe and Nicole Ari Parker, who cohosted Essence's Full Circle Festival, to everyday people, Black travelers were excited to return "home" to Ghana to celebrate heading into the New Year. On social media, even casual scrolling revealed glimpses of Ghanaian red, gold, and green flags that flew high above popular events like Afrochella, Afro Nation, and Detty Rave where artists like Davido and Rick Ross performed. Tina Knowles (Beyoncé's mother), rapper and actor Ludacris, and actress Erika Alexander were spotted around town.[24]

Interestingly, it was still not certain if with the promotion of the Year of Return campaign in Ghana would be lifted to another level with star power. Nevertheless, there is no doubt that President Nana Akufo-Addo of Ghana astutely planned it well.[25]A well thought-out tourism plan was put in place by Ghana officials as early as 2013.[26] Social media and star power brought it to new heights and its popularity is now the bulwark of the New Back-to-Africa Movement. Ghana previously put together a tourism development plan that seeks to increase the annual number of tourists to Ghana from one million to eight million per year by 2027. Ghana's *travel* industry is projected to raise $8.3 billion a year by 2027, plus associated benefits, according to the plan.[27] This is no small feat and soon other sub-Saharan African government officials will consider this success from its coverage in reputable and influential financial mainstream magazines such as *Forbes*.[28] Although Africa and the Diaspora are still arguably under the last remnants of Neocolonialism, "The New Back-to-Africa Movement" looks viable and is here to stay.

An important question that must be grappled with is whether this "New Back-to-Africa Movement" is sustainable or doomed to succumbing to white supremacy machinations as previous "Back-to-Africa Movements" have been subject to in the past. We are most familiar with the Back-to-African Movement led by the leaders Edward Blyden, Marcus Garvey, W. E. B. Du Bois, and Pan-Africanists Movements along with Trinidadian Henry Sylvester Williams and George Padmore. While documented, many people are unaware that Marcus Garvey was never able to set foot on the Continent of Africa as he caught the eye of Western colonial powers, and was accused of mail fraud or tax evasive, which was commonly used by racist American officials to rid themselves of so called trouble makers.[29] A more less well-known modern Africanist and Pan Africanist extraordinaire who ended up exiled in Ghana with W. E. B. DuBois was W. Alphaeus Hunton who was much more knowledgeable with data and details on how the Western powers who destroyed their nations in World War II planned to loot and exploit sub-Saharan African rich resources to restore themselves to power. Seen as a serious threat by CIA and other Western allies, Hunton wisely chose to live out his life in exile in various African nations just getting their independence. Interestingly, Hunton points out directly how Great Britain rebuilt London and paid off its tremendous war debts to the United States by using Southern African nations' mineral resources and exploiting Black African labor. France who had to rebuilt Paris did a similar "thiefing" using its various colonial holdings aptly named Francophone Africa.[30]

Other Back-to-Africa Movements occurred in the nineteenth century mainly to Liberia and Sierra Leone, West Africa. This movement was first put into place by Black sailor captain and businessman Paul Cuffe who sailed to Sierra Leone in 1810, which was then a barely established British beachhead colony viewed as a place to rid itself of Blacks residing in London. Also, this was seen as place to live for some Black Loyalists who sided with Lord Dunmore against the American colonists during the Revolution; to get their freedom, they ended up in Sierra Leone as well. Paul Cuffe, however, astutely turned his movements into an opportunity to offer oppressed free Black Americans who experienced Jim Crow anywhere an alternative to living in the Northern states. In fact, in his voyages during 1815–1816, he took nine Black families who voluntarily left the Jim Crow conditions of New England to live in Sierra Leone.[31]

Edward Blyden's granddaughter Dr. Nemata Blyden, professor of History at George Washington University, is today's authority on historic back to Africa movements.[32] Nemata Blyden has an online resource titled "In Motion: The African American Migration Experience" and has written a number of articles on the topic.[33] Dr. Blyden thoroughly covers the Back-to-Africa histories of important African American leaders such as Alexander Crummell, Martin Robison Delany, Henry Highland Garnett, and organizations like the African Civilization Society and the controversial American Colonization Society (ACS). Dr. Blyden argues that the migration of African Americans in what has come to be known as the "Back-to-Africa," or colonization movement was largely influenced by events and conditions in the United States:

> Emigration and emigration sentiments originated in the perception that oppressive conditions within the United States would not allow African Americans to live in a racism-free nation, enjoying the equality and liberty promised to all. Free Blacks in the nineteenth century frequently reconsidered their position as American citizens, while slaves hoped for emancipation and the ability to live their lives free of oppression. Another factor was the desire and determination of Black Americans to establish separate societies or nations that would be self-governing. Throughout the nineteenth century, therefore, small groups of African Americans left the shores of the United States, and Africa was the

site most often proposed. . . . This missionary spirit permeated the colonization movement.[34]

During the late eighteenth and the nineteenth centuries, Blacks in America faced many challenges. The South emerged as an extensive slave economy, and increasingly across the South, legislation was passed against the manumission of slaves. According to Dr. Blyden, as slave conditions deteriorated so did the opportunities for the small population of free Blacks living in the Southern states. Any ambiguity that had existed about the status of free Blacks in the South during the colonial period was gone entirely. The necessity for racial subordination in a slave society ensured that all those of color would be restricted economically, politically, and socially. When economic opportunity could be found, it was often limited. Although free Blacks in the North had a little more autonomy than their counterparts in the South, they, too, faced Jim Crow legislation and racism. Northern Blacks faced restrictions on voting while the justice system gave them little solace. By the 1830s, the prospects for free Blacks were grim. State and federal regulations, social customs, and popular pressure had relegated them permanently to a lower social, economic, and political position. The federal government passed the Fugitive Slave Act of 1850 and sanctioned the capture of a Black person anywhere in the United States.[35]

Edward Wilmot Blyden was a major spokesman for colonization and emigration to Liberia. He developed a close personal relationship with Liberia. Having immigrated to that colony in 1851, Blyden was influential in the emigration movement. He was an eloquent spokesman for the ACS, which put him at odds with some Black nationalists but especially with those African Americans who opposed colonization entirely. In his frequent writings, speeches, and visits to the United States, Blyden encouraged African Americans to immigrate to Liberia.[36] He also subscribed to the view that African Americans would bring progressive "civilization" to Africa and saw the positive role they could have in Liberia:

> And I am persuaded that when Liberia shall have passed through the struggles of infancy and the necessary drawbacks incidental to national inexperience, the regions beyond will be rapidly filled up with a thriving population composed of a fusion of American Blacks with the aborigines. And please hold it up continually as an axiom that there can never be any proper or healthful development of national life on that coast without the aborigines. This you must inculcate upon every emigrant you send out. They cannot transplant America to Africa and keep it America still.[37]

Many of the Black nationalists called for the settling of qualified, professional Blacks who could help develop the fledgling colony. Although Blyden was to qualify the type of African Americans suitable for expatriation to Liberia, he nevertheless saw the importance that all of them could play. In 1890, he supported a Congressional bill that would have provided transportation for any African American who wanted to move out of the South to another country. Several U.S. Senators supported the possibility of many Blacks leaving the country.[38]

Bishop Henry McNeal Turner was perhaps the most outspoken person for Black emigration in the late nineteenth century. At his urging, small numbers of African Americans, mainly poor Southern farmers, migrated to Liberia. These people, eager to leave the country in the past decade of the nineteenth century, experienced great hardships in their endeavor and sought passage wherever they could. Several organizations were created to encourage migration. In November 1891, the Liberian Emigration Company was formed. Seventeen people from Atlanta, Georgia, went to Liberia under its auspices in June 1893. Another forty-two left in March 1894.[39]

Unlike in Marcus Garvey's time in the twentieth century, when his Black star Liners to Africa and business ventures would be doomed by colonial white supremacy and the precursor to the FBI, in the twenty-first century, several independent African nations have their own airline businesses to travel worldwide. Most notable is Ethiopian Airlines, referenced earlier in this chapter, that not only boasts a twenty-first century modern plane fleet and airport in Addis Abba but also most importantly has a sustainable business model independent of European stopovers and fueling stations that regularly fly people (at reasonable prices) from the Diaspora in the Americas to most major cities in sub-Saharan Africa. Ethiopian Airlines, already a well-respected International Carrier, continues to expand at a rapid pace.[40] Thus, the ability for Africans and its Diasporic peoples now to travel externally and internally to physically visit each other without the past intrigue caused by colonial influence provides a positive role in buffering the New Back-to-Africa Movement. Most of the Diaspora Middle Class and College Travel Abroad Students currently can be on the African continent in most sub-Saharan nations within forty-eight hours of air travel. The fact that a sub-Saharan nation has a successful airline and pilots with modern fleets further decimates the perception of the underdevelopment of Africa.

Perhaps the most influential force in promoting the idea of the New Back-to-Africa Movement in the twenty-first century was Ryan Coogler's *Black Panther* (2018) movie.[41] Possibly no other popular culture genre has done more for promoting Africa, connecting it to modernity, and advancing progress toward challenging the pervasive concepts of African primitiveness and under development. Although fictional, the movie directed by Ryan Coogler is filled with metaphors that involve both past, present, time, and space, which address the African Diasporic peoples/ strained relationship with their estranged African relatives. This film interestingly did not focus on slavery or the white colonizer but rather on why those of the African Diaspora are not cooperating more to improve and advance all those within the Diaspora. In summary, the message forward is that Black Africans and Black African Diasporic peoples can no longer afford to leave anyone behind. Although both entertaining and subliminal in its messages, one clear theme that resonated in the movie audience is that "Wakanda" the secretly hidden Black African Homeland of the Black Panther purposely hid its advanced technology and skills as a race of people in order to protect them from an outside world, which was filled with generational strife and danger. This popular movie seen by hundreds of millions of people worldwide has arguably done more to promote sub-Saharan Africa and remove its stereotypes than any possible platform that could have been devised, consumed, and enjoyed by a massive audience. Just as Jackie Robinson's crossing the color barrier in the most popular sport baseball did for promoting civil rights on a large popular scale,[42] Coogler's *Black Panther* movie has promoted the idea that Black African nations have advanced and have skilled people that will regularly contribute to the world in the present and future. At times, this philosophy and genre have been referred to as Afrofuturism.[43] This does not mean that the movie does not have its critics as Coogler inserted many metaphors that could be interpreted various ways.

Ironically, the *Black Panther* movie might have opened wounds exposing the tensions and misunderstandings between the Africans on the continent that recently immigrated to the West by choice in the past twenty years[44] and the Older African Diaspora that was forced usually by enslavement to work in the Western Hemisphere under the must inhumane conditions.[45] Liberia and its sister colony Sierra Leone, although in Africa, are symbolic of these tensions as modern nation-states created with a mixture of the Africans already there, recaptives from other West African nations, and some misguided, psychologically distressed African Diasporans who either chose or were forced to return back to Africa. This latter group (for the most part) were distressed Blacks influenced by Western racist educational and religious institutions and denigrated by the chattel slave system in the New World.[46]

I recently had the opportunity to interview college students from the African American Diaspora about their Travel Aboard experience to Ghana, and it seems that this new generation will look at Africa much differently than some previous generations. I gave the students three questions to answer to assess their views of Africa: (1) Why did you decide to start traveling to Ghana? (2) Would you consider working in Ghana fulltime if the right opportunity came up? (3) Would you consider becoming a permanent citizen of Ghana and quitting America for good, and what would be your personal reasons for doing so?

Ms. Al-Shakinah Campbell, a senior at Ramapo College of New Jersey, traveled abroad to Ghana in spring 2019 and now works at Princeton University. Here is given her reflections on her life-changing experience:

1) Why did you decide to start traveling to Ghana?

"I decided to start traveling back to Ghana for reasons that contributed to my experience during my first visit. The first being the sense of belonging I got from the people. Reflecting back to how I felt when entering establishments, it was nothing short of feeling at *home*. The people were welcoming, and the idea of worrying about if 'I will fit in' or 'be seen as an outcast' had not crossed my mind once during my two-week stay. Comparatively, a feeling I often get when being 'home' in the United States. The second reason beyond me feeling a sense of belonging is seeing the opportunity to help others. Specifically, in any area regarding education, infrastructure development, or simply products and services that could enhance the inhabitants of the country's quality of living. Knowing that I possess a plethora of skills that can be useful in helping these areas far more than I do in the United States, pulls me in that direction to utilize my skills and exercises my abilities to their full extent while simultaneously challenging myself."[47]

2) Would you consider working in Ghana fulltime if the right opportunity came up?

"I would definitely consider working there fulltime if the right opportunity arose because I am willing to adjust the lifestyle I currently have in the states. Additionally, it would be an opportunity for me to live without constantly being under the pressure of racism woven into the structure of society, to define the Black American experience in the United States. To add on, not having the pressure of being scrutinized if you decide not to take the traditional route of wanting to adapt to the hustle and bustle lifestyle bred by capitalism. Consequently, limiting people from building genuine connections with others due to the scarcity of free time." [48]

3) Would you consider becoming a permanent citizen of Ghana and quitting America for good, and what would be your personal reasons for doing so?

"I would be open to a multiple or dual citizenship in America and Ghana only because I have family in the United States and due to the current political climate of government placing restrictions on the flexibility of others entering and leaving the country. I would definitely become a fulltime citizen in the country of Ghana while maintaining my citizenship in the United States to have the freedom to exit and enter the country anytime to visit family and friends."[49]

Mr. Stephan Lally, as a Sophomore and Junior at Ramapo College, and president of the Student Government Association, went to Ghana Travel Abroad multiple times from 2017 to 2019. His reflections on his life changing experience are as follows:

1) Why did you decide to start traveling to Ghana?

"I started traveling to Ghana because of the partnership between Ramapo and KNUST. At the time the subsidized price was too good to turn down for a trip of that length; little did I know I would return to the country for additional visits. I am also Jamaican, so I did have interest to see if there were similarities between Jamaican and Ghanaian culture."[50]

2) Would you consider working in Ghana fulltime if the right opportunity came up?

"I would work and live in Ghana fulltime if the right opportunity arose. But I do feel like Jersey is home to me, so I could not be in Ghana for too long."[51]

3) Would you consider becoming a permanent citizen of Ghana and quitting America for good, and what would be your personal reasons for doing so?

"I would not. I love Ghana, the culture, the food, the people, and the weather. I would do dual citizenship, but in my heart, I could not just leave America behind."[52]

Many views of Africa have changed in more positive directions as a result of popular culture and travel abroad opportunities for African Americans. For many young Black adults, Africa is no longer seen pervasively through Western eyes as the "Dark Continent." If anything, "Dark" now means *cool* and that Africa is a place that Black Americans can have opportunities to make a future living or at least visit. The West is no longer factually or perceptually the only viable land with the promise of opportunity (this includes the Americas and Western Europe).

Will African Americans/Blacks of the African Diaspora continue to accept second-class citizenship for the next generation?

NOTES

1. "Trump Alarms Lawmakers with Disparaging Words for Haiti and Africa," *New York Times*, January 11, 2018; "Uganda: 'Shithole' Countries—Is This a True Description of Developing Nations?," *AllAfrica.com*, January 26, 2018, http://all africa.com/stories/201801260085.html; "The African Union Finally Wakes Up to Trump," *AllAfrica.com*, January 17, 2018, http://allafrica.com/stories/201801180122 .html; "Daughters of African Immigrants Use the Stage to Tell of Two Worlds," *New York Times*, January 24, 2018.

2. The ambassador from the African Union Dr. Arikana Chihombori-Quao has made this point a number of times. See https://www.youtube.com/watch?v=WMC sQhMmgD8&t=1319s.

3. "Ethiopian Airlines to Start Building New $5 Billion Airport This Year: CEO," *Reuters.com*, https://www.reuters.com/article/us-ethiopia-airlines-airport-idUSKBN1ZE1W3.

4. Please see the African Diaspora Development Institute website for more details at https://ouraddi.org/.

5. Ramla Bandele, "Understanding African Diaspora Political Activism: The Rise and Fall of the Black Star Line," Journal of Black Studies 40, no. 4 (2010): 745–761.

6. Nemata A. I. Blyden, *African Americans and Africa: A New History* (New Haven: Yale University Press, 2019); Joseph E. Harris, "African Diaspora Studies: Some International Dimensions," *A Journal of Opinion* 24, no. 2 (1996): 6–8; 27–32; Edmund T. Gordon and Mark Anderson, "The African Diaspora: Toward an Ethnography of Diasporic Identification," *The Journal of American Folklore* 112, no. 445 (1999): 282–296; Robin D. G. Kelley, "But a Local Phase of a World Problem: Black History's Global Vision, 1883–1950," *The Journal of American History* 86, no. 3 (1999): 1045–1077; Paul Tiyambe Zeleza. "Rewriting the African Diaspora: Beyond the Black Atlantic," *African Affairs* 104, no. 414 (2005): 35–68; Obioma Nnaemeka, "Re-imagining the Diaspora: History, Responsibility, and Commitment in an Age of Globalization," *Dialectical Anthropology* 31, no. 1/3 (2007): 127–141; V. P. Franklin, "Introduction: Explorations within the African Diaspora," *The Journal of African American History* 95, no. 2 (2010): 151–156; Krista Thompson, "A Sidelong Glance: The Practice of African Diaspora Art History in the United States," *Art Journal* 70, no. 3 (2011): 6–31.

7. Cardi B. the most popular hip-hop woman star on the planet mentioned in regard to Donald Trump foreign policies that she was filing for her Nigerian Citizenship. See *NYDailynews.com*, https://www.nydailynews.com/snyde/ny-cardi-b-nigeria-citizenship-memes-are-fire-20200109-nyw4khu3zvf6xgrrgl3zoys6da-story.html; *CNN.COM*, https://www.cnn.com/2019/12/09/africa/cardi-b-moments-in-africa/index.html; "Everybody and their Momma was in Ghana from the Holidays," *Essence.com*, https://www.essence.com/lifestyle/travel/ghana-nye-.2019/.

8. "Akon & William Talk about the Rise of Afrobeats for the Questions," *Okay Africa*, https://www.okayafrica.com/akon-will-i-am-afrobeats-questions/, 2016; "How Davido became a Hit-Akon," *Punch*, https://punchng.com/video-how-davido-became-a-hit-akon/, 2019.

9. Carvell Wallace, "Why 'Black Panther' is a Defining Moment for Black America," *The New York Times Magazine*, Febuary 2018, https://www.nytimes.com/2018/02/12/magazine/why-black-panther-is-a-defining-moment-for-black-america.html.

10. Pew Research, "International Migration from Sub-Saharan Africa has Grown Dramatically Since 2010," https://www.pewresearch.org/fact-tank/2018/02/28/international-migration-from-sub-saharan-africa-has-grown-dramatically-since-2010/; Pew Research, "A Rising Share of the U.S. Black Population Is Foreign Born 9 Percent

Are Immigrants; and While Most Are from the Caribbean, Africans Drive Recent Growth," https://www.pewsocialtrends.org/2015/04/09/a-rising-share-of-the-u-s-b lack-population-is-foreign-born/.

11. Pew Research, "Sub-Saharan African Immigrants in the U.S. Are Often More Educated Than Those in Top European Destinations: Sub-Saharan Immigrants in the United States are Also More Highly Educated than U.S. Native-Born Population," https://www.pewresearch.org/global/2018/04/24/sub-saharan-african -immigrants-in-the-u-s-are-often-more-educated-than-those-in-top-european-destin ations/.

12. *New York Magazine*, https://nymag.com/intelligencer/2019/02/after-the-nypd-killing-of-amadou-diallo-whats-changed.html.

13. Carlos Echeverria-Estrada and Jeanne Batalova, "Sub-Saharan African Immigrants in the United States," *Migration Policy Institute*, November 6, 2019, https ://www.migrationpolicy.org/article/sub-saharan-african-immigrants-united-states.

14. "What Ever Happened to Chamillionaire?," 2017, http://mikesdailyjukebox. com/whatever-happened-chamillionaire/.

15. "How Ghana's Historic Homecoming is changing Africa," *CNN* online, https://www.cnn.com/travel/article/ghana-historic-homecoming-intl/index.html?fbc lid=IwAR2SRgN2uvSnlr9GhATOn2z5bBcW9w81gBXqHEimsEl8Hy_NDlYjdG 1o5VA.

16. "Ghana Among Africa's Fastest Growing Economies," https://m.peacefmonl ine.com/pages/business/economy/202001/399601.php?fbclid=IwAR0zt2_X4alZ AXjVK0_sXg8c7XVtcAUyDetWRq17o435m9S9NpCSIk4wxRA.

17. "Everybody and their Momma was in Ghana from the Holidays," *Essence* online, https://www.essence.com/lifestyle/travel/ghana-nye-2019/.

18. Kwame Lawson, "Africa Diaspora, Decade to Returning to Mighty Ghana," *YouTube*, 46,791 viewers, December 15, 2019, https://www.youtube.com/watch?v =onvjN2ZcAdk&feature=share&fbclid=IwAR1ppbA2oeLiGKiKvmCwUVFGCwpr p7iWVpd8l4mHKnt50izbENk24ZRP1OM.

19. Black Acres of the Gambia, *YouTube* Channel, https://www.youtube.com/c hannel/UCh7jmDz5MGZMvbZAt74NySg and its various family members spin offs.

20. "Ghana Makes 126 People from the Diaspora Citizens as Part of Year of Return Celebrations," *CNN* online, https://edition.cnn.com/2019/11/29/africa/ghana -foreign-nationals-citizenship/index.html.

21. "Rapper Ludacris Embraces African Identity with New Gabon Citizenship," *CNN* online, https://amp-cnn-com.cdn.ampproject.org/v/s/amp.cnn.com/cnn/2020 /01/06/africa/ludacris-gabon-citizenship/index.html?usqp=mq331AQCKAE%3D& amp_js_v=0.1&fbclid=IwAR2exC-M34utf1VAAf3iL5IGb9dFzId03_zzE-cHtlJ_ GEHT8JcWC6RgEZw#referrer=https%3A%2F%2Fwww.google.com&amp_tf=Fro m%20%251%24s&ampshare=https%3A%2F%2Fwww.cnn.com%2F2020%2F01% 2F06%2Fafrica%2Fludacris-gabon-citizenship%2Findex.html.

22. *CNN* online, December 29, 2019, https://edition.cnn.com/2019/11/29/africa/ ghana-foreign-nationals-citizenship/index.html.

23. *Daily News* online, https://www.nydailynews.com/snyde/ny-cardi-b-nigeria-ci tizenship-memes-are-fire-20200109-nyw4khu3zvf6xgrrgl3zoys6da-story.html; *CNN*

online, December 9, 2019, https://www.cnn.com/2019/12/09/africa/cardi-b-moments-in-africa/index.html.

24. *Essence* online, "Everybody and their Momma was in Ghana from the Holidays," https://www.essence.com/lifestyle/travel/ghana-nye-2019/.

25. *CNN* online, https://edition.cnn.com/travel/article/ghana-year-of-return-tourism-intl/index.html.

26. *Ghana Tourism Development Plan*, http://www.ghana.travel/wp-content/uploads/2016/11/Ghana-Tourism-Development-Plan.pdf.

27. Ibid.

28. Meghan McCormick, "How To Spark A Global Movement: Ghana's 'Year of Return' Welcomes 1M Visitors," *Forbes* online, December 10, 2019, https://www-forbes-com.cdn.ampproject.org/v/s/www.forbes.com/sites/meghanmccormick/2019/12/10/how-to-spark-a-global-movement-ghanas-year-of-return-welcomes-1m-visitors/amp/?usqp=mq331AQCKAE%3D&amp_js_v=0.1#referrer=https%3A%2F%2Fwww.google.com&amp_tf=From%20%251%24s&ampshare=https%3A%2F%2Fwww.forbes.com%2Fsites%2Fmeghanmccormick%2F2019%2F12%2F10%2Fhow-to-spark-a-global-movement-ghanas-year-of-return-welcomes-1m-visitors%2F%23referrer.

29. Ramla Bandele, "Understanding African Diaspora Political Activism: The Rise and Fall of the Black Star Line," Journal of Black Studies 40, no. 4 (2010): 745–761.

30. W. Alphaeus Hunton, *Decision in Africa* (International Publishers, Co., Inc., 1957).

31. Kwame Anthony Appiah and Henry Louis Gates, Jr., eds., *Africana: The Encyclopedia of the African and African American Experience* (New York: Basic Books & Perseus Books, 1999).

32. Nemata A.I. Blyden, *African Americans and Africa: A New History* (New Haven: Yale University Press, 2019).

33. Nemata A.I. Blyden, *In Motion: The African American Migration Experience*, http://www.inmotionaame.org/migrations/topic.cfm;jsessionid=f830478571254854203902?migration=4&topic=1&bhcp=1.

34. Ibid.

35. Ibid.

36. Ibid.

37. Ibid.

38. Ibid.

39. Kenneth C. Barnes, *Journey of Hope: The Back-to-Africa Movement in Arkansas in the Late 1800s* (Chapel Hill: The University of North Carolina Press, 2004).

40. "Ethiopian Airlines to Start Building New $5 Billion Airport This Year," *Reuters* online, https://www.reuters.com/article/us-ethiopia-airlines-airport-idUSKBN1ZE1W3.

41. Carvell Wallace, "Why 'Black Panther' is a Defining Moment for Black America," *The New York Times Magazine*, February 2018, https://www.nytimes.com/2018/02/12/magazine/why-black-panther-is-a-defining-moment-for-black-america.html.

42. Kwame Anthony Appiah and Henry Louis Gates, Jr., eds., *Africana: The Encyclopedia of the African and African American Experience* (New York: Basic Books & Perseus Books, 1999).

43. "Afrofuturism: The Next Generation," *New York Times*, December 12, 2016, https://www.nytimes.com/2016/12/12/fashion/afrofuturism-the-next-generation .html.

44. Pew Research, "International Migration from Sub-Saharan Africa has Grown Dramatically Since 2010," https://www.pewresearch.org/fact-tank/2018/02/28/intern ational-migration-from-sub-saharan-africa-has-grown-dramatically-since-2010/; Pew Research, "A Rising Share of the U.S. Black Population Is Foreign Born 9% Are Immigrants; and While Most Are from the Caribbean, Africans Drive Recent Growth," https://www.pewsocialtrends.org/2015/04/09/a-rising-share-of-the-u-s-b lack-population-is-foreign-born/.

45. John W. Blassingame, *The Slave Community* (Yale University Press, 1979).

46. C. Patrick Burrowes, *A History of the Liberian People Before 1800 and Liberia and the Quest for Freedom*; Appiah and Gates, Jr., eds., *Africana: The Encyclopedia of the African and African American Experience*.

47. Ms. Al-Shakinah Campbell, interview by Karl Johnson, February 17, 2020.

48. Ibid.

49. Ibid.

50. Mr. Stephan Lally, interview by Karl Johnson, March 4, 2020.

51. Ibid.

52. Ibid.

Part II

EXCLUDED OR INCLUDED?

AFRICAN AMERICAN, NON-CONFORMIST, AND TRANSGENDER

Chapter 4

(Re)Defining Hi-stories

Conducting and Preserving Oral Histories in Africana Studies

Catherine L. Adams

When Zora Neale Hurston first set out to interview Kossula "Cudjo" Lewis about his life as one of the last Africans to be captured in his native land, forced onto a ship, and enslaved in the state of Alabama, she was not the seasoned and prolific Hurston we think of today.[1] Due mainly to Alice Walker and other Hurston scholars' recovery work, Hurston is widely known generations after her death in 1960 for her collections of Africana folklore, plays, essays, and novels, such as *Their Eyes Were Watching God* (1937).[2] In 1927, she was a student who was close to finishing a baccalaureate degree and, much like students today, trying to take her formal training in anthropology from the classroom into the field. Hurston was to record Lewis, an octogenarian, at his home in Alabama for Carter G. Woodson's *Journal of Negro History*.[3] In her autobiography, she later reflects on her initial lack of success: "My first six months were disappointing. I found out later that it was not because I had no talents for research, but because I did not have the right approach."[4] Hurston returned to New York and her professor, Franz Boaz, with her "heart beneath [her] knees and [her] knees in some lonesome valley."[5] Like some students today, Hurston took short cuts to complete the journal article for Woodson; she borrowed excerpts from *Historic Sketches of the South* by Emma Langdon Roche, published in 1914, with inadequate citations to the earlier work. A few years before Hurston's first visit with Lewis, Alain Locke, a philosopher at Howard University, had collected two pieces of folklore from Lewis to include in a new anthology of philosophical declarations and literary effusions, *The New Negro* (1925). After some coaching from Locke, Hurston's return trip to Alabama in 1928 yielded the literary and historical bounty, *Barracoon: The Story of the Last "Black Cargo."*[6]

71

Hurston was collecting and writing in the early decades of the twentieth century, but how should we collect and preserve intergenerational stories like Lewis's in the twenty-first century? Ideally, in Africana Studies, we should always use the past to inform the present practices. This chapter uses the process described by Hurston as a point of departure for theorizing how Africana Studies might contribute to widely adaptable, culturally derived, and culturally relevant story gathering and sharing projects. Today, the academy is accepting of autoethnographic work, but not so much in Hurston's day. She decided to forego notions of pure objectivity, and readers are the richer for it. Hurston's transparency regarding her and Lewis's dynamic has powerful resonance when thinking of my own memories of sitting and listening to my grandmothers and grand-mentors. As a result, *Barracoon* has served as a cultural grounding text in my pedagogy on fieldwork, oral histories, and intergenerational transmission of wisdom since its publication.[7] The synergy between the written text, lived experiences, and academic discussions positions Hurston in the long-view genealogy of Africana storytellers from the most recent "as told to" biographers and amanuenses, back to the West African griots, and further back still to the classical African scribes.[8] Hurston's work and the ongoing work of oral history projects are imperative memory work—remembering who people of African descent were, are, and will be—collectively.[9]

With *Barracoon*, Hurston accomplishes four essential tasks in her memory work that should inform a ritualized approach to remembering, collecting, and preserving stories narrated by people of African descent.[10] First, she comes to the work prepared to "set down essential truth rather than fact of detail."[11] "Essential truth" means that Lewis's story may be representative or amalgamative and thus true for many African people in similar circumstances, which is consistent with the interest in the restoration of Africana collective memory. "Fact of detail" means that uncorroborated details may be devalued, dismissed, or deleted by people outside of Africana Studies, Africana-centered communities, and other Africana-centered spaces. Second, she permits Lewis "to tell his story in his own way without the intrusion of interpretation."[12] This lack of intrusion is in regard to both *what* Lewis remembers and *how* he remembers it. Hurston is like the amanuensis in recording Lewis's life memories, but she also writes his story in phonetic transcription of his lingua franca. By consistently capturing the sounds of his words as she hears them, Hurston engages readers in some of the much-needed work of collective identity forged in remembering and speaking in our own words.[13] Third, she includes tidbits of her own narration as a young interviewer. At the time, Hurston was a work-in-progress configuring academic training and experiential learning, which she intertwines in the writing of Lewis's story. This co-narration of the intergenerational transmission of wisdom is critical for thinking about the process of conducting oral history projects. Fourth, when Hurston refused requests from white publishers at Viking Press to translate Lewis's words into standard written English, she preserves the two stories—the story of the elder and the story of the young person entrusted with the story. In other words, Hurston's relationship to Lewis is more than that of an interviewer to the narrator. The ultimate success of *Barracoon* is cultural symbiosis. Hurston becomes a part of Lewis's village. As evident in Hurston's work, in Africana Studies, conducting and preserving oral histories must be rooted in Africana memory work, ways of knowing, and cultural meaning-making.[14]

CONDUCTING ORAL HISTORIES AS "MEMORY WORK" IN AFRICANA STUDIES

It is common for African Americans to lament about lost and forgotten culture, but the cultural practices we do remember need immediate attention. Individual stories may seem incomplete, but when assembled as part of a larger mosaic—there is no memory or story too insignificant. The first step to conducting oral histories that draw out memories and stories is to explore culturally specific context and content in preparation for memory and story collection. The development of Africana context begins with exploring macro-level questions about what people of African descent did during the time when a narrator (the person telling stories and sharing memories) was born, grew up, and now lives. For an elder who is an octogenarian, like Lewis was when Hurston sat with him, a student in 2020 might read about local, regional, national, or international events from the 1930s or 1940s to the present. Macro-level questions might include: How did Black people respond to economic conditions in the 1930s to1940s before/during/after the Great Depression? What were people doing in the 1940s to 1960s during enforced racial segregation of neighborhoods, employment, public accommodations, and educational institutions? What strategies or resources did people develop and employ in the 1950s to 1970s to address racism and white supremacy before/during/after the Civil Rights Movement? What was the state of Black America in the 1970s to 1990s? How has Black America fared, so far, in the twenty-first century? These questions are not exhaustive but suggestive of a way to build Africana context at the macro-level.

The questions of context help to give shape to the search for content. In Toni Morrison's essay, "The Site of Memory," she writes of Africans in America: "no slave society in the history of the world wrote more—or more thoughtfully—about its own enslavement."[15] On this literary foundation rests subsequent generations of African Americans writing about their experiences in America after the ending of enslavement. Therefore, in Africana Studies, first, we read what people of African descent wrote about their own lives (post-enslavement narratives, journals, letters, memoirs, autobiographies, memorabilia). Then, we read what they wrote about indirectly- or directly observed circumstances (essays, newspaper and journal articles, and nonfiction books). We also read their creative works (poetry, short stories, and novels) at various historical moments and markers.

Additionally, with the institutionalization of Black studies at Predominately White Institutions (PWIs) in the late 1960s, scholars of all racial and cultural identities have produced a wealth of secondary literature about African Americans. So, we read inside and outside perspectives on Africana historical moments. Lastly, we intertwine traditionally and digitally archived primary texts such as speeches, presentations, interviews, other audio/visual materials, and newspaper/magazine/journal articles with the books. The timeline of the project usually dictates the amount of these materials consumed from start to finish. For example, a semester-long project for students at a college or university might include as few as two or three assigned books and a much longer list of articles and internet-archived videos.

BARRACOON AND TEACHING WAYS OF KNOWING

Since 2018, *Barracoon* has proven to be an exemplary central text for teaching how to collect memories and stories in Africana spaces. The text illuminates the intergenerational transmission of wisdom and ways of knowing—between Lewis and Hurston. Hurston begins the first chapter with some preliminary observations and essential details about her return to get Lewis's story: "It was summer when I went to talk with Cudjo so his door was standing wide open. But I knew he was somewhere about the house before I entered the yard, because I had found the gate unlocked. When Cudjo goes down into his back-field or away from home he locks his gate with an ingenious wooden peg of African invention."[16] Hurston is using her previous meeting with Lewis to develop a "right approach" on the second attempt. She is mindful of the season—in the American South, summer is the midpoint between last and first frosts, and gardens have to be carefully tended for the best harvests. She acknowledges his use of the African peg that secures his gate—which means she is curious about tools and technology that he learned to make and use before he was captured and brought to America. Lewis's story is Hurston's priority; the garden—how best to secure it and cultivate it—is Lewis's priority. There are days when he sends her away to focus on his work in the garden, and there are days when Hurston makes his priority, her priority. Sometimes he narrates during their work together, and some days are days of work and no recorded talk. Lewis is not just narrating; he is teaching Hurston how to work and spend time with him, and she is a willing student.

After chronicling the preliminary observations, Hurston demonstrates the practice of "correct entrance" in African culture.[17] According to Robert Farris Thompson, correct entrance is the observation of clear boundaries and established patterns for entering a space, which would include Hurston's entry into Lewis's home. Hurston writes:

> I hailed him by his African name as I walked up the steps to his porch, and he looked up into my face as I stood in the door in surprise. He was eating his breakfast from a round enameled pan with his hands, in the fashion of his fatherland.
>
> The surprise of seeing me halted his hand between pan and face. Then tears of joy welled up.
>
> "Oh Lor', I know it you call my name. Nobody don't callee me my name from cross de water but you. You always callee me Kossula, jus' lak I in de Affica soil!"[18]

While there is so much that can be unpacked in Hurston's greeting, the significant point is that she uses the name given to him by his mother. It is a sign of recognition and respect for his Africanness. However, the greeting is not over with hailing him by his name. When he asks the purpose of her visit, Hurston's response is, "First, I want to ask you how you feel today?"[19] Correct entrance includes respectfully calling the elder's name and then inquiring about his state of well-being as the first order of business.[20]

After performing the correct entrance, Hurston demonstrates the "how" in sitting with an elder. She poses her open-ended interview questions that express interest in Lewis's life, and then she patiently waits for him to begin answering:

> His head was bowed for a time. When he lifted his wet face again he murmured, "Thankee Jesus! Somebody come ast about Cudjo! I want tellee somebody who I is, so maybe dey go in de Afficky soil some day and callee my name and somebody dere say, 'Yeah, I know Kossula.' I want you everywhere you go to tell everybody whut Cudjo say, and how come I in Americky soil since de 1859 and never see my people no mo'. I can't talkee plain, you unnerstand me, but I calls it word by word for you so it won't be too crooked for you."[21]

Lewis, the elder, senses that this time his story will be truly valued by the younger Hurston. He then shares his memories as his legacy to his family, his village, and subsequent generations of Africans on the continent and in the Diaspora.[22]

In this first chapter, Hurston includes a real-time "teachable moment" with her as the student and Lewis as the elder teacher. Hurston has some knowledge to draw on from her previous visit(s) and her "prep" work, but she is not immune to impatience. Lewis begins his story with how he gave himself the name "Cudjo" in America, but how his mother gave him the name "Kossula" in Africa. Then he tells the story of his lineage, which begins with his grandfather's story. Hurston interjects: "I was afraid that Cudjo might go off on a tangent, so I cut in with, 'But Kossula, I want to hear about you and how *you* lived in Africa.'"[23] Lewis responds to her impatience with nonverbal and verbal instruction: "He gave me a look full of scornful pity and asked, 'Where is de house where de mouse is de leader? In de Affica soil I cain tellee you 'bout de son before I tellee you 'bout de father; and derefore, you unnerstand me, I cain talk about de man who is father (et te) till I tellee you bout de man who he father to him, (et, te, te, grandfather) now, dass right ain' it?"[24] Hurston did not understand but learns in real-time that Lewis's individual story is not separate from his people's story.[25] Hurston uses her academic training as an interviewer, but allows the elder to teach what she did not learn in academia about African culture and ways of knowing.

At the end of the first chapter, Hurston includes her observations and exchange with Lewis; she performs a "correct exit," which complements her correct entrance.[26] After an initial recounting of his grandfather's memories, Lewis is emotionally spent. He decides to end his storytelling for the day with instructions for Hurston: "he said brusquely, 'Go leave me 'lone. Cudjo tired. Come back tomorrow. Doan come in de mornin' 'cause den I be in de garden. Come when it hot, den Cudjo sit in de house." Without urging him to continue or answer one more question, Hurston leaves him to return the next day "about noon."[27]

Additionally, throughout her time with Lewis, Hurston practices the art of "seeing after an elder." She is not only respectfully chronicling his story and learning from his wisdom. She is also providing support to Lewis in ways expected of a family or a village member—not as an objective observer or interviewer. As the editor of *Barracoon*, Deborah Plant notes, "Over a period of three months, Hurston visited with Kossola. She brought Georgia peaches, Virginia hams, late-summer watermelons, and Bee Brand insect powder."[28] She spends time with him in his home, she drives him to Mobile to get seeds for planting, and she helps him clean the church for Sunday morning service. Hurston waits for him and on him—ready to resume the memory work when he is. She continues to "see about him" until he has finished.[29]

THE RIGHT APPROACH: A STUDENT ORAL
HISTORY PROJECT AT ALLEN UNIVERSITY

In the early iterations of assigning this memory work, oral histories and projects were inserted into upper-level English courses taught at Historically Black Colleges and Universities (HBCUs). At the start of fall 2018, in an "Advanced Composition" course, we started the semester with the following framing questions: What might become lost in the twenty-first century if one does not write? What histories do African Americans forget when we do not commit our culture to memory, fail to record it, or fail to write it down? We discussed how previous generations of African Americans had to rely heavily on the oral tradition, especially in times of instability, when enslavement made literacy illegal, and when post-enslavement access to education was fraught with racialized limitations. The oral tradition (or griot tradition) was how Lewis was narrating his story to Hurston.

By grounding the composition course with *Barracoon*, a reflection essay assignment on oral histories became the precursor to a student-driven oral history project. Valencia James transformed her reflection essay into a research proposal funded by the South Carolina Humanities Council.[30] In her submission, James took an autoethnographic approach to doing memory work:

> As a child, I remember the stories that my grandmother used to tell me of her grandfather, which no one ever thought to write down. Now that she is gone, the richness of those stories seemed to die with her. It may be too late for me to record the stories of my once enslaved ancestor from my grandmother's mouth, but not too late to record the stories women of my grandmother's generation are still able to tell.[31]

In collaboration with her faculty mentor, James put *Barracoon* in conversation with *Mama Day* by Gloria Naylor, a novel depicting three generations of African American women rooted in the sea islands off the coast of South Carolina and Georgia. James connected the texts in her proposal:

> I would like to critically examine *Mama Day*, set off the coast of the sea islands, and collect oral histories of African American women who may resonant with Miranda "Mama" Day who represents memory, culture, and wisdom for her grandniece, Cocoa Day. Instead of wondering what we lose when we do not record our stories, I want to answer what we gain when students like me read the world created by Naylor and compare it to the memory, culture, and wisdom of the grandmothers who are still with us. They are waiting for someone to listen and believe their stories are important enough to be read for generations to come.[32]

James also read literary criticism, like Susan Millar Williams's article "'Something to Feel About': Zora Neale Hurston and Julia Peterkin in Africa Town" and Tara T. Green's book, *Reimagining the Middle Passage: Black Resistance in Literature, Television, and Song*. The work by Green, notably her chapter titled, "Acts of Redemption through Forgiveness: Remembering Charleston in the Post-Middle Passage Era," inspired the pursuit of interviews with church grandmothers from Emanuel A. M. E. Church in Charleston, South Carolina.[33]

James focused closely on the places in *Barracoon* where Hurston inserts herself or co-narrates, and she used them as an outline for her fieldwork. In February 2020, she interviewed two church grandmothers at Emanuel.[34] The dynamic of the interviews, in many ways, was consistent with Hurston's model. For example, James greeted the grandmothers with gifts of small palmetto plants (correct entrance); she was respectful in using "Ma'am" as an honorific title in the American South.[35] She asked prepared questions, and then she "sat at their feet" to listen. Still, very sparingly, she also interjected remembrances of her grandmother, which seemed to cement the church grandmothers' stories to James's ancestor grandmother. The grandmothers talked at length about growing up in integrated neighborhoods with segregated schools.[36] The women have been life members of Emanuel, so they spoke about the church over many decades. They talked about their children and grandchildren. And just like Lewis did with Hurston, they spoke of their ancestral lineage—their mothers, "other mothers," and grandmothers.[37]

James also improvised on the structure of the interview. Instead of conducting two separate interviews, she interviewed the grandmothers simultaneously, which enhanced the interview experience. When one narrator was a bit fuzzy on memory, the other narrator completed sentences and filled in details. When listening to the audio recording of the interview, each woman utters audible signs of agreement while the other is speaking. Both women co-narrated memories of events such as attending Buist Elementary School, youth choir rehearsals with Reverend Hilda Scott at Emanuel, and eating Charleston staples such as red rice and Hoppin' John. There are moments when the voices are passionate, overlapping and words are indistinguishable, but there is as much meaning in the emotion of the co-narration as in the words.

The last question James asked was: To whom are the memories and cultural stories being passed? It was the question of legacy. One woman named a granddaughter; the other woman shared memories of children gathering at her house when she was a child. When she became a mother, her home was the place where her children and their friends gathered. In her answer to the question, she named a daughter who is taking up the mantle: "Well, you know, my daughter . . . she is taking that role. Planning things. Having gatherings.

That's her love. And she does that a lot. And a lot of times when they have things planned, she loves to put things together." She even provided a few examples:

[My daughter] always do the Christmas Day, they normally do—I used to do all of that, but now [my daughter does] Christmas. I used to do Thanksgiving every year after my mother died, and then my son and his wife, they started picking it up. And you know, Mother's Day, [my daughter] started something for me and all of my siblings, she got their daughters involved . . . [my daughter] would be the person that I feel would pick up and carry things on.[38]

James listened and recorded the wisdom of the two grandmothers who have daughters and granddaughters watching them and training to carry on family traditions. The interview ended with a church tour and a commemorative picture of James and the church grandmothers, smiling, in front of the Emanuel chapel.[39]

While James did not have the luxury of repeated visits over a three-month period, as did Hurston, James was able to replicate Hurston's "right approach" to foster trust from the church grandmothers. She performed correct entrance and exit. She was able to bring academic knowledge into the field and also improvise.

This chapter is the first attempt to make the process of this memory work available to wider audiences. More of these histories need to be collected and preserved in and for African American families, communities, and institutions like Emanuel and Allen.[40]

CULTURAL MEANING-MAKING: STUDENT ORAL HISTORY PROJECTS AT CLAFLIN UNIVERSITY

The most recent iteration of memory work occurred during the fall semester of 2020. In the "African American Oral History" course at Claflin University, the semester's topic aligned with the 2020 Black History Theme: African Americans and the Vote.[41] We used *Barracoon* as a text to help theorize about how we might study African Americans' experiences regarding the vote. Using Hurston's co-narration and interview notes, during the first few weeks of the semester, we discussed Lewis's story as a way to think about the multiple sites of identity for Africans at home and in the Diaspora. In other words, what happens when narratives of African Americans begin with freedom in Africa and not slavery? How does Lewis's individual story alter our understanding of governance in African societies before European intervention?[42] Lewis's memories, in the chapter titled "Freedom," are illuminating:

We make Gumpa (African Peter) de head and Jaybee and Keebie de judges. Den we make laws how to behave ourselves. When anybody do wrong we make him 'pear befo' de judges and dey tellee him he got to stop doin' lak dat 'cause it doan look nice. We doan want nobody to steal, neither gittee drunk neither hurtee nobody. When we see a man drunk we say, "Dere go de slave whut beat his master." Dat mean he buy de whiskey. It belong to him and he oughter rule it, but it done got control of him. Now dass right, ain' it? When we speak to a man whut do wrong de nexy time he do dat, we whip him.[43]

He narrates the establishing of Africa Town as a way for Africans to govern themselves in America. The formation of all-Black towns like Africa Town in Alabama was one way for recently emancipated individuals and families to resist racism and white supremacy in America.[44]

Organized campaigns to challenge racial segregation and inequity were another way to resist. When Representative John Lewis passed away during the semester, we reflected on his lifetime commitment to such organized campaigns. The recording of the John Lewis funeral was a timely shift to the semester's theme. In particular, we used the requiem delivered by Reverend James Lawson to talk about African American resistance to dehumanization and denied citizenship rights in America. Just as Kossola Lewis's story provides previously unknown details about the Africana experience, Lawson's words serve as a corrective action when he talks about John Lewis and the Nashville Movement of the 1950s and 1960s:

I've read many of the so-called civil rights books of the last 50 or 60 years about the period between 1953 and 1973. Most of the books are wrong about John Lewis. Most of the books are wrong about how John got engaged in the national campaign of 1959–60 . . . when Kelly Miller Smith and the Nashville Christian Leadership Council met in the fall of 1958, and we determined that if there's to be a second major campaign that will demonstrate the efficacy of Satyagraha, of "soul force," of love truth, that we would have to do it in Nashville.[45] John Lewis did not stumble in on that campaign. Kelly Miller Smith, his teacher at ABC, invited John to join the workshops in the fall of 1959, as we prepared ourselves to face violence and to do direct action, and to put on the map, the issue that the racism and the segregation of the nation had dammed. So, in the 60th anniversary of that sit-in campaign, which became the second major campaign of the Nonviolent Movement of America, John Lewis called what we did between 1953 and 1973 the Nonviolent Movement of America—not the CRM. I think we need to get the story straight. Because words are powerful. History must be written in such a fashion that it lifts up truly the spirit of the John Lewises of the world. . . . The media makes a mistake when John is seen only in relationship to the Voting Rights Bill of '65.[46]

This extended excerpt from Lawson's requiem is an elder's memories and narration challenging what historians have often written about John Lewis and his contributions to the African American freedom struggle. For students, hearing and discussing Lawson's firsthand accounts of John Lewis raised questions, such as, why is Lewis often portrayed as someone who "stumbled" into the movement or merely as an understudy of Reverend Martin Luther King, Jr.? What are we to make of the consistent choice by historians to use "Civil Rights Movement" versus Lewis's use of "Nonviolent Movement of America" to describe the nonviolent resistance work of the 1950s and 1960s? Why are the names and roles of African American women and men of the Nashville Movement—including Lawson's—overshadowed or unspoken? Then, we used Lawson's requiem as the next guiding text in the prep work for collecting oral histories. Students were assigned a project to map stories of activists from the Nashville Movement mentioned in Lawson's tribute, including Kelly Miller Smith, Andrew White, Johnetta Hayes, DeLois Wilkerson, Diane Nash, C. T. Vivian, Marion Barry, James Bevel, Bernard Lafayette, Pauline Knight, and Angeline Butler.[47]

About one-third of the course focused on social structure—the cultural relationships between people of African descent.[48] The next third was dedicated to operationalizing the interview process. Students studied the form and content of widely accessible oral history interviews with African Americans: Lawson, Claudette Colvin, and C. T. Vivian.[49] Then, as a group, they developed interview questions based on the theme of voting and assembled a manual of "best practices" for conducting African American oral history interviews.[50] Finally, students identified two narrators—an elder and a peer (for comparison)—to interview about voting.

Due to COVID-19 restrictions, the course met using digital platforms, and students met with their narrators in the same format. Like Hurston, students were out in the "virtual" field, collecting stories, honing academic skills, and improvising as needed. They interviewed a pastor, grandmothers, grandfathers, and other family members. All of the elders spent significant time referencing racial inequality and a desire to have it end. Some narrators had participated in protests, politics, and the Afrocentric homeschool movement. All of the elders remembered voting and remembered who impressed upon them the importance of voting. One elder, recently re-elected to the county school board and active in the Democratic Party, was asked what should be the role of young people. He said, "I think they need to be involved, more involved at a local level—period—you know, when it comes to school board, county council, maybe a state representative, state house. I think they need to be more involved in these . . . where it really helps us . . . at the grassroot[s]." When asked about the role of the elders, he replied, "Guidance." These last two responses speak to the importance of elders and young people having additional opportunities to connect, learn, and guide.

In hindsight, we will have to amend some steps for virtual fieldwork, but so much was unknown and unanticipated during the semester. For example, we have to consider the following virtual fieldwork questions: How should we recreate the performance of correct entrance and exit, which establishes a tone of trust between narrator and student before the storytelling begins and after—when the work of preserving the story begins? What cultural cues and instruction do we miss when students are not face-to-face with elders? How might we have to reinterpret or expand memory work when there is a shift from an interview (focus on the narrator's uninterrupted stories) to a conversation (back-and-forth between student and narrator)? For example, one student's interview was mostly a conversation versus an interview. The disruption to the elder narrator's storytelling pattern was noticeable. However, this inaugural teaching of the African American Oral History course was instructive regarding the meaning students derived from the memory projects—even with a global pandemic's challenges.

PRESERVATION AS CULTURAL MEANING-MAKING

The preservation of *Barracoon* is as vital as Lewis's willingness to narrate his story and Hurston's steadfastness to tend to the story. Many African Americans pass remnants of stories told from one generation to the next without context or a plan for preservation. Preservation is critical not just for repetition but for collective, cultural meaning-making that comes from learning customs, traditions, memories, and identities. Preservation can positively impact families, but it can also reverberate throughout communities across the Diaspora. In the past century, members of the Hurston family and estate had the presence of mind to preserve the co-narrated text at Howard University in the Moorland-Spingarn archival repository. What might we be able to recover collectively if African American families donated their oral histories to one of the more than one-hundred HBCUs in America? There was a time when archival materials were expensive to purchase and maintain. However, there are more ways to preserve individual and family stories in the twenty-first century—oral tradition (griot tradition), writing (scribal tradition), and the newer digital tradition (use of digital technologies).

At the end of the fall 2020 course, students reflected on their knowledge of African American oral history, their understanding of the complexities of African American culture and history, and their knowledge of digitized, archived projects for preservation and access (digital humanities).[51] In other words, how did they make meaning from the course's memory work? One student reflected on the viewing of source interviews in preparation for her interviews:

> Sources that stood out to me in this course were the oral histories from Reverend James Lawson, Reverend C.T. Vivian, and Claudette Colvin. These oral histories have unknown information in them that should be accessible to all Black students. The oral history interview of C.T. Vivian with Roland Martin has charges in it that will guide us into our future. Sources like these are important to have because they are the stories of our recent past. Meanwhile, the fact that it is recent is challenged and attacked. It is our responsibility to record and understand complex truths of our history so that it will be retold to our next generation.[52]

Some students included the challenges of the COVID-19 pandemic in their reflections. One student wrote:

> My elder interview created circumstances that were out of my control. The pandemic made it difficult to communicate face to face, so using technology proved complex for my grandmother. Unfortunately, I could not get a signed release form but used FaceTime to record her verbal consent. Through trial and error, I learned that collecting oral history is about reevaluation and adapting when necessary.[53]

A second student wrote:

> While there is still much more to learn about the African tradition of oral history, the best part is understanding that the tradition is all around us. From the interviews with family members to civil rights activists, my definition of oral history is, at its essence, the preservation and documentation of our history. Although COVID-19 significantly affected my beloved Claflin University, I think there is much to be learned and appreciated from having an accessible and versatile space facilitated through Zoom.[54]

Another student reflected on why African American oral histories matter:

> This class gave me much perspective on why African American Oral History is a necessity. Collecting the stories of others in our lives is a must because these stories carry truths and lessons. When you sit down and speak with this person, you become amazed at their memories, and you see another side to them. Everyone has a story and . . . it is a part of history. Their words matter, and we should take the time to capture those words.[55]

One student reflected on the duty of African Americans to collect and preserve oral histories:

With the increasing interconnectedness of the world, different people and their cultures are interacting more than ever. I believe this has a net positive impact on our global society, but we must be careful to preserve the culture that we have now in some form that will be accessible in the future. Now that we have the tools to easily do so, it is our duty as members of the African Diaspora in America to value our experiences just as much as we are taught to value whiteness. This comes in the form of recording our culture and experiences as a people with an emphasis on preserving its integrity.[56]

Lastly, another student interviewed her grandmother for the project and expressed a desire to continue the work of collecting the stories of her family:

This semester was highly informative about the importance of oral history and the process to preserve oral history. Digital humanities will continue to evolve as there are many ways to preserve oral history. African American oral history is a prominent aspect of African American culture. I hope to continue oral histories in my family and start a tradition. This class allowed me to see that all oral histories are important, and my family is quite large with deeply rooted history.[57]

The excerpts from the reflection essays mitigate the criticisms of the approach during the pandemic. The reflection essays also provide actionable data for improving the course for the next fall semester. The goal will be to increase the meaning-making for the elders as well as the students.

(RE)DEFINING ORAL HI-STORIES IN AFRICANA STUDIES

Reflections of the classroom and field experiences of teaching oral history projects invite the question: How might oral history be (re)defined in Africana Studies? Instead of traditional ways of centering "history" as a discipline, Africana Studies should be thinking about defining oral "hi-stories" based on three components: (1) voiced, firsthand accounts of an elder narrator; (2) direct questions asked by a younger interviewer who "sits at the feet of the elder"; and (3) communal ways of knowing informed by spoken answers of the past.[58] The three components combined allow African elders to transmit wisdom to younger generations and for younger generations to interpret that wisdom in a larger context of past hi-stories to inform the present and the future.

The break between "hi" and "stories" is to culturally foreground (and in some cases re-establish) the "high" position of elders and their stories of long, lived experience, particularly among members of Africana communities who revere earned eldership. According to Moriba Kelsey on the African(a) life cycle, elders ages fifty-five through sixty-five perform the critical role of making a "commitment to provide support, guidance and nurturing to the entire village or family."[59] For elders sixty-six and beyond, spiritual connections heighten, and the principal responsibilities are "peacemaking, reconciliation, and harmony."[60] The more senior elders "should be held in high esteem" for their memory and vision—both of which are vital to capture for family and community continuity before they make their transition.[61] The collection and preservation of the hi-stories of "junior" and "senior" elders, as defined by Kelsey, should be a priority for majority Black spaces including, but not limited to families; community-based organizations (CBOs), public and private educational institutions from middle schools to colleges and universities, Africana Studies programs, HBCUs, and Historically Black Institutions (HBIs).

The definition of oral hi-stories in African studies also should be cemented to what Ayi Kweh Armah calls "cycles of remembrance."[62] The cycles include culturally relevant events with regular occurrences such as family reunions, birthdays, holidays, anniversaries, seasons, historical remembrances, cultural observances, or academic cycles. For example, a fall semester African American Oral History project or course could be in the rotation for Africana Studies programs every fall to coincide with the annual conferences and Black History Month themes of the Association for the Study of African-American Life and History (ASALH).[63] Another example would be asking families to conduct memory work during July—National Black Family Month.[64] The employment of unified themes and intervals would provide a wealth of support, resources, and collaborations at the family, community, organizational, and institutional levels.

CONCLUSION

Through trials and tribulations, Hurston found her "right approach" to collecting and preserving Africana stories. Certainly, Hurston's collection and preservation of Lewis's story proved to be enduring. Despite the rejection of publishers who insisted that Lewis's words be "written in language," Hurston never consented. Her vision—recreating those summer months in Alabama, at the feet of an elder entrusting her with his legacy—came to fruition. After reading *Barracoon*, we have to ask—how can we continue Hurston's legacy of collecting Africana stories to be experienced for future generations? The work has to be grounded in concepts that will unlock the memories of elders who thought they had forgotten their elders' customs and practices when they were young. Despite the trauma of separation, capture, enslavement, and mourning, Lewis remembered the hi-story. Despite her unsuccessful first attempt, the shame of intellectual dishonesty, and the impatience of youth, Hurston recorded and preserved the hi-story. With the right approach—an Africana-centered approach—there is much more memory work to do.

NOTES

1. Lewis's given name was Oluale Kossola, from the Yoruba tradition. Oluale was his father's name, and Kossola was the name his mother gave him. Deborah G. Plant discusses the meaning of his names in her introduction of Zora Neale Hurston's *Barracoon: The Story of the Last "Black Cargo"* (New York: Amistad, 2018). The spelling of "Kossola" varies across texts, reflecting the name's sound more than spelling in English. For example, in 1914, Emma Langdon Roche spells his name "Kazoola" in *Historic Sketches of the South* (New York: Knickerbocker Press, 1914); Hurston spells his name "Kossula." In this chapter, I follow the spelling that Plant uses: "Kossola."

2. LeRhonda S. Manigault-Bryant notes, "The increased attention to Hurston's life and work has resulted in her subsequent veneration to that of a sacred ancestor figure . . . who has become, by all contemporary accounts, a Black literary grand-matriarch." "'I Had a Praying Grandmother': Religion, Prophetic Witness, and Black Women's Herstories," in *New Perspectives on the Black Intellectual Tradition*, eds. Keisha N. Blain, Christopher Cameron, and Ashely D. Farmer (Evanston: Northwestern University Press, 2018), 119.

3. Hurston, *Barracoon*, 6; Robert E. Hemenway, *Zora Neale Hurston: A Literary Biography* (Urbana: University of Illinois Press, 1980), 88–89.

4. Hurston, *Dust Tracks on a Road: An Autobiography* (Urbana: University of Illinois Press, 1984), 174.

5. Ibid, 175.

6. Note that Hurston and Locke first crossed paths on the campus of Howard University, a historically Black university in Washington, D.C. Hurston spent a year and a half as a student at Howard University before moving to New York to attend Barnard College. In her autobiography, Hurston remembers her membership in the Stylus, a small, influential literary society at Howard, which included Locke as one of its two faculty members. Ibid, 167.

7. I am indebted to Beverly Fields Burnette, storyteller, poet, and president of the North Carolina Association of Black Storytellers, Inc., for urging me to read *Barracoon* during the summer of 2018. Her enthusiasm for the book was contagious. After my first reading, I immediately added it to the reading list for one of my fall courses at Allen University in Columbia, South Carolina.

8. According to Greg Carr, chair of Africana Studies at Howard University, it is "on the basis of long-view genealogies of Africana intellectual work" that Africana Studies as an academic endeavor theorizes about the translation and recovery projects central to the discipline/field. "What Black Studies Is Not: Moving from Crisis

to Liberation in Africana Intellectual Work," *Socialism and Democracy* 25, no. 1 (2011): 178.

9. Ayi Kweh Armah warns " memory, enduring memory, is a social acquisition, not a natural gift; that time and the natural decay of all that lives both tend to work against memory, so that a society that wishes to remember its values must work out deliberate ways of countering the normal, inertial slide into forgetfulness," *Eloquence of the Scribes* (Popenguine: Per Ankh, 2006), 196.

10. In this chapter, I use various names—depending on context—to refer to people of African descent: Africans, African Americans, Black people, and Black America.

11. Hurston, *Barracoon*, 3.

12. Ibid.

13. In Michael Gomez's chapter titled "Talking Half African: Middle Passage, Seasoning, and Language," the layers of identity (de)construction from African to African American are stated poignantly: "When I speak a word, I am extending myself to the listener. I am drawing from that which I understand about myself and my relationship to my reality and sharing it with another person. My isolation, my separateness, my aloneness, is transcended by means of language; I have the power to break out of my insularity when I utter a word meant to be heard. In this way, I affirm and reaffirm my essential humanity and identify myself with my community. I engage that community, link with it, merge with it in the very process of speaking through space into the receptive capacity of the community. That I can speak a word and have it understood, and can in turn understand the words of others in my community, constitutes a celebration of my belonging to other of like mind. Our words represent us, for they are our words. Our words declare our vision of the world and our relationship to it. We are our words." *Exchanging Our Country Marks: The Transformation of African Identities in the Colonial and Antebellum South* (Chapel Hill: University of North Carolina Press, 1998), 172–173.

14. For at least a decade, Carr has been presenting, workshopping, and implement-ing into curricula six African conceptual categories for framing work in Africana Studies: social structure, governance, ways of knowing, science and technology, movement and memory, and cultural meaning-making. In the interest of space, the current study explicitly mentions three of the six categories—memory, ways of know-ing, and cultural meaning-making; however, we explore all six during a fourteen- to sixteen-week semester. Delivered at Clark-Atlanta in November 2012, I attended his presentation titled "The Impact and Implications of the Maafa: Africana Studies, the HB[M]CU and Acts of Remembering." In December 2020, I attended his virtual pre-sentation at the Association for the Study of Classical African Civilizations (ASCAC) Mid-Atlantic Regional Conference titled "The African Worldview in These Times."

15. Toni Morrison, "Site of Memory," in *Inventing the Truth: The Art and Craft of Memoir*, ed. William Zinsser (Boston: Mariner Books), 190.

16. Hurston, *Barracoon*, 17.

17. Robert Farris Thompson explores the African concept of "correct entrance and exit" as one of ten canons of African form present in many West African cultures. *African Motion in Art* (Los Angeles: University of California Press, 1974), 18–20. Additionally, Greg Carr (in "Impact and Implications") suggests that Thompson's ten

canons can be used as "tools for identifying extensions, translating, and recovering" evidence of African ways of knowing in Africana Studies.

18. Hurston, *Barracoon*, 17.

19. Ibid, 18.

20. According to Moriba Kelsey, when the elder is well, his/her wisdom should be "sought, valued, and used." *Being Healthy and Wealthy: A Process for African People: A Guide for Successful Growth and Development for Africans* (United States: Publishing Associates, Inc., 2008), 148.

21. Hurston, *Barracoon*, 19.

22. For further discussion of African elders "crystallizing legacy" at the age of sixty-six and beyond, see Kelsey *Being Healthy and Wealthy*, 155–156.

23. Hurston, *Barracoon*, 20 (author's emphasis).

24. Ibid, 20–21.

25. Armah discusses ancestral narratives: "When I lived with my mother and grandmother . . . the narratives I most often heard were narratives of lineage and origin. Such narratives follow a pattern found in other parts of Africa. They begin with a statement of identity, indicating to the people as audience *Who We Are.*" *Eloquence of the Scribes*, 55 (author's emphasis).

26. Thompson, *African Motion*, 18–20.

27. The ending of the first chapter in *Barracoon* is in aesthetic alignment with Thompson's discussion of correct exit: "The 'kill' of the Diola song, the 'cut' of the dancer's phrasing in the ring, the 'end gesture' among the Akan, and 'lining' in the final stages of Ekiti Yoruba carving—each is an instrument by which to realize the perfected sequence." Ibid, 22.

28. Hurston, *Barracoon*, xiv.

29. The practice of "seeing about elders" will resonate particularly with grandchildren who lived with a grandparent, spent extensive time in the home of a grandparent, or were charged with "being the eyes" or "being the legs" of an elder. For example, when I lived with my grandmother, Lucille Terry, I watched her sewed lots of dresses and quilts. She had a handheld needle threader, but when I was with her, she would ask me to thread her needles with my "young eyes."

30. As a South Carolina Humanities Fellow, funding from the South Carolina Humanities Council generously covered James's research. She purchased books, supplies, and contractual services for research and fieldwork. She registered and traveled to two conferences—the Massachusetts College of Liberal Arts (MCLA) Diversity, Equity, and Inclusion Conference in June 2019 and the Southern Modern Language Association (SAMLA) in November 2019—to present various stages of her work. She traveled to Emanuel A. M. E. Church to interview church grandmothers. I served as James's faculty adviser for the entirety of the project.

31. From an application submitted by Valencia James to the South Carolina Humanities Council during the fall semester of 2018 in the author's possession.

32. Ibid.

33. Emanuel A. M. E. Church is a cultural treasure in Africana Studies, also known as "Mother Emanuel." Allen University, where James completed her baccalaureate degree in 2020, was founded by the A. M. E. Church and named for the church's

founder, Richard Allen. Every year on Founder's Day at Allen University, A. M. E. clergy and members come from across South Carolina to attend workshops, exhibits, and dine with the students. Allen has a special relationship to Emanuel in that three of the church members who were victims of white supremacist violence in 2015 were also alumni of Allen: Reverend Daniel Simmons (Class of 1967), Reverend Clementa Pickney (Class of 1995), and Tywanza Sanders (Class of 2014). However, James's work cites Emanuel as a locus for cultural histories in Charleston and surrounding communities in the low country of South Carolina.

34. The interviews with the church grandmothers would not have occurred if not for the church historian, Lee Bennett. I am grateful to Bennett for his patience as we passed emails and text messages to each other. He was protective of the members of Emanuel—and rightly so. Ultimately, he understood that Valencia James was interested in cultural memories and traditions—not retraumatizing church members who suffered unimaginable losses in 2015. I am withholding the names of the two narrators to protect their privacy until the archival process for the interviews is complete.

35. James conducted the interviews during a scheduled appointment that lasted two hours and two minutes on February 15, 2020.

36. The neighborhood was integrated, but one narrator remembers not being allowed to enter white homes or yards. However, white children were permitted to play in Black children's yards. Interview with church grandmothers, February 15, 2020.

37. James's prepared questions included the following: What was the world like during your childhood? What are some of the holidays or traditions you remember from your childhood? What is your favorite childhood story or your favorite memory of a story you heard? Growing up, who was the person who served as "mother" to the community? (Someone who everyone respected?) Can you think of a time when you or a loved one was sick and modern medicine failed but home remedies helped or saved a life? What remedies do you remember or are you known for? What recipes do you remember or are you known for? Who was the strong female role model in your life and how was she related to you? Who is the person in your life who seems to be the most interested in your wisdom and lived experience, like a child, grandchild, niece, or neighbor's child? Who do you think is most likely to pass on your cultural traditions?

38. Interview with Emanuel A. M. E. church grandmothers, February 15, 2020.

39. Hurston includes a photograph of Lewis in from of his home in Alabama. Lewis dressed in "his best suit and removed his shoes: 'I want to look lak I in Affica, 'cause dat where I want to be'" *Barracoon*, 113.

40. The digitized materials from the church grandmothers' interview are being shared with the archivist at Allen University and the historian at Emanuel.

41. The website for the Association for the Study of African-American Life and History (ASALH)—ASALH.org—lists the annual themes from 1928 to 2023.

42. Students in the course noted "how emotional Kossula is with Hurston" when reflecting and mourning his life in Africa. They also commented on the "detailed information" on African familial and societal experiences and "intricacies" of the capture and enslavement derived from Lewis's memories.

43. Hurston, *Barracoon*, 68.

44. According to Norman L. Crockett, "At Least Sixty Black Communities Were Settled Between 1865 and 1915," *The Black Towns* (Lawrence: The Regents Press of Kansas, 1979), xii. Many of these freedom towns still exist and include, but are not limited to: Africatown and Hobson City in Alabama; Eatonville, Fort Mose, and Rosewood in Florida; Nicodemus in Kansas; Davis Bend and Mound Bayou in Mississippi; Bethania, Hayti, James City, Princeville, and Roanoke Island in North Carolina; Boley, Brooksville, Clearview, Grayson, Langston, Lima, Redbird, Rentie Grove, Rentiesville, Summit, Taft, Tatums, Tullahassee, Vernon, and Greenwood (Tulsa) in Oklahoma; and Barrett Station, Douglass Community, Deep Ellum, Ellis Alley, Elm Thicket, Freeman's Town in Fourth Ward (Houston), Independence Heights, Kendleton, Little Egypt, Moore Station, Mosier Valley, Pelham, Saint Johns Colony, Shankleville, Tamina, and Tenth Street Historic District (Dallas) in Texas.

45. In "Rev. James Lawson Speaks at John Lewis' Funeral" uploaded on *YouTube* by CBS News on July 30, 2020, Lawson cites the bus boycott in Montgomery, Alabama, as the origin of the Nonviolent Movement of America, commonly referred to as the Civil Rights Movement.

46. Ibid.

47. Since Claflin is located in South Carolina, students were also given the option to map stories of activists who resisted in the state during the same period. A student who is a South Carolina native mapped stories of "ten prominent civil rights activists from my home of South Carolina": Septima Clark, James Clyburn, Joseph Armstrong DeLaine, Cassandra Maxwell, Benjamin E. Mays, Bernice Robinson, Modjeska Simkins, Charles Gomillion, Isaiah DeQuincey Newman, and Annie Belle Weston. The student also noted, "many of them were first from their families to attend college," and "most of them chose HBCUs."

48. Carr, "Impact and Implications."

49. Mary Elizabeth Moore, Dean of the School of Theology at Boston University in 2011, conducted the interview with Lawson; Rachel Windsor, a student at American University in 2019, conducted the interview with Colvin; and Roland Martin, an African American journalist, conducted the interview with Vivian. All of the interviews were available for viewing on *YouTube*.

50. The interview questions were categorized into pre-interview questions, background questions, deeper questions, and thought questions. A sample of the questions included: Why is the vote important? Tell me about the first time you voted. Describe a time when you had difficulty voting. What do you think about local candidates and the issues you care about? How involved are you with local elections and community politics? What was it like for you when Barack Obama was on the ballot? How do you feel about the general election this year (2020)? When it comes to voting, what do you think is the role of elders? Of young people? *Documenting Treasures of AKA Spirit: A "How-To" Manual for Conducting Oral History Interviews* printed in 2002 by the National Archives/Heritage Committee of Alpha Kappa Alpha Sorority, Incorporated, and "Writing Interview Questions and a Script for Interview" uploaded on the Minnesota History YouTube Channel in 2010 served as templates.

51. During the semester, our working definition of digital humanities was "collaborative collecting, curating, and disseminating interviews and projects using digital technologies with a focus on social and community responsibility."

52. Student reflection essays (Claflin University, November 18, 2020) in author's possession.

53. Ibid.

54. Ibid.

55. Ibid.

56. Ibid.

57. Ibid.

58. This definition was compiled with history and African and African American Studies students in the African American Oral History course during the fall semester of 2020. The selected course textbook, opens with "it is the voice, the first-hand accounts, and the privilege and opportunity for scholars to ask direct questions and grapple with spoken answers of the past that the historian seeks." *Oral History and Digital Humanities: Voice, Access, and Engagement* (New York: Palgrave McMillan, 2014), 1. However, this project seeks to de-center history as a discipline in favor of recovering and restoring equity to modes of African storytelling. The de-privileging of western proprietary modes of narrative production and analysis is intentional and necessary to encourage and expand meaningful exchanges between elders, youth, and community in developing content and understanding.

59. Kelsey, *Being Healthy and Wealthy*, 133.

60. Ibid.

61. Kelsey, *Being Healthy and Wealthy*, 155.

62. Armah, *Eloquence of the Scribes*, 196.

63. As previously stated, during the 2020 fall semester, the African American oral history course at Claflin University was centered around the ASALH 2020 theme, which was "African Americans and the Vote." Next year's theme for ASALH and the course at Claflin is "The Black Family, Representation, Identity, and Diversity." Greater attention to the 2021 theme could possibly ignite a national youth movement to collect elders' stories for Black family histories.

64. In 2006, the Black Women's Agenda (BWA) established National Black Family Month. According to bwa-inc.org, the celebration is to "promote the enrichment of families through education, health, and self-improvement. This observance also encourages us to support our loved ones, reflect with one another, and invest in and inspire our young." What better way to inspire young people than to have them conduct memory work during a time when Black family reunions are prevalent?

Chapter 5

Did You Bring Me Here to Be Like You?

Philosophizing about Diversity, Equity, and Inclusion

Anthony Sean Neal

Mainstream, in principle or at face-value, seems like such an exclusive term yet one that is so American. There are mainstream movies. There is mainstream music. There are mainstream ways of dress. There is mainstream education. There are mainstream foods. There is even the mainstream church or religious practices. To not be in the mainstream is exhausting. It requires constant explaining and resistance to conform or assimilate. This is a great drain on energy. Americans are taught to find similarities and to jettison anything that does not fit. There are the lessons in school that train us to find which one is not like the other one. There are also commercials that cater to Americans with "discriminating taste." It seems that one of the most important skills a person can gain is how to "fit in" or swim in the mainstream. It seems so obvious that a true American virtue that frees one from oppression or discrimination is to become "like." Put another way, to become "like" is to be liked. To be liked is also a type of inclusion, but everyone is not liked, often due to no fault of their own, and because of this (dis)like, something else is needed.

In this chapter, diversity, equity, and inclusion (DEI) will be narrowly defined through philosophizing such that, based upon the definition put forth, a speculative argument[1] will be made for what elements might be necessary in order that DEI can exist. After this analysis, the definition acquired will be accessed for its adequacy and applicability. Once the definition has been shown to be adequate and applicable, it will be used to first offer a critique of ineffective examples of inclusion and then it will be used to put forth some an account of how DEI function at a high level of purpose example might appear. Lastly, an explanation will be offered as to why it is necessary to revisit and reframe our working models of DEI over time.

The questions that could be raised or introduced at this moment is why not perform the work of analyzing DEI while using notions of DEI already established by existing institutions?[2] Fundamental to this project is the very process of thinking. It is the thought process that grounds this project in its development, and it is the thought process that I am making central to DEI. In using preestablished DEI notions, there are assumptions taken for granted concerning the general efficacy of the notion taken and the future adequacy of the same notion for any other given institution or scenario that arises. To apply a previously crafted DEI statement as a ready-made notion of DEI as if it were acceptable for general use simply reduces the ability to avoid the very thing that this paper seeks to circumvent and the very thing that this author finds to be problematic with existing conceptions of DEI.

This does not imply that this project seeks to create a discipline of how DEI projects should be carried out from start to finish. This philosophical study is related to DEI in much the same way as the scientific method is related to the sciences. One would not expect a book on scientific method to do the work of science itself; and one must not expect to find here any conclusions of what specific conduct is right or wrong. The purpose of any methodological study, whether of science or of DEI, is always indirect and of a second order nature.[3] The intent of this study is to send others to their tasks with clearer heads and less wasteful habits in their practices. This necessitates a continual scrutiny of what others are doing in the work of DEI, and, if not, analyses of methods become useless.

Any substantive thought given to the realization of goals as they pertain to DEI within the context of the United States must consider structurally that visible manifestations of these ideals have only had a short and obscure existence. However, this realization may be evident only after a rigorous analysis of what must be reasonably intended by the words DEI. Before the reasonable intent of the terms can be put forth, the question(s) to be answered by the words DEI must be brought to bear. One question that could be engaged by the intent of the words DEI might be, "who can participate?" If this can be taken to be an adequate example of the kind of question DEI work might reasonably pose, then one way to understand DEI is as a limiting or delimiting response as to who can participate in both the work and the results of this work.

In a truly philosophical manner, it becomes necessary to address any presuppositions that may inherently inhibit this search for adequate and applicable notions of DEI. The obvious and most glaring presupposition has to do with the status or value attached to DEI in all attempts to improve the incorporation of such work and practices into any organizational or institutional structure. Any talk of improvement assumes the improvement as a necessary condition, or, if not, then the question must be asked toward why have any discussions of DEI at all. This moves far beyond the improvement of these conditions to some sort of retraction or regression toward the path of least resistance for which to do business regardless of the organizational structure. An organizational leader who thinks like this might assume that following the path of least resistance might mean that no attention is needed where DEI work and best practices are concerned. In countering such a claim, history becomes a reasonable means to provide relevant pushback to such a position.

In the modern era of the African American Freedom Struggle (1896–1975),[4] protests, boycotts, sit-ins, elections, marches, and riots were all aimed at overcoming problems caused by the lack of DEI in the United States, which exists as a heterogeneous space. The prevailing assumption by the majority is that DEI should be left to the preference or whim of organizations, governments, or institutions. This type of thought and practice is prevalent in the United States owing to the fact that just thirty years back, violence was used to secure these conditions for the mainstream of people (Caucasians), within the institution of slavery. Even in the face of horrible violence and brutality, eventually slavery gave way to a form of freedom.

Struggle within the system from those who were being oppressed required more and more violence from the oppressors so that the system could be maintained, until eventually the system became unsustainable. In 1896, the case of *Plessy v. Ferguson* was adjudicated by the Supreme Court upholding legislation aimed at continuing the systems that operated in the blatant absence of DEI.[5] This absence remained legal, although incurring many impairments until the adjudication of *Brown v. Board of Education* in 1954, yet the absence was slow in its recession. Indeed, there are existence vestigial components even now. The point is this, the absence of DEI is difficult to examine and alter without extreme measures when considering the presence and proximity of so much diversity in a heterogeneous population; therefore, it can be posited that it is of increasing value to engage in DEI work and practices than to ignore the need for its activation.

Definitions for each of these concepts are multitudinous, but not all definitions approach adequacy. Because there exists a fundamental philosophical aim of clarity, capturing the essence of the concepts of DEI requires sober thinking about what kind of atomistic or minimalist description can create consistency in a defining agreement among reasonably sincere individuals. A definition of this sort requires thinking that begins apophatically and focused on what DEI *is not* and then moves toward a cataphatic description, or what can be adequately embraced within DEI work and implementation of best practices. Thinking in this fashion, which is usually referred to as categorical thinking, creates the proper separation from other concepts thereby reducing the opportunities for confusion. To this end, when something is not diverse or is uniform, there exists any number of one type of thing.[6] This alone is not truly an expression of non-diversity or uniformity. To be truly uniform, there must exist any number, more than one, of the same expression, or predicative form, of one thing. So then, uniformity hinges upon whatever predicative expression of a thing that qualifies, includes, or excludes a category of membership into a group. In a similar manner, diversity hinges upon removing whatever predicative expression of a thing that disqualifies or excludes a category of membership into a group. So then, in diversity, there must exist any number, more than one, of a different expression or predicative form of a category. In a mathematical sense, diversity might be conceived as an infinite set and expressed as such: diversity=d; d=$\{a, b, c, d...n\}$;[7] with each variable representing the differing or diverse members of a group or institution.

The aforementioned definition has adequacy with reference to space but has no potential with reference to time. Whatever might count as diversity should refer to time as well as space. The title of this article is a reference to this necessity. Time is important because many contemporary institutions have stringent policies upon entry/hire with reference to diversity. These policies are confusingly *open* with "come as you are" implications. An analogy might be made to the institution of the church wherein the presupposition exists that (all) members will assimilate over time. This may work well to a degree in the church environment but not so much in the work environment, educational institutions, or any organization where individuals are supposedly admitted because of abilities and not their willingness to assimilate. This approach to diversity does not even bode well in families. Freedom of thought, conformity, or assimilation does not seem to play well together.

The foundational question that must be asked within spaces that purport to embrace DEI is, *"Did you bring me here to be like you?"* The weight of this question cannot be easily dismissed because it cuts straight to the heart of the underlying time factor necessary in creating and implementing any policy concerning diversity. Many want diversity upon entry into work and other institutional spaces but instead eventually settle for uniformity over the duration of time. This creates unwritten policies about person's hair, speech patterns, weight, complexion, childbirth practices, religious beliefs, political affiliations, and beyond. Individuals responsible for policies that address diversity must consider whether their aim is assimilation or the embrace of difference and make that aim clear in both policy and practice. Anything short of this approach seems at best to be deceitful. For example, the military is clear that you will enter with your uniqueness, yet uniformity is the goal. This is why they wear uniforms and take oaths. One might note in another "uniformed arena" that sports teams wear uniforms, yet they do not take oaths perhaps owing to the challenges team members often have with leadership's attempts to move members toward assimilation.

EXPOSING THE QUESTION MORE PLAINLY

This question is not only relevant for policy-makers but also extremely important for the individual expected to be an adherent to both the written and unwritten policies. This individual must be cognizant of the perceptual frameworks and prevailing culture of the institution being entered. This cognizance assists in making determinations about the totality of what is expected in terms of conformity or in terms of finding room for an individual to find their own lane in this space. For example, in most organizations, the existent members usually have few to no overt intentions in being oppressive to newcomers who are different in some degree from the dominant group within the work or other institutional spaces. The prevailing and frequent thought of the "insiders" is that newcomers will simply somehow "fit in."

This phenomenon can even be observed at dinner parties. In the nineties, I was vegan, and I let as many of my friends and family know as possible; however, I was always being placed in situations to simply "fit in." For example, people would send me an invitation for a gathering such as Thanksgiving. I should add that I am a Southerner, which is necessary because in the 1990s, there were not many vegans in the South. I would say to my friends and family, "You do remember that I am vegan, right?" I would get a reply such as, "Of course!" I would then proceed to provide a detailed explanation of what I did not eat and even offer to bring my own food if necessary. The reply would always be, "Please don't bring anything, there will be something just for you." It never failed that I would leave the gathering hungry. Every dish would be made with meat or animal byproducts, even the gravy. Truly, my friend and family had no overt intentions to be oppressive to me, but they simply thought with all the food that was present, surely, I would find something and simply "fit in." I would, consequently, in this "food diversity scenario" either conform or go hungry. For this type of scenario, I want to be clear that solutions are not as complicated as those in a work environment or academic institution beginning DEI work and implementation of best practices. The pressure to conform in the latter of these environments is much greater than simply visiting a friend for a meal.

Another point of consideration, with reference to this food diversity scenario, is equity. Let us define equity as any number (more than one) of a different expression or predicative form (of a thing) all valued the same or equally. Suppose that I was told that I could bring my own food or it was agreed upon that I should eat before I came. If this were to be the case, in many cultures, it would not be looked upon favorably. Many would think that it was an offense to do such engage in both bringing food and pre-eating and thereby devalue whatever freedom I had to be different. This is not equity. Equity requires—even demands—difference. Singularity cannot include difference and therefore cannot be equitable. If the expectation of equity is sincere, then in this scenario difference would simply go unnoticed or, more appropriately, garner celebration.

Inclusion, in a like manner, is also in need of definition, but it does require building a case in the same sense as diversity and equity. In this sense, I take diversity and equity to be a more robust description of inclusion. For it is possible, to have some level of inclusion in an organization without having a conspicuous notion of diversity and equity. All organizations technically have a degree of inclusive practice, but it is their notion of diversity and equity, which determines their exclusivity or participatory inclusion. This points to our earlier and foundational question, "Who can participate?". Inclusion as a modus operandi for an institution is a good starting point in terms of institutional policy, but leaders should not consider it to be the final performance of actions aimed at the creation of a space that produces a viable existence for any and all. There must be more. Consideration should be given to the types of people in a particular pool or society who are both available and desirous of participation. When this is both recognized, sought, and cultivated as a practice then the expansion of inclusion such that diversity and equity are also woven together as a requisite thread of the institution is a must and a reality. Otherwise, inclusion will exist without equity or diversity.

To elaborate on the possibility of inclusion existing without diversity or equity, I will expose a presentation of this matter found in the novel *Kindred*, by Octavia Butler.[8] For those aware of the *Kindred* novel, the example may seem a bit crude at first glance but what must be kept in tension is that many of the customs initially used, with some continuing to remain, in terms of the treatment of Blacks and other under-represented groups in American society, post-slavery, derived from the social terrain of the plantation. Also, such an egregious example serves to stimulate the understanding of the possible depths of negativity, which can be experienced while participating in an inclusive environment where diversity and equity are not present.

In the narrative, Butler uses a broad array of character types to assist the reader in imagining the vast and complicated world of a Southern plantation. As an analogue, the plantation is applicable for the purposes of demonstrat-ing institutional inclusion without the presence of its higher forms (diversity and equity) because of the connection to the notion of participation. Relying upon earlier definitions in this chapter of DEI, the aim here will be to use the plantation as a source of an analogue to demonstrate its commensurability with modern institutions that focus singularly on inclusion while ignoring diversity and equity. Each entity, the plantation and the modern-day institution, has certain components which share similarities, such that their qualities can be mapped onto the other entity. This can be easily detected when reducing each of these entities to their three essential components: a location, a system of governance, and workers.

Also, as with most institutions of today, most plantations were inclusive in the narrow sense mentioned earlier. This is owing to the idea that the plantation was a microcosm of the society of that time, and it was also integrated into society in such a way that all levels of society were impacted socially, politically, and economically. In terms of the situated nature of the characters in *Kindred*, the story exists as many other stories having a central plot of slavery. The exception or twist in the plot comes with the appearance of a time-traveling writer named Dana who happens to be the great-great grand-daughter of young master Rufus Weylin, the son of Tom Weylin. Also, her great-great grandmother, Alice, was a slave on the same plantation. Beyond this, there is not any need to say more about the plot, with only one addition. The owner, Tom Weylin, was not considered a wealthy or prominent slave owner. In a summative statement concerning the story, as it pertains to the purpose of this paper, there were few, if any, types of people who were excluded from participation in the population of the plantation. People of color, those who usually find barriers to their participation in the institutions of today, were certainly included in the population of the plantation. The only limits were set by Tom Weylin's resources, yet and conspicuously, diversity and equity were nonexistent.

At first glance, an argument could be made for diversity, especially in a strict sense with respect to the definition provided earlier, which was given as any number, more than one, of a different expression, or predicative form, of a thing. Upon closer inspection, however, it is plain to see the social barriers that existed on the plantation, which created separate worlds of existence: master/slave, male/female, and Black/white. Because of the existence of separate worlds, the possibility to change one's station in life or interact outside one's station simply did not present itself. This phenomenon can historically and currently be witnessed in strict observance and application with respect to the Black/white relationship. So, if the argument is made that the plantation as an institutional space was diverse, this would only have validity if the major concern is visual, yet humans do not only exist at a visual level. Community life within social institutions, inclusive of plantations, consists of interactions. The plantation, as a social institution, simply did not have intentional diverse participation across all human interactions.

Even if I were to acquiesce to the notion that diversity is as diversity appears, a problem according to earlier goals remains. That is to say, if a space includes any number, more than one, of a different expression, or predicative form, of a thing, and the institution's policy on diversity is satisfied by optics alone, then it becomes necessary to climb the next rung upon the inclusion ladder to also incorporate equity. Earlier, equity was defined as any number, more than one, of a different expression, or predicative form, of a thing, all valued the same or equally. Given this definition of equity, it is difficult and maybe impossible to determine that all individuals were valued the same on a plantation. So, what significance does this example of the plantation in *Kindred* have when considering DEI in contemporary institutions? The physical punishments that existed during slavery in general and in Butler's novel, to keep the walls of separation in place, simply do not exist today; however, in terms of social interactions and social mobility, institutions that are not intent on being inclusive at all three levels are usually just as restrictive in an experiential manner; therefore, policy statements alone should not only serve as fulfilling the requirement of DEI but also must be assessed experientially. If this is not done, just as the experience of the workers in both the contemporary institution and the plantation are similar (but certainly not equal), their responses may be likewise, similar but not equal.

In order to create any working reality of DEI, the individuals tasked with such duties as conceptualization, implementation, and assessment must give thought to how these tasks must be thought about before engagement. If not, there is always the possibility that whatever processes they develop will always be subject to an ideological disruption upon their presentation to those who are prone to ask, are you sure about the efficacy of this work and implementation, in terms of best practices. Of course, even if the response is in the affirmative, the natural rejoinder to this response is how are you sure. The type of thinking that should occur may begin simplistically at first, such as what things would an individual need to know before they can adequately answer questions about DEI? Then, the more complex discipline specific queries arise such as, what statistical gauge can best assess a social construction designed to maintain DEI within a 500-member corporation? Or, what mechanisms are best suited for producing a cognitive change geared toward understanding the necessity of DEI? These are just a few of the possible examples; however, due to the limitations of space, I certainly cannot consider all queries that might arise, but it is wise to consider a few, so that the type of deliberation necessary to put forth a solution might be demonstrated.

As stated earlier, one of the concerns of this chapter is the thinking involved when considering DEI. This type of reflective activity assists in gaining clarity of thought on the matter. Clear thought on the matter begins with clearly identifying what we intend to seek in understanding a truthful approach to DEI work and implementation. Once this is done, we can then concern ourselves with should be known in order to begin the process of conceptualization. One key question stems from considering whether DEI are of a "natural kind"? From this question, defining the concept, *natural kind* (primary or first order) while questioning the relationship between knowing whether DEI exists as a natural kind within how a DEI initiative might be conceptualized is secondary. In order to dispense with the possibility of this section becoming a mini-disputation, either proving or disproving a particular definition to be correct on the concept of natural kind, I will simply take as adequate the definition offered in the *Cambridge Dictionary of Philosophy* for the intent of demonstrating that defining concepts is necessary before assessing the justification in the belief of their existence.

The definition provided for *natural kind* (in the encyclopedia) states that it is a category of entities classically conceived as having modal implications or having sortals that apply to an entity, classifying it as a particular kind.[9] Quine[10] and others clarify this definition by equating natural kind with being identifiable as belonging to a class of things. In order to be a natural kind, it must be able to be separated, enumerated, and classified as part of a group or set. This cannot be said of DEI, but it can be thought of as a naturally occurring phenomenon one that is akin to a type of decision. This type of decision rests upon a beneficial outcome or positive aim for those involved. In this sense, DEI can be thought of as a cooperative agreement, an intentional decision to cooperate for the common good, which is a type of moral decision. This type of decision does qualify as a natural kind, for moral decisions can be classified into categories.

It is now that I will assess the adequacy and applicability of the earlier definition(s) as well as the relevancy of the previous question regarding the relationship between deciding whether DEI exist as a natural kind and how a DEI initiative might be conceptualized. In order to address the adequacy and applicability of such an initiative, the question should be asked: Why isn't the institution [already] demonstrating diverse, equitable, or inclusive behavior? What barriers exist to prohibit the presence of populations that would show the entity capable of these behaviors?

Whatever the barriers are this is what must be understood to be the thing or phenomenon addressed by a DEI initiative. DEI cannot be either adequate or applicable if barriers to such either exist presently or have in the past. In this sense, the barrier(s) to be addressed can be seen as a prohibitive force "x." The reason this becomes an appropriate analogy is because DEI initiatives are usually brought to the fore as necessary owing to a situation where there already exist populations desiring these behaviors. Therefore, these initiatives can also be seen as a force "y," which can and must overcome the barriers, which prevent the presentation and existence of these behaviors. The mathematical representation of these forces in a successful or adequate and applicable DEI initiative must assume the following form: "$x < y$." That is to say, whatever the form the initiative assumes, it must be a force greater than the barrier "x" to effect positive change. If it is equal, "x = y," it will effect no change and if it is less than, "x > y," there will be a negative change. In this sense, then these initiatives cannot be standard but instead must address the barriers of the institutions where they are to be implemented. This has to be the aim of highly effective DEI work or it cannot be thought of as either adequate or applicable. *"Good enough" is only good enough if there is positive change.*

In the conceptualization of DEI, the aim of positive change must be kept in view. Positive change, or in this case increased participation, is understood to be in contradistinction to static change and negative change. Another factor that must be kept in view is the essence or core of the work of DEI. Previously, "who can participate" was the question that was put forward to focus the discussion concerning the definition of DEI. From a reduction of this question, we can focus our attention on participation as an essential concept described by this work. The conceptualization of a positive and postured initiative of DEI must keep participation central. One suggestion on how this might be done is to use a simple utilitarian notion—the greatest good for the greatest number of participants. This approach has an enormous upside; however, for those barred from participation by a utilitarian decision the downside can be just as steep.

Again, earlier in this essay, DEI were conflated as being analogous to inclusion, with diversity and equity being thought to be better forms of the same concept. In order to separate the terms, I gave attention to essential differences. In this sense, the definition for diversity is distinguished on the basis of difference while the definition of equity is separated on the basis of value. This means in the apophatic sense, those who are not allowed to participate are ultimately not valued or undervalued by members of the group. And, in American society of the past, this point was demonstrated as having the ability to be internalized by the out-group.[11] The significance of the internalization of an outer-derived value proposition is found in the possibility of the institution as being thought of as destructive to the community-at-large. Even when this destruction is not the case, the accountability hypothesis must also be considered. "The accountability hypothesis claims that the presence of racially diverse members in a working group of equals widens the range of people to whom each participant must justify their opinions and conduct and so motivates the participants to think more carefully about what they say and do from what they anticipate are the perspectives of racial out-group members."[12] As an adjustment to the aforementioned utilitarian approach, the accountability hypothesis can be added such that instead of thinking only of the greatest good for the greatest number of people, the consideration should be expanded to include the greatest good for the greatest number of people to whom the institution should be accountable. This adjustment forces the institution to reconsider how conception of the notion of the greatest good.

In conjunction with the previously mentioned conflation of DEI to the notion of inclusion, the lens of a cooperative decision or agreement can also be added as a mode of functioning, under the assumption that inclusion means to be included in or allowed to participate in the activity of the group. Participating in this manner must not only be horizontal but must also have verticality. Allowing this type of participation provides the measure by which the distinction between belief and commitment can be determined. Belief by this measure has no required performative function. Commitment must be actionable thereby able to be measured through observation. When this lens of a cooperative agreement is added, an assessment also becomes possible concerning the moral nature of a conceived DEI initiative. One presupposition attached to the notion of any cooperative agreement is the aim of a common good from which is derived a notion of moral conviction.

An assessment becomes possible owing to the description of a cooperative agreement as being a decision based on an intended mutually beneficial aim. The fundamental question that forms the basis upon which the morality of DEI rides is once again, who can participate? Participation, or the willingness to allow participation, becomes a measure by which the morality of an institution can be assessed. The determination can be made about the present status of an institution and predictions can also be made about the future status of that same institution by performing an analysis that addresses the willingness of current and incoming employees to establish and maintain a DEI initiative. A consideration of note is the realization that any such initiative is always already contingent on population, proximity, and the intended impacted community.

With respect to mutually cooperative agreements, it should be noted that here again assimilation should not be the requirement for participation. This consideration must be kept in tandem with conceptions of moral community cooperation. Given these requirements, even democratic processes may be a hindrance to certain levels of DEI. John Stuart Mill's analogue, the tyranny of the majority,[13] is a useful construct toward gaining understanding of how democratic decisions can obfuscate the benefits for those in groups outside the majority. The fundamental logic used here to ground the concepts of DEI within space and time stand apart from any notion of political ideologies or processes. These logics rest upon an ontological notion or conceptual model, which includes the sustainable nature of an institution in a heterogeneous environment. This simply means that all organizations interested in optimal work environments must look toward creating better scenarios, but not necessarily best-case scenarios, which are usually understood to be ideal and that can endure over time. In a plural society, regardless of the affinities of the majority, there should be little, if any, consideration given toward creating exclusive organizations and institutions.

The fragile nature of any institution dependent on and subject to change from the outside must always consist of reflective thinking and periodic maintenance of its core values and commitments. DEI should not be assumed but should exists as an actionable processes fundamental to an institution's core values and occurring extensively within the functions of all institutions. In this chapter, the aim was to demonstrate the type of thinking that should take place at the beginning of a DEI initiative. After addressing the presuppositions, a definition of DEI was offered as a heuristic to demonstrate how philosophical investigation could be used to determine the elements necessary for the existence of DEI in an organizational space. An assessment was then performed using adequacy and applicability as objective measures. Some areas for future research could further investigations into determining effective DEI strategies; however, the aim here is only to demonstrate the type of thinking necessary in the conception of an initiative to allow wide participation in an institution that exists in a heterogeneous community or society, particularly in the American context.

NOTES

1. Speculative philosophy here is used here in the sense that A. N. Whitehead defined its use in his work *Process and Reality*. Alfred North Whitehead, *Process and Reality: An Essay in Cosmology* (New York: McMillan, 1967), 9.

2. Many philosophers subscribe to the belief that when beginning a project such as this, it is beneficial to clarify the concept through a history of the use of the term. However, fundamental to this project is the understanding that in the process of recovering the use of the terms in history, the temptation is to form a new DEI initiative through combining and trimming statements that are already in use. The aim here is to point out the type of thinking in which the interested parties should engage before acting under the presupposition that the previous statements are adequate.

3. R. C. Collingwood, *An Essay on Philosophical Method* (Mansfield, CT: Martino, 2014), 1–7.

4. Ibid.

5. The segregation instituted by the adjudicated by *Plessy v. Ferguson* necessarily disrupted all attempts toward DEI.

6. "Thing" here is to be understood as the substantive category that includes one in a group. Different expressions are qualitative differences such as color, size, weight, and so on.

7. This formula should be understood as a representation of maximal available diversity in tension with a good faith effort toward this measure as opposed to

requiring infinite diversity. The good faith effort should be measurable in terms of those to which the institution is responsible or could possibly be responsible.

8. Octavia Butler, *Kindred* (Boston, MA: Beacon, 2003), 18–52.

9. If Socrates is a member of the natural kind *human being*, then he is necessarily a human being.

10. Ibid.

11. Kenneth Clark and Mamie Clark perform the famous test that helped in the feasibility of passing *Brown v. Board of Education*.

12. Elizabeth Anderson, *The Imperative of Integration* (Princeton, NJ: Princeton, 2010), 130.

13. John Stuart Mill, *On Liberty* (New York, NY: Dover, 2002), ch.1.

Chapter 6

Missing the Whole Picture

A Content Analysis of Transgender and Gender Non-Conforming Characters in Children's Literature

Saisha Manan and Eden-Reneé Hayes

As a popular source of cultural knowledge, children's books are often recalled by adults as agents that defined their worldviews, with the messages as well as the fantastical excitement of favorite bedtime stories and afternoon pleasure reads resonating with them for the rest of their lives.[1] Apart from the entertainment value of children's books that leads adults to reminiscence fondly, children's literature, from its conception, has been utilized as an instructional and socializing tool,[2][3][4] a field which developed alongside the growing recognition of a developmental period named childhood.[5] The established purposes of children's books as instructional and educational tools lend them significance as sources of knowledge and vehicles for presenting children with complex societal constructs packed into more accessible allegorical tales of animals, toys, fantastical creatures, and more, in order to aid their development.

However, the issue of gender presents a gap in the cultural knowledge available within children's literature, due to a lack of transgender and gender non-conforming (TGNC) representation. In a study evaluating standards of diverse children's books library collections in over 5,000 libraries in the United States,[6] there was found a general trend of greater availability of racially/ethnically/culturally diverse literature than availability of gender and sexuality diversity. Even among the more diverse collections, one-third of the libraries that were examined[7] did not meet minimal standards for racial and ethnic representation and only half met the minimal requirements for LGBTQ+ representation.

Moreover, the representation of TGNC individuals in LGBTQ+ specific literature continues to be sparse. For example, in the 2018 Rainbow Book List, an archival list curated by an LGBTQ+ American Library Association group noting LGBTQ+ children and teen literature, the top-ten choices from 260 evaluations across target age and identity groups included only one story about a gender non-conforming individual, wherein the character identifies as agender.[8] From the larger pool of forty-eight finalist books, only two more titles addressed and represented TGNC individuals.[9] Thus, compared to the already minimal representation of other marginalized groups such as lesbian, gay, and bisexual people, as well as marginalized racial and ethnic groups, TGNC representation pales in the field of children's literature.

Naidoo[10] further comments that TGNC individuals and representative stories in children's literature are virtually invisible across levels of publishing and distribution (through points of access such as public libraries and schools), and when such representation is available, TGNC individuals are portrayed stereotypically, and in negative light (i.e., morally incorrect, sexually promiscuous, "mentally ill," laughingstocks). This invisibility is of particular note when it comes to a marginalized group such as TGNC individuals, seeing as mere exposure to positive and authentic representation of a group can lead to reduced prejudice and greater support for said group.[11][12] To explore the implications of the noted lack of TGNC representation as it intersects with the significance of children's literature as an educating and informing tool accessed by children in periods of gender schema development, the present study entails a content analysis of K–5 children's books representing TGNC individuals.

TERMINOLOGY

Comprehending the gender terminology used in this study is crucial to understanding the design, methods, and findings. *Transgender* is an umbrella term for people whose gender identity or gender expression differ from what is typically associated with the sex they were assigned.[13] *Trans* is short-hand for "transgender." *Gender non-conforming* is a term used to describe some people whose gender expression is different from "traditional" expectations of masculinity and femininity. It is important to note that while the terms *transgender* and *gender non-conforming* are not mutually exclusive, not all gender non-conforming people identify as transgender, nor are all transgender people gender non-conforming.[14] *Transition* or *transitioning* refers to a person's process of developing and assuming a gender expression to match their gender identity (Trans Student Educational Resources 2016). There are several ways that one may transition. These methods can be categorized into acts of *social transition* or *medical transition* and other categories. A social transition can include coming out to one's family, friends, or coworkers, changing one's name or sex on legal documents, and a medical transition can include hormone therapy and surgery.[15] *Cisgender* refers to people who are not transgender; that is, people whose gender identity or gender expression aligns with the gender typically associated with the sex they were assigned.[16] *Cisnormative*, *cisnormativity*, or *cissexism* refers to the enforcement of harmful gender binary systems and the assumption that all people identify with the gender identity they were assigned at birth.[17]

The researchers acknowledge that individuals may identify using a wide variety of terms that may not be used within the present study, though are equally valid as distinct identities, and that may overlap with identifying as transgender or gender non-conforming (i.e., genderqueer, agender, gender-fluid, and non-binary). Based upon the available sample of children's literature and the available definitions and terminology, as well as the purpose of this study, the terms *transgender* and *gender non-conforming* provided the best conceptual fit.

TRANSGENDER AND GENDER NON-CONFORMING MEDIA REPRESENTATIONS

TGNC communities have long been disenfranchised, ostracized, and persecuted in cisnormative societies, as evidenced by laws and policies that fail to protect these vulnerable groups and fail to provide their fundamental human rights as decreed by the United Nations, such as the right to medical care, freedom of expression, and the right to life.[18] As societal structures are often reflective of and further perpetuate the prejudices and biases of majority groups (in the case of gender, cisgender individuals), animosity, prejudice, and hatred for TGNC people proliferate in our legal and social practices, as well as the cultural stratosphere, which includes various types of media representations through movies, television, social media, music, and books.[19][20] Despite an increase in frequency of TGNC representation in media since the 1970s, several of these depictions remain unfavorable, painting transgender individuals as "mentally ill," sexually promiscuous/deviant, or other such characteristics indicative of trans-negative and otherwise prejudiced ideologies,[21][22] save for the increasingly relevant platform of social media and other online forums, where greater positive depictions of TGNC individuals circulate, perhaps due to the fact that social media allows for individuals to create their own images and take control of perceptions.[23] Since individuals utilize media and its representations as a source of cultural knowledge, especially with regard to gaining knowledge on outgroups that may be rendered invisible in one's social network,[24][25] TGNC representations in media hold a position of influence in shaping people's perceptions, attitudes, and behaviors toward said groups.

One study found that such perceptions and attitudes do in fact impact support for policies intended to protect trans and gender non-conforming individuals and support for trans rights. Prejudice reduction was found to be a significant influential factor in garnering public support for trans rights, and in order to reduce prejudice, conditions in which participants were encouraged to develop a humanized understanding of TGNC populations through mere exposure and education were most successful.[26] On the basis of the current research on TGNC media representation and its implications, it is imperative to note that positive education and exposure through media forms can indeed yield positive and supportive attitudes, not only within the observing cisgender public, but also for TGNC individuals who may receive validation and experience a sense of affirmation from seeing positive, authentic depictions of their group within the media, a finding that holds true across several marginalized groups with regard to media representation.[27][28][29] However, as the primary sources of positive representation of TGNC people are social media and other online platforms, which are primarily utilized by and target the youth population,[30] the question of TGNC representation of and for the younger populations, such as children in elementary school, remains. What might be the content and frequency of TGNC representation among their relevant forms of cultural knowledge, and what is the impact of such representations for this age group?

CHILD DEVELOPMENT AND GENDER SCHEMA

As Trepanier-Street and Romatowski[31] posit on the basis of gender schema theory[32] and social cognitive theory,[33] the early childhood years are crucial for the development of gender schema, or the framework by which children organize information about gender differences, gender roles, and attitudes regarding gender. Such a period marks the first step in understanding theory of mind in several aspects of social life and gender is no exception from this learning. An understanding of gender for children arises not only from various contributors and teachers, such as families and role models, but also from less direct means such as television, games, clothing, and children's literature. As children all over the world typically acquire reading skills in early childhood,[34][35] a period coinciding with gender schema development, children's literature occupies a unique space as a cultural influence to the socio-cognitive development of children, as everything one reads does impact their self-concept and concept of others.[36]

This crux of gender schema development and the developmentally ascertained acquisition of reading places children's literature and its representation of gender roles, gender stereotypes, and other social messaging regarding gender identities as an important influencer to their worldviews.[37] [38] [39] A study examining the portrayal of women's roles in children's literature and its impact on attitudes and beliefs among children about women's roles in society found that while outdated and stereotypical portrayals are still prevalent within children's literature, books with non-stereotypical portrayals, more positive and more diverse depictions of women's roles can help shape the attitudes and beliefs of the young consumers,[40] in line with Flores et al.[41] findings regarding attitude and belief change with exposure to positive and authentic representations of an identity group.

Another study analyzing children's reflections on the Rwandan fairytale, Ndabaga, further reinforces this power of stories and representation, wherein it was found that a positive role representation of a woman helps children to realize the inequalities of traditional gender roles and the impact such roles could have on women.[42] Furthermore, such representation also garnered positive reactions to and support from children of several genders and varied socioeconomic backgrounds for a woman protagonist who defies gender roles, which is an untraditional and typically non-accepted response.[43] While this particular fairy tale was expressed, received, and discussed verbally, the findings corroborate with the notion that stories of any kind allow us to connect and explore what may not be deemed acceptable to explore within societal norms[44] [45] and engage in learning within new territory. In the case of Ndabaga, the points of exploration include affirming gender equality, and perceptions of women's roles.[46] However, little is known in the literature presently regarding the representation, prevalence, and general trends of themes and social messaging with regard to non-binary and gender non-conforming identities in children's books.

Children's literature also holds a history of using anthropomorphism, the attribution of human characteristics to nonhuman entities such as animals.[47] Animals and personified objects are used in order to convey social messaging, which is one core purpose of children's literature.[48] [49] [50] Yet, the use of anthropomorphism in literature can hold specific implications in the unpacking of complex social concepts, such as gender. Burke and Copenhaver[51] argue that the use of animals can create psychological and emotional distance from concepts that we may not be willing to grapple with directly, allowing for the critical exploration of complexity. The authors posit that all of us, including children, must contend with societal complexities, and the distance provided by the use of anthropomorphism for such stories allows for readers to explore the topics at hand while retaining the ability to save face as they observe characters making mistakes that they may have made prior to the newfound understanding gained through the messages in the book.

The use of anthropomorphism and the psychological and emotional distance it creates from the messages of the story may present pitfalls in representing marginalized groups, such as TGNC people. Encouraging empathy and evoking the humanity of group members can lead to reduced prejudice toward a group.[52] Since anthropomorphizing by virtue distances any subject from the concept of humanity, using animals and personified objects to represent TGNC individuals might contribute to a further dehumanized understanding of TGNC individuals. In such cases, the use of anthropomorphism, while useful as a tool to create a safe and accessible exploratory space for the child audience, could potentially backfire and fail to create the necessary mechanisms for reduced prejudice.

Based on evidence within the extant literature regarding the educational impact of children's literature and the media representations of TGNC individuals, the content analysis in the present study was designed to examine the current trends of TGNC representation in K–5 English-language children's literature. The aim of the present study is to contribute to the understanding of how such populations are construed and constructed for children from available cultural knowledge, thus impacting their perceptions of such populations, which can hold implications for the real world. The age range of focus is based on Trepanier-Street and Romatowski's[53] analysis of gender schema theory and social cognitive theory wherein they claim that the early childhood years are especially crucial for the development of gender perceptions.

THE PRESENT STUDY

This content analysis of children's literature with representation of TGNC individuals focuses on four broad facets through the coding of several variables regarding the story: the extent to which the TGNC characters and their identities are central to the story, the demographic makeup of the TGNC characters, what type of support, if any, the TGNC characters receive from others, and what elements of transition are depicted. These categories reflect a line of questioning that aligns with the concepts of interest regarding media representation of TGNC people, such as the question of authentic, positive representation, with the recognition that such representation holds the potential to decrease discrimination and increase support for a marginalized group.[54] Due to the issue of anthropomorphism and its potential effects on representation-related perception, this content analysis also aims to document frequency of TGNC representation using nonhuman characters.

Though the issues of oppression, discrimination, and victimization certainly impact the lives of TGNC individuals, there is more to the experiences and lives of TGNC individuals than their oppression, and their identities are more than a facet of oppression, and are not a matter to be pathologized. While the representation of TGNC individuals contributes to the attitudes and beliefs within society that can either perpetuate negative stereotypes and pave the way for discrimination, the same representation can provide helpful knowledge for creating more positive and authentic perceptions and reducing prejudice.[55][56][57]

In an effort to take a more holistic perspective, the present content analysis focuses on the types of support, if any, that the TGNC characters in these children's books receive, and how support is portrayed within the general literature representing TGNC individuals as opposed to focusing on the many ways that the characters are depicted as oppressed. This support focus is not intended to erase the realities of oppression faced by the population in question, but to examine whether the education that children are receiving through their significantly relevant cultural resources are also depicting positive actions one can take and modeling how one can support and view TGNC individuals in a positive and authentic light. In addition to evidence examining how children do shift perceptions and stereotypes when presented with positive depictions in their books,[58] it is known that mere exposure, and even more significant, mere positive exposure can encourage not only support from majority outgroups, but also affirm and validate those within the ingroup.[59][60] For these reasons, TGNC representation within children's literature can be an impactful force in perceptions of gender and consequent real-world implications of such perceptions, making such representation a prime subject for content exploration.

METHOD

Materials

Criteria for inclusion in this content analysis exploring TGNC identities within children's literature were that (1) the book be at an assigned reading level of K–5, (2) the book be published in English, (3) the story features at least one transgender or gender non-conforming individual or one character who represents transgender or gender non-conforming identities, and (4) that the content of the story have some relevance to gender identity (specifically TGNC identities).

Children's picture books meeting the aforementioned criteria were acquired through local public libraries. The books were identified based on parenting blogs and online research, as well as availability through the local public library systems. Out of the twelve books examined, all TGNC characters were main characters. Almost all books in the sample involved only one TGNC character, though one book featured a TGNC side character in addition to the TGNC main character. Four books featured TGNC main characters who were nonhuman (i.e., animals, personified objects, etc.), seven books featured TGNC main characters who were human, and one book featured a TGNC main character who was both human and nonhuman. Of the human characters, featured racial or ethnic groups included white (three characters), Indian (one character), Latinx/Hispanic (two characters), and East Asian (one character), with one multiracial individual (white and Latinx/Hispanic).

Procedure

All books included in the study were coded for twelve uniform items based on the themes within the extant literature regarding children's literature and gender and media representation of TGNC individuals. Due to the subjective nature of certain items, a second coder's input was also recorded for those variables in order to ensure interrater reliability. When discrepancies were presented in the ratings of the first and second coders regarding the subjective items, a third coder's input was recorded as a determining factor.

Variables for coding included the total number of named characters in the book including TGNC individuals, the number of TGNC characters present in the story, whether the TGNC individuals in the book are main or side characters, and the relevance of the TGNC individuals' identities to the arc of the story. These four variables were determined by counting the number of named characters, making determinations through visual and story cues which characters are TGNC, and making determinations regarding the centrality of the TGNC characters and their gender identity to the overall story of the book. For example, if the story was about a TGNC individual transitioning and coming out to their social support network (i.e., family), finding social support and community, and so on, the gender identity was deemed central to the story arc. On the other hand, if the plotline held a different focus though still featured TGNC individuals, gender identity was deemed peripheral to the overall story. Additionally, it was noted as a variable whether the themes of the story are applicable to identities other than gender (i.e., sexual orientation, race, ability/disability, etc.), determined by the level of metaphorical or figurative tone embodied in the children's book with regard to the subject material, wherein the more abstract the link to the theme of TGNC identities, the more applicable the message and story would be to identities other than gender.

Further variables of interest were the supporters of the TGNC individuals (i.e., parents, friends, family members, siblings, peers, teachers, etc.), and how many of those supporters were also named characters. Support was qualified as an acceptance and reaffirmation of the TGNC individuals' identities (i.e., using correct names, helping the TGNC character express identity outwardly, and celebrating these individuals) as depicted by the end of the story arc; and, if such support came from a named character, they were counted in the tally of overall supporters. Relationship of supporter to TGNC individual(s) was recorded categorically.

Other aspects of gender identity and the experience of TGNC individuals were accounted for in the coding, such as whether or not there were elements of social or medical transition depicted in these stories (i.e., a name change, using appropriate pronouns, expressing gender identity outwardly through clothing, etc.), whether the TGNC individuals face pressure to conform to cisnormativity (i.e., called name assigned at birth, made to wear clothes inconsistent with gender identity, and explicitly told that they are wrong), and if/when the TGNC individuals experience social acceptance within the story (at the beginning, toward the middle, and toward the end of the story), determined by the actions of those in their social networks with regard to the TGNC individuals' gender identities.

Finally, a coded variable for intersecting demographic information presented earlier in this section examined whether the TGNC individuals in the book are human or nonhuman characters (i.e., animals and personified inanimate objects), and if human, the racial/ethnic background of the TGNC individuals. The human/nonhuman and race/ethnicity variables were coded by first identifying the TGNC individuals, next determining if they are portrayed as human characters, or nonhuman characters, and then identifying their race/ethnicity through visual and story cues regarding the individual, the family, and the community, depending on the information available in each story.

RESULTS

Identity Relevance

A factor of interest in the present analysis included what relevance a TGNC character's gender identity has to the story arc in the book, and whether the story is relevant only for TGNC identities and gender identities in general, or if the story could be relevant/apply to other types of identities (i.e., race, sexual orientation, ability/disability, etc.). Coding results demonstrate that all books except one present a story in which the TGNC characters and their identities are central to the story, as opposed to peripheral (i.e., the character is a background/side character, whose gender identity is not a facet of exploration, etc.). Furthermore, eight of the twelve books in the sample did not present stories that were applicable to other identities; in other words, eight of the twelve stories were gender identity-specific. The remaining four books in the sample presented stories with themes applicable to other identities (i.e., being part of a family).

Number and Category of Supporters

Another examined variable was the number of supporters that the TGNC characters had in the story who also were named characters (see table 6.1). While a select few stories representing TGNC characters depicted support from less than 50 percent of named characters, the majority of stories in the study sample depicted support from more than 50 percent of the named characters, with seven of the twelve stories featuring support from 100 percent of named characters. Furthermore, the relationship of supporters to the TGNC characters was noted categorically, with trends presented across the sample of twelve children's books. Supporters were mostly parents, family members, siblings, select friends/peers, and teachers, with parents depicted most frequently as supportive.

Transitioning, Acceptance, and Conformity

Finally, areas of inquiry for this content analysis included determining whether elements of social or medical transition were present in the story, determining if and when TGNC characters receive social acceptance (i.e., from the beginning, during the story, and by the end of the story), and determining if the TGNC characters in the sample books face pressure to conform to cisnormativity. Analysis shows that while there were no elements of medical transition presented in these books, almost all of the books (two exceptions) represented elements of social transition, such as the utilization of clothing and accessories that embody and express gender identity, as well as TGNC characters' adoption of new names and supporters' recognition and use of those names.

Coding also demonstrated relatively equal distribution among these books regarding points of acceptance: all books presented stories in which TGNC individuals were accepted by some or all of their social spheres eventually, and the points at which such acceptance was demonstrated in the stories overall varied equally from the beginning, during the story, or at the end. Several books also provided a multilayered depiction of acceptance, wherein some named characters supported their respective TGNC characters from the beginning, and others came to accept by the end.

Table 6.1 Number of Supporters for Transgender and Gender Non-Conforming (TGNC) Characters

Title of Book, Year Published	Author(s), Illustrator(s)	Total Number of Named Characters (Including TGNC Characters)	Number of TGNC Characters	Number of Named Supporting Characters Excluding TGNC Characters (%)
Red: A Crayon's Story (2015)	Michael Hall	23	1	2 (9%)
The Boy & the Bindi (2016)	Vivek Shraya, Rajni Perera	2	1	1 (100%)
Julián Is a Mermaid (2018)	Jessica Love	2	1	1 (100%)
Neither (2018)	Airlie Anderson	11	1	6 (60%)
Bunnybear (2017)	Andrea J. Loney, Carmen Saldaña	4	2	2 (100%)
From the Stars in the Sky to the Fish in the Sea (2017)	Kai Cheng Thom, Wai-Yant Li & Kai Yun Ching	2	1	1 (100%)
I Am Jazz (2014)	Jessica Herthel & Jazz Jennings, Shelagh McNicholas	7	1	4 (67%)
Introducing Teddy (2016)	Jessica Walton, Dougal MacPherson	3	1	2 (100%)
One of a Kind, Like Me/Único Como Yo (2016)	Laurin Mayeno (translated by Teresa Mlawer), Robert Liu-Trujillo	8	1	2 (29%)
Jacob's New Dress (2014)	Sarah and Ian Hoffman, Chris Case	6	1	4 (80%)
Morris Micklewhite and the Tangerine Dress (2014)	Christine Baldacchino, Isabelle Malenfant	8	1	3 (43%)
Sparkle Boy (2017)	Lesléa Newman, Maria Mola	5	1	4 (100%)

Conformity variable analysis revealed that a majority of these stories (eight out of twelve) included pressure on the TGNC individuals to conform, though on a range of varying levels and consistency of such pressure. For example, some stories depicted initial pressure to conform with a removal of such pressure in the duration of the story, typically once the TGNC characters' gender identity is made known to surrounding individuals. Other forms of pressure to conform were coded as more direct, wherein TGNC characters were asked to perform more cisnormative activities (i.e., play "boy sports," go catch fish, and dress like a boy). Some stories that depicted no pressure to conform were due to the fact that within the story, TGNC characters were simply ostracized from the beginning, whereas other *no-pressure-to-conform* stories simply included no unsupportive characters in the TGNC character's life. Significantly, around half of the books identified and placed peers as the primary source of pressure to conform.

DISCUSSION

Findings from the present content analysis indicate that among the sample, nearly all books depicted the TGNC characters as main characters and maintained the gender identities of these characters as central to the story arc. The majority of these books provided stories that were specifically meant to address gender identities. Furthermore, a significant number of the books included in this analysis portrayed all named characters within the story as supportive of the TGNC characters, with a larger majority portraying support from at least half of the remaining characters who are typically parents, family, and friends of the TGNC characters. Elements of social transition were present in nearly all books, as were varied levels of pressure to conform to cisnormativity. All books included acceptance of TGNC characters and their identities by other characters eventually in the story arc.

Implications

Considering the age range of the target audience, these findings shed light on the potential education about TGNC individuals that is available to children at a crucial moment of gender schema development through representation in children's books. For example, while all TGNC characters in the sample books experienced acceptance, validation, and support from those around them, thus modeling positive modes of engagement that can influence the perceptions and attitudes of children, almost all books also showcased TGNC characters experiencing pressure to conform within the story arc, mostly from peers in the story. Such representation of peers of TGNC characters may allow for what Burke and Copenhaver[61] and Tsao[62] put forth as the space for children to explore potentially unfamiliar territories, such as the concept of TGNC identities, as well as the prospect of making mistakes and engaging in consequent learning without the psychological and emotional risk of enacting the same mistakes in reality. If children's books such as the ones included in this study provide this function, then the learning offered through these books could promote perspective-taking and empathy for an outgroup as well as validation for those within the ingroup,[63 64] which can strengthen acceptance and support for TGNC individuals within those who engage with such literature and other educational efforts, thus fortifying potential support networks for TGNC individuals. The likelihood for developing a supportive stance on trans rights is further increased when the representation of TGNC individuals in modes of education is positive, gender-affirming, and authentic.[65] This effect is true for all of the books in the sample through the inclusion of supportive characters in their lives, inclusion of gender transition elements, and the centrality of TGNC characters and their gender identities to the story. Children specifically have been shown to respond positively and shift previously prejudiced attitudes about gender when presented with positive and authentic representation through children's books and stories.[66 67] The content, quantity, and availability of children's books such as the ones included in this study are of importance in their potential to change attitudes, augment support, and validate a marginalized group from an early and crucial age of development.

Another implication of these findings is the frequency of anthropomorphism within children's literature representing TGNC individuals. The sample within this study demonstrated greater human representation than nonhuman representation, which may reflect an understanding in the children's literature field of the importance of positive, authentic, and engaging representation of this marginalized group. As Burke and Copenhaver[68] posit, anthropomorphism has been used in children's literature consistently as a tool for providing psychological and emotional distance to allow for the critical exploration of socially complex constructs (e.g., gender). The psychological and emotional distance created by anthropomorphism[69] in the context of representing marginalized groups may, however, take away from invoking empathy, which is helpful in shifting prejudices, and, when present, may instead lead to a dehumanized understanding of such groups. The results on the human/ nonhuman character divide thus suggest recognition of the need to humanize, and not dehumanize TGNC individuals in children's literature to perhaps allow for the promotion of a supportive, gender-affirming, and validating culture among children. Further analysis could provide greater clarity on this apparent trend, and perhaps provide comparison with evidence of the human/nonhuman representation divide in books representing other types of marginalized individuals.

Limitations and Further Directions

The findings of this content analysis are placed within the parameters of certain limitations. For one, this study only examines children's literature printed in English, which means that findings on the effects of such literature would only hold for those who are literate in English, as well as those who have access to such literature. The question of educational access and literacy also contextualizes the findings of this study as applicable only to those holding socioeconomic statuses that enable them to orient their education around the written word. Further directions for this research could address this issue by examining alternate forms of learning commonplace among children of this age group for TGNC representation such as oral histories, television shows, children's gendered play, toys and board games, role models, and direct familial beliefs. While the present sample included significant cultural, racial, or ethnic diversity intersecting with gender diversity, most of the books analyzed were published within North America, which may lend these books and consequently the present analysis a Westernized orientation to gender. Further avenues for research on this subject might include a comprehensive cross-cultural examination of TGNC representation within children's literature across the world.

Though the early childhood years are especially formative with regard to gender schema development;[70] [71] another opportunity to explore TGNC representation and its implications may lie in the literature for those in other formative periods of development, such as older children and teenagers. The present study focused on literature identified as appropriate for the K–5 age group. Literature for older ages may present other dynamics, levels of support, and less anthropomorphism than K–5 literature. Learning about those around us and diversifying our social knowledge is certainly not limited to childhood, and individuals who may have learned certain prejudiced attitudes toward marginalized persons such as TGNC individuals can also unlearn such beliefs through mere exposure to positive and authentic representation;[72] [73] [74] at several points beyond early childhood.

Lastly, while the present research examined the dimensions of support both in content of children's literature and in its implications for the real world, as a contrast to an oppression-focused analysis for a marginalized group, the shift in conceptualizing how the social sciences study TGNC people could be further developed to include elements of identity celebration as well as the facets of oppression, discrimination, and support.

Conclusion

TGNC rights have long remained under attack, and recently, their governmental recognition, their legal existence, has been put in jeopardy in the United States. The Trump administration considered narrowing the definition of gender to "biologically determined sex assigned at birth" for all federal programs, a move that would effectively eliminate and provide new obstacles to accessing medical care, provisions of safety in educational settings, and other civil rights for TGNC individuals.[75][76] This attempt to eradicate gender identities that do not align with cisnormativity highlights that the United States is at a crucial point with regard to a societal understanding of gender, transgender, and gender non-conforming identities. Although Trump did not earn a second term, those that subscribe to this unsupportive mindset continue in their political careers. The threat to erase rights indicates a real need for continued education, and a need to continue efforts to bring the existence of TGNC individuals to the forefront in a positive and authentic manner such that TGNC individuals will not be erased in society. Stories, such as children's literature, are one such mode of resistance, and it is imperative that such stories are told, heard, and not forgotten.

NOTES

1. Carolyn Burke and Joby Copenhaver, "Animals as People in Children's Literature," *Language Arts*, 81, no. 3 (January 2004): 206.

2. Burke and Copenhaver, "Animals as People," 208–210.

3. Angela Gooden and Mark Gooden, "Gender Representations in Notable Children's Picture Books: 1995–1999," *Sex Roles*, 45, no. 1/2 (July 2001): 89–93.

4. Jean Mendoza and Debbie Reese, "Examining Multicultural Picture Books for the Early Childhood Classroom: Possibilities and Pitfalls," *Early Childhood Research and Practice*, 3 no. 2 (Fall 2001): 155–156. http://ecrp.uiuc.edu/v3n2/index.html.

5. Burke and Copenhaver, "Animals as People," 208.

6. Virginia Kay Williams and Nancy Deyoe, "Diverse Population, Diverse Collection? Youth Collections in the United States," *Technical Services Quarterly* 31, no. 2 (March 2014): 112. 10.1080/07317131.2014.875373.

7. Williams and Deyoe, "Diverse Population, Diverse Collection?" 116.

8. "2018 Rainbow List," *American Library Association*, accessed January 03, 2019, https://glbtrt.ala.org/rainbowbooks/archives/1270.

9. "2018 Rainbow List."

10. Jamie Campbell Naidoo, *Rainbow Family Collections: Selecting and Using Children's Books with Lesbian, Gay, Bisexual, Transgender and Queer Content* (California: ABC-CLIO, 2012), 39.

11. Robert Zajonc, "Attitudinal Effects of Mere Exposure," *Journal of Personality and Social Psychology* 9, no. 2 (1968): 1–27. https://doi.org/10.1037/h0025848.

12. Lauren McInroy and Shelley Craig, "Transgender Representation in Offline and Online Media: LGBTQ Youth Perspectives," *Journal of Human Behavior in the Social Environment*, 25, no. 6 (April 2015): 615. 10.1080/10911359.2014.995392.

13. "GLAAD Media Reference Guide—Transgender," *GLAAD*, accessed December 6, 2019. https://www.glaad.org/reference/transgender.

14. "GLAAD Media Reference Guide."

15. "Definitions," *Trans Student Educational Resources*, accessed December 13, 2018, http://www.transstudent.org/definitions.

16. "GLAAD Media Reference Guide."

17. "Word of the Week: Cisnormativity," *Center for Sexual Pleasure and Health*, accessed December 13, 2018, http://www.thecsph.org/wotw-cisnormativity/.

18. UN General Assembly (1948).

19. Jessica Jobe, "Transgender Representation in the Media," (Honors Thesis, Eastern Kentucky University, Kentucky, 2013), 30.

20. McInroy and Craig, "Transgender Representation in Offline and Online Media," 606.

21. Jobe, "Transgender Representation," 13.

22. McInroy and Craig, "Transgender Representation in Offline and Online Media," 607.

23. Ibid., 608.

24. Jobe, "Transgender Representation," 7–8.

25. Ya-Lun Tsao, "Gender Issues in Young Children's Literature," *Reading Improvement* 45, no. 3 (Fall 2008): 108–109.

26. Andrea R. Flores, Andrea R., Donald Haider-Markel, Daniel Lewis, Patrick Miller, Barry Tadlock, and Jami Taylor, "Transgender Prejudice Reduction and Opinions on Transgender Rights: Results from a Mediation Analysis on Experimental Data," *Research and Politics,* 5 (January–March 2018): 7.

27. Flores, Haider-Markel, Lewis, Miller, Tadlock, and Taylor, "Transgender Prejudice Reduction," 7.

28. McInroy and Craig, "Transgender Representation in Offline and Online Media," 608.

29. Mendoza and Reese, "Examining Multicultural Picture Books," 157–158.

30. McInroy and Craig, "Transgender Representation in Offline and Online Media," 608.

31. Mary Trepanier-Street and Jane A. Romatowski, "The Influence of Children's Literature on Gender Role Perceptions: A Reexamination," *Early Childhood Education Journal* 26, no. 3 (1999): 155.

32. Sandra Bem, "Gender Schema Theory: A Cognitive Account of Sex Typing," *Psychological Review,* 88, no.4 (July 1981): 354–364.

33. Albert Bandura, *Social Foundations of Thought and Action: A Social Cognitive Theory* (New Jersey: Prentice-Hall, 1986).

34. Tsao, "Gender Issues in Young Children's Literature," 109.

35. Mendoza and Reese, "Examining Multicultural Picture Books," 156.

36. Tsao, "Gender Issues in Young Children's Literature," 109.

37. Burke and Copenhaver, "Animals as People," 208–210.

38. Tsao, "Gender Issues in Young Children's Literature," 109.

39. Trepanier-Street and Romatowski, "The Influence of Children's Literature," 155–156.

40. Gooden and Gooden, "Gender Representations," 97.

41. Flores, Haider-Markel, Lewis, Miller, Tadlock, and Taylor, "Transgender Prejudice Reduction."

42. Pierre Canisius Ruterana, "Using Children's Literature to Promote Gender Equality in Education: The Case of the Fairy Tale of Ndabaga in Rwanda," *Rwanda Journal of Arts and Humanities* 2, no. 2 (2017): 36–38.

43. Ruterana, "Using Children's Literature to Promote Gender Equality in Education," 36–38.

44. Jobe, "Transgender Representation," 30–31.

45. Tsao, "Gender Issues in Young Children's Literature," 113.

46. Ruterana, "Using Children's Literature to Promote Gender Equality in Education," 36–38.

47. Burke and Copenhaver, "Animals as People," 207.

48. Burke and Copenhaver, "Animals as People," 206.

49. Gooden and Gooden, "Gender Representations," 89.

50. Mendoza and Reese, "Examining Multicultural Picture Books," 155–156.

51. Burke and Copenhaver, "Animals as People," 207.

52. Flores, Haider-Markel, Lewis, Miller, Tadlock, and Taylor, "Transgender Prejudice Reduction," 7.

53. Trepanier-Street and Romatowski, "The Influence of Children's Literature," 155–156.

54. Flores, Haider-Markel, Lewis, Miller, Tadlock, and Taylor, "Transgender Prejudice Reduction," 7.

55. Flores, Haider-Markel, Lewis, Miller, Tadlock, and Taylor, "Transgender Prejudice Reduction," 7.

56. McInroy and Craig, "Transgender Representation in Offline and Online Media," 615.

57. Gooden and Gooden, "Gender Representations," 97.

58. Trepanier-Street and Romatowski, "The Influence of Children's Literature," 158.

59. Flores, Haider-Markel, Lewis, Miller, Tadlock, and Taylor, "Transgender Prejudice Reduction," 7.

60. McInroy and Craig, "Transgender Representation in Offline and Online Media," 608.

61. Burke and Copenhaver, "Animals as People," 210.

62. Tsao, "Gender Issues in Young Children's Literature," 108–109, 113.

63. Flores, Haider-Markel, Lewis, Miller, Tadlock, and Taylor, "Transgender Prejudice Reduction," 7.

64. McInroy and Craig, "Transgender Representation in Offline and Online Media," 608.

65. Flores, Haider-Markel, Lewis, Miller, Tadlock, and Taylor, "Transgender Prejudice Reduction," 7.

66. Gooden and Gooden, "Gender Representations," 90–91.

67. Ruterana, "Using Children's Literature to Promote Gender Equality in Education," 36–39.

68. Burke and Copenhaver, "Animals as People," 210–212.

69. Burke and Copenhaver, "Animals as People," 212.

70. Trepanier-Street and Romatowski, "The Influence of Children's Literature," 155.

71. Tsao, "Gender Issues in Young Children's Literature," 109.

72. Flores, Haider-Markel, Lewis, Miller, Tadlock, and Taylor, "Transgender Prejudice Reduction," 7.

73. McInroy and Craig, "Transgender Representation in Offline and Online Media," 615.

74. Bandura, *Social Foundations of Thought and Action.*

75. Erica L. Green, Katie Benner, and Robert Pear, "'Transgender' Could be Defined Out of Existence Under Trump Administration," accessed October 23, 2018, https://www.nytimes.com/2018/10/21/us/politics/transgender-trump-administration-sex-definition.html.

76. Dan Diamond, "Trump Moves to Scrap Protections for LGBTQ Patients," accessed May 7, 2020, https://www.politico.com/news/2020/04/24/trump-team-moves-to-scrap-protections-for-lgbtq-patients-206398.

Chapter 7

Organizational Culture

Pivoting on Diversity, Equity, and Inclusion

Willette Neal

INTRODUCTION

Culture should always maintain a point of reference in discussions and dialogue around diversity, equity, and inclusion (DEI). Who we are, what we believe, how we exist, and how we operate and interact are outward responses to our individual culture. Our very essence is consumed with experiences that pile one on top of the other in an effort to help us navigate different spaces and encounters. We see, we respond, we react, we suppress, we hold back, we release, we tolerate, we express all based on our culture. This response is not a singular idea of culture but one that embodies our interactions, experiences, and our conversations. Some conversations were given to us just this morning while other conversations have been with us since childhood, and they are continuously locking and unlocking to create our individual culture. We see ourselves in the literature, and we see "how" you see us in the literature; we see ourselves in pictures, and we see "how" you see us in pictures. And we—this world of humans—are unable to remove or to put aside the deepest parts of our culture when we seek to understand DEI in culturally mixed settings.

The understanding of DEI is aided by the gathering of different cultures together to reach a common goal. When culture becomes the foundation of the DEI conversation, elements such as race, ethnicity, age, and gender can be reframed. The reframing of these elements offers the opportunity to expand the conversation to include more than the general knowledge of these elements to reach a common goal and, instead, offers the opportunity for an extensive and intentional dialogue to erupt. The intended recipients of the dialogue must be central to the conversation. For instance, if the DEI dialogue is about race relations and the path, the transmitter of the conversation will be taking references race relations, then the intended recipients should be integral in the dialogue. Recipient feedback on the path being taken can be integral in determining the success of the DEI effort. Adding cultural intelligence (CQ) to the dialogue changes the diversity conversation from passive to active, because at this point, the "actors" are engaging in an activity that seeks to transform the DEI dialogue. DEI transformation involves more than mere diversity statements.

This chapter provides a method to introduce CQ as a viable tool to review perceptions associated with DEI. CQ is defined as "the capability of an individual to function effectively in situations characterized by cultural diversity."[1] CQ can suggest more dynamic ways to address DEI by creating a space to examine culture as foundational in dialogue about DEI. Schein views culture more as shared experiences and patterns that have proved viable in enough instances to be passed from generation to generation.[2] However, culture is not static but instead is continuously changing and adapting. Traditions and culture are often intertwined when referring to a group of people; however, both traditions and cultures can change over time while existing statically as a fixture in the cultural dialogue. Therefore, dialogue around diversity and inclusion could and does change over time. Throughout this discussion, culture will reflect the ability to change. In addition, it will reflect culture as being associated with a group of people with learned behaviors, with a clear understanding that behaviors can change.

Although there are several methodologies that can be used to address DEI, CQ offers a guide for using culture as the grounding force. CQ is a learned skill; therefore, it enables individuals to adjust perceptions in an effort to develop a differently constructed and expanded mindset in reference to DEI initiatives. This learned skill is used to enable societal and behavioral adjustments in culturally diverse settings. DEI dialogues are saturated with attempts to impact or influence different cultures creating the need for adjustment.

There are four components of CQ, and they can be used to explore the perceptions or tools needed for adjustment in the DEI dialogue. The components are *cognitive* or how we think about DEI; *metacognitive* or how much we know about DEI; *motivation* or what propels us to explore DEI; and finally, *behavioral* or how we behave during culturally diverse encounters. Behavior is the outward response to the three prior CQ components. Behavioral CQ is what can be seen, heard, and referenced in cultural interactions. Behavioral CQ is usually that part of the cultural dialogue that intrudes in the conversation.

Cognitive CQ, which is the knowledge one possesses about another culture, can be a point of reference when the dialogue around diversity is initiated. How much does one know about the cultural interaction that is about to take place? More importantly in the cognitive spectrum is how the issue of cultural knowledge will influence the outcome of the dialogue. Next of concern is metacognitive CQ, which consists of more than the general knowledge one possesses and delves deeply into the ability to intentionally seek the opportunity to learn more about another culture. In other words, how much preparation went into preparing for the cultural dialogue? And, then, there is motivational CQ, which delves deeply into the incentives or intrinsic and extrinsic factors that propel the cultural dialogue. In this scenario, the item or thing that encourages the pursuit to learn about another culture is evaluated. Finally, with behavioral CQ, the actual outward acts are explored in an effort to understand another's culture. The key takeaway here is that outward acts of the DEI conversation should not stop at the diversity statement but must intentionally link the statement to demonstrable actions.

Communication will be defined for this chapter as dialogue that is not only transmitted but also is understood by the intended audience. Intercultural communication enters the narrative as an additional tool to address the verbal and nonverbal communication that occurs during intercultural interactions. CQ explores intercultural interactions or the way culture is understood and expressed during intercultural interactions. CQ is a learned skill and therefore analogous with culture; it is fluid.[3] Therefore, utilizing culture as a foundation overlaid with the ability to successfully communicate in culturally diverse situations is an essential frame in the cultural dialogue. Cultural understanding and cultural awareness are the core of CQ.

Organized thinking about people, places, and events leads to (a) cultural script about a group of people.[4] "A cultural script is best thought of as a routine that describes how events and people are expected to interact over time."[5] Although these definitions allow one group to become easily identifiable, it has the same potential to accentuate the differences in another group using these same parameters. CQ is not a tool that is designed to link these similarities and differences but instead is a tool that will allow for a deeper understanding of how the two ideals of similarities and differences can exist simultaneously. CQ gives a pathway to dynamics that is inherit in the diversity discussion. For instance, culturally intelligent individuals are often able to "anticipate social rules across cultures."[6] Additionally, CQ enables conversations around dynamics that are not often discussed.

DEFINING DIVERSITY, EQUITY, AND INCLUSION

DEI involves integrating the underprivileged group into the larger group or the more dominate group by enacting and dividing DEI initiatives with a common goal of inclusivity.[7] Diversity in the literature has been defined using several variations. One can safely assume that there is not a clear cut, across the board approval on the definition of diversity. In the

Concept of Diversity by Dr. David Washington, he begins the conversation by explaining that although one would think there is a singular definition that clearly defines diversity, it is, in fact, the opposite; diversity carries several different meanings. "The definition of diversity differs from person to person, from organization to organization, and from author to author."[8] Gardenswartz and Rowe describe the different layers of diversity as personality, internal dimensions, external dimensions, and organizational dimensions.[9] In continuation, cultural diversity, a sub-aspect of diversity, is not only recognizing these differences but also appreciating the fact that these differences make us all unique.

There is a consensus that there are several meanings and definitely several different interpretations for the word diversity. The meanings that have been associated with diversity continuously increase throughout the years. For instance, not only can it apply to race, gender, ethnicity, age, and religion but also it can apply to (diversity of) thought, marital status, and socioeconomic status, to name just a few diversity touchpoints. The theory of the layers of diversity proposed by Gardenswartz and Rowe interjects several of these dimensions as a part of the diversity wheel. The looming issue with the loose definitions associated with diversity is that it allows organizations and especially individuals to self-define diversity; consequently, organizations and individuals are able to form a range of possible remedies or solutions to address the internal actions springing forth from diverse situations. In other words, individuals with the capacity to act or ability to act can decide to give access or create the necessary conditions needed to be inclusive based on self-defining or self-benefiting definitions of diversity. Each of these behaviors contributes in some manner to the DEI dialogue. The truth is that oftentimes diversity dialogues do not translate into including all the necessary "actors" inside the cultural dialogue. Additionally, oftentimes those "acted upon" or those who are the intended recipients of DEI statements or initiatives are often visibly absent from the dialogues and the DEI decision-making process altogether.

The Society for Human Resource Management (SHRM) defines diversity as "the collective mixture of differences and similarities that includes, for example, individual and organizational characteristics, values, beliefs, experiences, backgrounds, preferences, and behaviors."[10] Legal ramifications lead the way in some organizational conversations about the need for this level of defined diversity. Increased numerical measures are yet another way diversity is defined. In other words, the myriad of definitions associated with diversity allows an acceptance of statements such as "be at ease when we tell ourselves that we are not bigots or sexists because at least we admit that racism, sexism, and other inequalities still exist."[11] Therefore, due to the existence of (some) inequalities, organizations or individuals should act to address and rectify the areas that remain unequal. These actions must extend beyond the diversity statement and inclusion should be considered.

INCLUSION

Inclusion is considered equal/the same as diversity in some literature; it is simply considered as the replacement word for diversity. Looking at inclusion another way would be situations wherein the existing environment makes space, seeks, and appreciates the myriad of differences in individuals and utilizes those differences to meet the organizational goals. Inclusion should aptly be viewed as only one yet essential tool used to increase employee engagement and employee retention. Inclusion works by fully engaging the employee in the processes, procedures, and practices of the organization. Engagement in the diversity dialogue creates opportunities to express cultural differences as well as similarities. There are several studies that link the employee perception of inclusion to commitment and job performance.[12] Perception of inclusion experienced by the employee builds a level of trust between the employee and the organization.

Inclusion requires an organization to become intentional about the strategies that are in place reducing bias in access to resources and creating opportunities to advancement.[13] Inclusive strategies must be intentional and will require an understanding of the barriers that are currently in place that contribute to the decreased opportunities. Inclusive programs within an organization can take on several different methodologies, yet the organization must be culturally intelligent in deciding on these strategies. Why is this important? Simply put, one program cannot be the fix for an all "inclusive" experience. Inclusivity requires the organization to understand the cultural diversity that is present in the organization before it can take fundamental action beyond a DEI statement. A foundational imperative to inclusivity at an organization as stated by Davidson and Purdue-Greenway must "eradicate the perception that race will be a barrier to advancement."[14] Inherently, inclusion must be a consideration during the cultural dialogue.

Inclusion links the employee to the organization in a bond that is similar to a bond with a relative. The employee builds a sense of trust with the organization and therefore translates this level of trust into buy-in of the organization's goals and mission. Once the trust is established in the employee organizational relationship, the employee is endeared to the organization in a manner that encourages a sense of belonging. Belonging then translates into a paradigm of connection. The employee is connected to the organization and the possibility of building longevity together exists. In turn, the organization reaps a prospective employee retention scenario from what started as an inclusion campaign. "Engaged employees provide companies with crucial competitive advantages such as higher productivity, greater revenues, and lower employee turnover."[15] However, when the strategy does not address inclusivity at its very core, the company fails and employee engagement is reduced or in some cases erased. Erasure or reduction halts the cultural dialogue conversation.

When employee engagement or the level of inclusion is increased, the more productive the employee becomes thereby increasing the performance leading to increased cultural dialogue. Increased performance is a direct link to the organizational benefit of inclusion. Employee engagement is a type of emotional relationship between the employee and the organization. The employee evokes a sense of "caring" for the organization. Inclusivity requires a knowledge, a sense of knowing, that is invoked when organizational decisions are made about inclusion. This sense of knowing will be apparent that the decisions being made will have a direct impact on individuals. The decisions should link to the need to invoke equalization in the processes of the organization. Is equalization a simple split (half and half) or does equity require a more in-depth analysis?

EQUITY

What may seem equal to you may not seem equal to another, and this difference is often situated within cultural differences. Equity as a component of diversity and inclusion is not the outlier but instead becomes the tie that binds. Equity or equality rests on the outcome that diversity and inclusion seek to gain. In other words, diversity and inclusion set forth the blueprint for a finished product that depicts an equitable situation. In the reverse manner, when equity is missing, diversity and inclusion must be addressed. Equity is equal access to the opportunities that exists within a structure.[16] What creates equal access to opportunities? This is not a simple and even divide but a more intentional focus on creating opportunities that reduce barriers to an inclusive environment. Diversity statements or diversity intentions in an organizational structure often miss the mark by refusing to identify barriers that prohibit the equalization phenomenon.

In instances where the barriers are known, the next logical step is to remove the barriers. This action would require behavioral CQ. Organizations would have to act on knowledge gained from a deeper understanding of knowing another's culture. I will use the field of aviation as an example. Aviation is not considered a diverse field, therefore, if we were to examine what barriers exists to contribute to this lack diversity, we would need cultural knowledge or understanding. Environment, education, and race are contributors in the lack of diversity in the field of aviation. Delving deeper requires a commitment or an action to go beyond identifying these barriers but taking decisive action to eliminate the barriers. If we move this a step forward into applicant examples, the picture clears. Applicant A has never flown on an airplane nor knows anyone who has flown previously. Applicant B flies every summer and has participated in several aviation camps along with close friends. Applicant A and Applicant B will most likely have different barriers. There is a process needed to reach the equalization phenomenon of inclusivity. Inclusion is directly related to the individual's feelings of "having equal access to opportunities and resources so that they can fully contribute to the organizations success."[17] Inclusion offers opportunities at two different levels—the individual level and the organizational level—to address inequalities in organizations.[18]

ORGANIZATIONAL CQ

DEI are not necessarily the new buzz words, but instead have become the new *imperative* for organizational survival. Business success is chained to and weighed down with the urgency and impending requirement of creating an environment that is either "perceived" as diverse, equitable, and inclusive or at the very least "accepted" as diverse, equitable, and inclusive. "Perceived" and "accepted" each hold one end of the spectrum but in many ways are considered in a similar and positive light in the world of DEI "watchers." Perception and acceptance of DEI both yield some accolades due to the effort businesses put into being recognized or *perceived* as being diverse, equitable, and inclusive or being *accepted* as being diverse, equitable, and inclusive. When peeling back the onion, the questions remain: What is diversity, what is equity, what is inclusion, and is there a difference in the organizational understanding and the individual understanding? Importantly, how is this understanding linked to CQ?

For the most part, DEI are a staple in the business community. Williams and Wade-Golden state that "every institution needs to achieve access and equity for racially and ethnically diverse individuals."[19] Language and literature are saturated with the benefits associated with diversity and the need to have a diverse and inclusive work environment. Businesses latched onto the idea of diversity in combination with inclusion as a model of "doing" business—a model that without small amounts of variance increases the bottom line for the business. Oftentimes the diversity and inclusion environment that is professed is not always perceived in the same manner. CQ can contribute positively to the dialogue around DEI and can add meaning to the conversation around barriers to successfully achieving access and equity for racially and ethnically diverse individuals. Lack of CQ provides foundational evidence of the rationale for the differences between the organizational understanding of DEI and the individual understanding of DEI. For example, when the company states something similar to "we value all employees," the individual may not understand this dialogue because the actions of the company are not synchronous with the statement. *Noise* is the result of this lack of understanding; it is the part of the dialogue that prevents the transmitter from reaching the receiver in the intercultural dialogue.

PERCEPTIONS OF DIVERSITY AND INCLUSION IN THE ORGANIZATION

Perceptions are how one chooses to view a situation using personal encounters, experiences, and word-of-mouth narratives as the foundation for analysis. Interestingly enough, these personal encounters, experiences, and word-of-mouth narratives are not always perceived as intended due to these narratives. For instance, my sibling has the capacity to pass along a word-of-mouth experience that happened to her that could greatly impact my perception of the situation. We all embody unique experiences, and occasionally these experiences guide our vision toward an encounter; with the same impact our vision can be guided by the encounter and our vision can be widened by the encounter. Williams explores the individual understanding of diversity from a participant:[20]

> It is almost impossible for most people to come up with the same meaning of diversity. Because it means you give your own interpretation. And some people really don't want you to know what they think. I know for me diversity had had a profound impact on me. I turned down job opportunities and friendships that may have developed into something good because of my viewpoints on diversity. I am aware of my personal biases and prejudices toward cultural groups different from mine and don't mind acknowledging them. Many decisions I had to make in my professional life have held me back because of that one word—diversity. I cannot say I am dissatisfied. Because I knew what I was doing. I never met any people I did not like; I just did not understand them.

Diversity is difficult to put into meaning at the organizational level, and it can be just as difficult to define diversity on an individual level. The literature on diversity is not inundated with examples of how individuals seek to understand or apply the concepts or definitions associated with diversity. There are several narratives around diversity that give credence to how the organization links the mission of the organization and the diversity and inclusion initiative, but it is not often that the mission of the organization delves into how diversity will impact and operate on the more personal level of the individual. Williams continues the exploration of the perception of diversity in the following response when asking an individual to explain their understanding of diversity:[21]

> I take time to reflect on one coworker at a time that I consider to be just like me and see if I can identify ways in which the coworker is different from me. Also, I reflect on the coworker I consider to be different from me and see if I can identify ways in which the coworker is like me. In my mind, I am happy even if I'm not doing it perfectly. I am a well-rounded healthcare professional sensing diversity is about understanding cultural differences.

Diversity has become and possibly has always been a business imperative. Diversity contributes or detracts from what is considered the bottom line in the business world. It makes good business sense in most literature to have a diverse and inclusive workforce. It also shares insight for clients and employees about the company's stance on issues related to diversity. Diversity and inclusion lead to less turnover, better employee engagement, and better-recruiting targets. Businesses seek opportunity to make the bottom line more profitable, and diversity may be the answer to this dilemma. The Towers Watson 2010 Global Workforce report found that "companies with engaged workforces demonstrate an average of 19 percent higher operating income and 28 percent higher growth in earnings per share than the average employer."[22] Numerical benefits such as these have a positive impact on the bottom line of the organization and become a great encourager in persuading companies to become active about initiatives that support diversity. The business imperative behind the diversity initiatives rarely consider the perception that diversity has on the employee or the actual recipient of the diversity and inclusion mission.

In a random search of companies and federal agencies on their public declaration of diversity statements, both private and federal diversity statements (with the exception of a few) centered on the benefit diversity can offer to the bottom line of the business. If diversity and inclusion have such variance in their meanings, how can the individual understand the message that is being transmitted? Individual CQ on the part of the receiver can sift these messages through each component of CQ. It is rare that companies consider the impact via positive or negative impacts that diversity initiatives will have on the individual.

CQ at the individual level gives us avenues to explore the individual CQ of decision-makers. Organizational CQ allows the dialogue to transcend beyond the individual level and expand to the organizational level. Organizational

CQ is in the infancy stage in the literature, yet there are possibilities to have the link between individual and organizational CQ identified into a framework to address DEI. Organizational CQ is the top-down approach to the processes that exists within an organization that either promotes DEI or creates barriers to DEI.

There are five factors associated with organizational CQ: leadership behavior, adaptability, training and development, organizational intentionality, and organizational inclusion.[23] CQ at the individual level gives insight into the ability of the individual to operate in an environment that is culturally diverse. Organizational CQ is the view of the organization's processes and practices that encourage success when operating in a culturally diverse environment. "Organizational CQ will facilitate effective management of cultural diversity within the organization as well as cross-cultural environments in which the organization engages."[24] Organizational CQ takes a deeper look into what is really happening in the organization whether those things are contributing positively or negatively in the creation of a culturally intelligent environment. A culturally intelligent environment is an environment that is successful in culturally diverse situations and is the impetus behind the need for DEI.

As noted earlier, this type of view requires a look at the organization that goes well beyond the view of the diversity statement. This view gazes into the leadership and the process that would encourage success or failure in culturally diverse settings. External and internal factors are also a consideration for a culturally intelligent organization. Leadership is the first factor of organizational CQ. Oftentimes, when discussing DEI internal initiatives, leadership is reviewed as a whole, but organizational CQ allows leadership to be viewed as an individual construct that has impact on the entire organization. An example of this occurs when *Leader A* block attempts at creating an internal system that addresses barriers for women and minorities, then *Leader A* becomes the focus of attention for the culturally intelligent organization.

Leadership is oftentimes explored in the DEI environment as very broad, and its direct association to the DEI initiative is often limited. For example, the responsible entity for upholding the initiative associated with DEI belongs to which leadership position? The DEI initiative is commonly "owned" by the organization as an entity and assumed ownership is "someone" in leadership without specifics. This lack of ownership or accountability could contribute to "many Black professionals having little evidence that diversity and inclusion initiatives actually help them advance in their organization and careers."[25] But what if key leaders were aware of the cultural difference within the organization when they were interacting with people from different cultures? This could give insight into why some Black professionals are not able to link the organization's DEI statement to the actions that occur within the organization. What if the key leaders of the organization were confident in working with other cultures and were able to identify that the DEI statements were not actually addressing inequalities or exclusions? Linking the individual in the position, the leader, to the leadership position gives a viable path to view the organization's CQ. The next factor of organizational CQ is adaptability.

Organizations must be able to adapt in culturally diverse environments. *This is the way it's always done and therefore this is the way it always will be* is an old adage that creates a solid barrier to adaptability. Cultural fluidity is implicit in its reference to the ability to adapt. Adaptability requires leaders to be able to have a level of confidence when working with other cultures.[26] Adaptability in organizational CQ requires adjustment of structure and process in order to interact more effectively in culturally diverse settings. This type of adaptability requires a shift in the normal operating process and procedures of the organization. Key leaders are instrumental in driving the adaptability of the organization. Adaptability implies that when DEI statements are not positively linked to internal processes and procedures, change to the internal processes and procedures should occur. Changing internal processes and procedures shows a commitment on the leadership level to address barriers. Organizational CQ explores the international experience of the key leaders.[27] International experience is a critical component in increasing CQ due to the leader's ability to interact with several cultures. Additionally, leaders will have a broader view of other cultures when they possess international experience. The next factor for a culturally intelligent organization is training and development.

Training and development under organizational CQ align key leadership characteristics with cultural interactions. For instance, is the organization committed to producing leaders and employees who are bicultural or multicultural in their skill set?[28] Commitment on this level once again requires more than the DEI statement. DEI statements can be the beginning of the process to address the lack of real inclusivity, but training and development are essential in forming an environment that embraces DEI initiatives. Companies have succeeded in training their employees and managers on the company's expectations or views on DEI. However, this training may be effective in some instances, but it may not be effective in increasing diversity or addressing the lack of cultural awareness needed to address DEI.[29] Training and development in the organization must go beyond the DEI statement and address the associated barriers. Training must be specific to the issue or barrier it is intended to address. Specificity at this level requires measurable attainment. If the training is designed to increase diversity, there should be a clearly measured method detailing how diversity training is attributed to increased diversity within the organization. Linking the training and development of DEI requires intentionality.

Intentionality is the next factor in the culturally intelligent organization. Organizations must be intentional in linking the process and activities to address barriers to DEI. Intentionality deletes the haphazard training and development activities that are basically checking the box. Intentionality in organizational CQ views feedback as an integral part of developing an organization that seeks to have a strong and viable DEI culture.

Are the individuals in key leadership positions asking for feedback after communication? Feedback gives leadership a deeper understanding of what is occurring at the individual level; however, this feedback must go beyond the standard end of training survey. Feedback is not your basic end of training survey but a more intentional feedback process. Feedback alone does not guarantee a change in leadership behavior toward DEI.[30] This is where intentionality must be central in the feedback received. Intentionally seeking to eliminate barriers to effective DEI gives feedback its proper place in the DEI dialogue. Leadership must be willing to take the feedback and address the feedback in relation to barriers to DEI. Intentionality can be accomplished by having inclusive practices.

Inclusion is the last stage of organizational CQ. Inclusivity requires the organization to "give equal opportunity to employees regardless of gender, ethnicity, religion, race and so on."[31] Giving equal opportunity in the organization links to the identification of barriers in the organization that cripple DEI initiatives. Barriers can be identified through feedback from the impacted employees. Giving equal opportunity in the organization requires intentional actions from the key leadership officials. Key leaders must understand the dynamics of diversity and inclusion. In order for key leaders to gain this level of understanding they must be culturally intelligent on the individual level about the cultural diversity that exists within the organization. Addressing DEI through the usage of CQ on the individual level and the organizational level delves into the ability of key leaders to be culturally intelligent and the organizations in which they lead to also be culturally intelligent. Key leaders enact policies and practices that impact DEI initiatives and link the beliefs of the leaders to the process and practices that can address DEI in a more holistic approach.

Individual level CQ is the ability to adjust in culturally diverse settings and organizational CQ explores the organization's processes and practices in culturally diverse settings. Both are viable tools to address DEI in organizations. CQ specifically relates to culture and how an individual relates or reacts in situations characterized by cultural diversity. Understanding cultural similarities and cultural differences are essential in the understanding of DEI. Key leaders must possess cultural awareness of the cultures that are at play in the dialogue. The following feedback is part of a case study based on the resignation of Michael Johnson, the first African American CEO of the United

Way of Greater Cincinnati. This occurred only four months after Mr. Johnson assumed the position; however, Mr. Johnson wrote a letter to the board prior to leaving that included this excerpt:[32]

> I have never been micromanaged and disrespected the way I am being now. . . .
> She is placing undue pressure on our team to do things her way, overreaching
> her authority. One example is the hiring of our Chief Development Officer that
> currently reports to me. . . . She also told me to shut up and put my head down.
> She told me that I was nothing more than an angry man and referred to me as
> a boxer in a ring.

Cognitive CQ or the general knowledge a key leader knows about another culture is the beginning of the process. We know that Mr. Johnson is an African American male, but there are several cultural assumptions that are not evident in this statement but may be evident to the board to which he is writing. Metacognitive CQ requires actively thinking about cultural differences. It "triggers critical thinking about habits, assumptions, and culturally bound thinking."[33] Key leaders must be critical about their assumptions and intentional about changing those assumptions. Motivational CQ addresses key leader's desire to see DEI initiatives work. Motivational CQ is influenced by both extrinsic factors such as the business model for success, but it also includes intrinsic motivation.

Finally, on the individual level is behavioral CQ. Behavioral CQ is the ability to "exhibit both appropriate verbal and non-verbal actions when interacting in culturally diverse situations."[34] Mr. Johnson (in his earlier-given statement) mentioned "she" told him to shut up and put his head down. This implies a lack of behavioral CQ based on the spoken communication, but key to the understanding of DEI is "she" was a key leader in the organization. In this scenario, the key leader's CQ must be addressed because their function within the organization can be toxic to the success of the DEI program and the overall functioning of the organization.

Organizations can use individual CQ and organizational CQ as tools to review, address, and change DEI programs. Leadership behaviors are the impetus in DEI programs. Adaptability is directly linked to the leader and the behaviors of the leaders. Leaders must intentionally seek to understand cultural differences that are present and have the culturally intelligent motivation to change when necessary. Training cannot be viewed as a checkbox exercise in an organization that is seeking success with DEI initiatives. Instead, training must be directly linked to the identified barriers and measured regularly. Finally, individual leaders must be intentional in the processes and procedures utilized to develop an equalized phenomenon in the work environment.

FUTURE RESEARCH

In conclusion, CQ and organizational CQ can be linked to address the work of DEI key leaders on the individual level. Key leaders drive processes and practices within the organization. Organizational CQ is a tool that views the process and practices of an organization that are linked to the successes and failures that directly reference DEI practices. Future research with a closer look at DEI in organizations through interviews utilizing the CQ assessment from the Cultural Intelligence Center and the Organizational Cultural Intelligence Scale presented by Lima (2016) [35] could be revealing toward new best practices in this essential work for individuals and organizations striving for measurable success in the DEI environment.

NOTES

1. Linn Van Dyne and Soon Ang, "Conceptualization of Cultural Intelligence: Definition, Distinctiveness, and Nomological Network," *Handbook of Cultural Intelligence: Theory, Measurement, and Applications* (Routledge, New York, 2018): 3.

2. Edgar H. Schein, *Organizational Culture and Leadership Second Edition* (Jossey-Bass, San Francisco, 1992): 12.

3. Linn Van Dyne and Soon Ang, "Conceptualization of Cultural Intelligence: Definition, Distinctiveness, and Nomological Network," *Handbook of Cultural Intelligence: Theory, Measurement, and Applications* (Routledge, New York, 2018): 3.

4. Soon Ang, P. Christopher Early, and Joo-Seng Tan, *CQ Developing Cultural Intelligence at Work* (Stanford University Press, 2006).

5. Soon Ang, P. Christopher Early, and Joo-Seng Tan, *CQ Developing Cultural Intelligence at Work* (Stanford University Press, 2006).

6. Detelin S. Elenkov and Joana R. C. Pimentel, *Handbook of Cultural Intelligence: Theory, Measurement, and Applications* (Routledge, New York, 2018): 296.

7. Osman Ozturgut, "Internationalization for Diversity, Equity, and Inclusion," *Journal of Higher Education Theory and Practice* 17, no. 6: 84.

8. David Washington, *Concept of Diversity*, 2008, www.dwashingtonllc.com.

9. Anita Rowe and Lee Gardenswartz, *Managing Diversity: A Complete Desk Reference and Planning Guide* (McGraw-Hill, 1998).

10. "Introduction to the Human Resources Discipline of Diversity, Equity and Inclusion," July 21, 2020, http://shrm.org.

11. David G. Embrick, "Thinking Diversity, Rethinking Diversity," *Humanity & Society* (2016): 40.

12. Aneesya Panicker, Rakesh Kumar Agrawal and Utkal Khandelwal, "Contentious But Not Optional: Linking Inclusive Workplace to Organizational Outcomes," *Drishtikon: A Management Journal* 8, no. 2 (2017).

13. Martin N. Davidson and Valarie Purdie-Greenaway, "Is D&I about Us? How Inclusion Practices Undermine Black Advancement and How to Design for Real Inclusion," *Race, Work, and Leadership: New Perspectives on the Black Experience* (Harvard Business School Publishing, 2018), 315.

14. Martin N. Davidson and Valarie Purdie-Greenaway, "Is D&I about Us? How Inclusion Practices Undermine Black Advancement and How to Design for Real Inclusion," *Race, Work, and Leadership: New Perspectives on the Black Experience* (Harvard Business School Publishing, 2018), 315.

15. "Employee Engagement and Commitment: A Guide to Understanding, Measuring and Increasing Engagement in Your Organization," www.shrm.org/hr -today/trends-and-forecasting.

16. Osman Ozturgut, "Internationalization for Diversity, Equity, and Inclusion," *Journal of Higher Education Theory and Practice* 17, no. 6: 84.

17. Martin N. Davidson and Valarie Purdie-Greenaway, "Is D&I about Us? How Inclusion Practices Undermine Black Advancement and How to Design for Real Inclusion," *Race, Work, and Leadership: New Perspectives on the Black Experience* (Harvard Business School Publishing, 2018), 315.

18. Martin N. Davidson and Valarie Purdie-Greenaway, "Is D&I about Us? How Inclusion Practices Undermine Black Advancement and How to Design for Real Inclusion," *Race, Work, and Leadership: New Perspectives on the Black Experience* (Harvard Business School Publishing, 2018), 315.

19. Damon A. Williams and Katrina C. Wade-Golden, "The Complex Mandate of a Chief Diversity Officer," *The Chronicle of Higher Education* 55, no. 5 (September 2008): B44.

20. Williams and Wade-Golden, "The Complex Mandate of a Chief Diversity Officer."

21. Williams and Wade-Golden, "The Complex Mandate of a Chief Diversity Officer."

22. *Introduction to the Human Resources Discipline of Diversity, Equity and Inclusion,* July 21, 2020, http://shrm.org.

23. Bruce E. Winston, G. R. Bud West, and Joanna E. Lima, "Measuring Organizational Cultural Intelligence: The Development and Validation of a Scale," *International Journal of Cross- Cultural Management* 16, no. 1: 9–31.

24. Bruce E. Winston, G. R. Bud West, and Joanna E. Lima, "Measuring Organizational Cultural Intelligence: The Development and Validation of a Scale," *International Journal of Cross- Cultural Management* 16, no. 1: 9–31.

25. Martin N. Davidson and Valarie Purdie-Greenaway, "Is D&I about Us? How Inclusion Practices Undermine Black Advancement and How to Design for Real Inclusion," *Race, Work, and Leadership: New Perspectives on the Black Experience* (Harvard Business School Publishing, 2018), 315.

26. Bruce E. Winston, G. R. Bud West, and Joanna E. Lima, "Measuring Organizational Cultural Intelligence: The Development and Validation of a Scale," *International Journal of Cross- Cultural Management* 16, no. 1: 9–31.

27. Bruce E. Winston, G. R. Bud West, and Joanna E. Lima, "Measuring Organizational Cultural Intelligence: The Development and Validation of a Scale," *International Journal of Cross- Cultural Management* 16, no. 1: 9–31.

28. Bruce E. Winston, G. R. Bud West, and Joanna E. Lima, "Measuring Organizational Cultural Intelligence: The Development and Validation of a Scale," *International Journal of Cross- Cultural Management* 16, no. 1: 9–31.

29. Anthony J. Austin, Patricia G. Devine, Patrick Forscher, and William T. L. Cox, "Long-Term Reduction in Implicit Race Bias: A Prejudice Habit-Breaking Intervention," *Journal of Experimental Social Psychology* 48, no. 6: 1267.

30. London, Smither, and Wohlers, 1995.

31. Bruce E. Winston, G. R. Bud West, and Joanna E. Lima, "Measuring Organizational Cultural Intelligence: The Development and Validation of a Scale," *International Journal of Cross- Cultural Management* 16, no. 1: 9–31.

32. Lucy May, "United Way CEO Michael Johnson on Leave after Alleging 'Subtle Threats, Hostile Work Environment,'" October 29, 2018, http://wcpo.com.

33. Linn Van Dyne and Soon Ang, "Conceptualization of Cultural Intelligence: Definition, Distinctiveness, and Nomological Network," *Handbook of Cultural Intelligence: Theory, Measurement, and Applications* (Routledge, New York, 2018): 3.

34. Linn Van Dyne and Soon Ang, "Conceptualization of Cultural Intelligence: Definition, Distinctiveness, and Nomological Network," *Handbook of Cultural Intelligence: Theory, Measurement, and Applications* (Routledge, New York, 2018): 3.

35. Bruce E. Winston, G. R. Bud West, and Joanna E. Lima, "Measuring Organizational Cultural Intelligence: The Development and Validation of a Scale," *International Journal of Cross- Cultural Management* 16, no. 1: 9–31.

Chapter 8

Approaching Diversity, Equity, and Race Work in Twenty-First Century America

Gwendolyn VanSant

Education and work are the levers to uplift a people.

—W. E. B. Du Bois

Over the past fifteen years, I have developed a methodology to approach equity, inclusion, and justice work with corporations, universities, and communities. This approach appeals and applies to our common humanity and need for belonging. It also reflects the evolution and emergence that we find in nature.

Meaningful diversity, equity, and race work fundamentally requires cultural humility and cultural competence in our organizations. Cultural competence is a framework of mutual respect that is the foundation of all equity, inclusion, and justice work. As a leader-practitioner, I start cultural competence work by helping teams build a foundation of shared language, concepts, and frameworks. I work with leaders to prepare themselves and their team members for integration. To integrate an "other" is to embrace the needs, values, and value of the person and their perspectives being *invited in*. This work begins with understanding our historical and cultural context, and its legacy of privileges of access or systemic barriers that deny access. Every team has to commit to consistently reckoning with those biases and truths.

Specifically, I work with organizations in three areas:

PERSONAL VISION AND AUTHENTIC LEADERSHIP

The leader's first step is to name one's values, identify one's own biases, and begin to practice self-awareness. I guide leaders in honest conversations about how to use a "power, privilege, and poverty" analysis to understand the resources that are available to them for equity and inclusion work (up to and including financial resources). Leaders gain new concepts and tools to lead with more authenticity and power, practice better self-care, and tell meaningful stories to teams about their personal "why" for leading this work. Leaders help teams learn where their organizational culture is at *now* so they have a much better chance at arriving where they want to go. According to Laurence Overmire, "Our individual power to effect change may not seem like much, but remember, we are all interconnected. We are One. Powerlessness itself is an illusion. Every positive action we take, no matter how small, will have an impact."[1]

Here is where positive psychology, rooted in global wisdom, becomes useful in advancing equity. It provides leaders with a way to embody growth mindset, resilience, and grit. I leverage positive psychology not only for positive transformation but also for self-care in the work of equity and justice. It is useful for many different purposes but essential when it comes to inspiring and stewarding transformational change in workplace cultures. In our organizations, cultural groups, and as a nation, we have the fortitude to deconstruct and build anew. We need to build from that strength. We will have to learn from our mistakes with a discerning eye (resilience) and co-create a shared vision for the future. We will have to know why we are doing what we are doing and use the grit of deliberate practices to keep going. I apply Barbara Frederickson's concept "broaden and build" here.[2] For many teams, starting with what is already working is the critical missing link for cultural change work that needs to take place. I personally practice authentic and adaptive leadership in my own leadership work in the world (and encourage the same in my clients and colleagues).

SHARED VISION AND MOMENTUM
FOR CULTURE CHANGE

I introduce the concept of "cultural reflexivity" (a step beyond "cultural competence"), which teams use to improve organizational performance and more effectively meet the needs of an expanding community (and often, evolving mission and vision). This involves learning what I call "The Four Pillars of Integration and Justice:" Inclusion, Diversity, Equity, and Access (IDEA). It is critical to break down these terms and concepts in order for (a) teams to have shared language for what the work actually is and what it requires and (b) all team members, especially senior leaders and "influencers" to communicate the value of these different types of work to employees, partners, board members, and community members. The IDEA framework supports teams in clarifying their goals, builds muscle around using new language, and fosters accountability in the integration of new concepts in their work.

INCLUSION, DIVERSITY, EQUITY, AND ACCESSIBILITY

Inclusion: The process of integrating individuals of diverse talents and backgrounds successfully and equitably without fear, perception, or threat of harm (i.e., retaliation, no upward mobility, isolation, etc. for members and employees).

Diversity: Representation and reflection of the community on the staff, board, and member base (i.e., a reflection of diversity of community and target communities for a specific program) and representation of identified diverse talent, training, and experience needs.

Equity: Shifting the concept of "fair and equal" to the concept of meeting the needs of individuals (e.g. members/community externally and employees internally).

Accessibility: Physical and socioeconomic access to programs and services for the diverse members of a community and workplace; access to a quality of life that meets the overall well-being of team members in a thriving community and workplace; opportunities for promotion and career development within a work environment.

BUILDING EQUITY AND ACCOUNTABILITY THROUGH SYSTEMS AND NEW PRACTICES

For many teams, a large part of equity work is to build trust through authentic relationships and the practice of accountability. In our organizations, we are accountable to each other's humanity, each other's trials, and each other's individual experiences. With a growing sense of living accountably, we are compelled to act when we see evidence of systemic, historical, or cultural injustices as well as microaggressions. By practicing accountability, communities and organizations create a safer, more just, and more equitable society for Black, indigenous, Asian, and all other people of color and marginalized groups as well as for people who have been historically underrepresented due to race, religion, and ethnicity. This accountability should extend to newly arrived immigrants, people living in poverty without access to resources, for elders, for people who are not neurotypical, and for individuals living with differing abilities or chronic illnesses. Accountability is about using voice, influence, and power for positive social impact.

To design accountability into organizational work, I work with teams to create IDEA plans as an integral component woven into larger strategic plans and agendas including clear outcomes and measures of success. Together, we look at how to measure and sustain progress (relational, cultural, and organizational). I share practices for results-based accountability (to constituents, staff, and mission). We use clear tracking and problem-solving tools informed by design thinking and lean thinking. The goal is to leverage those best practices *that are most suitable to each organization* to advance equity and inclusion, solve problems, and transform culture.

An integrationist approach to equity and justice work is ideal, yet almost every organization I encounter starts with an attempt at inclusion and "inviting in" with insufficient regard to the power differential embedded within that very invitation. With inclusion, teams run the risk of tokenism if they aren't also doing the intentional work on how to identify, listen to, and integrate differences. In short, an organization that truly aims to better "include" members of marginalized communities within its ranks and leadership, decision-making, and operational processes will develop a culture of authentic, emergent leadership with a commitment to safety. This is about respecting all team members' individual humanity at work and back in their community.

When is an organization on the path to true integration?

Simply put, authentic inclusion is the first step. And this work requires dismantling the legacy of oppressive power structures and capitalism and supplanting it with the new currency of humanity and mutuality. Leaders work to intentionally create new systems and processes that *integrate* the diverse talent, skill, and life experience of individuals across race, generation, ethnicity, gender, and professional training. At minimum, a starting point occurs when a leadership team can demonstrate commitment and process toward understanding the cultural and historical literacy of sexism, classism, and racism (and their overlapping impacts) *within* their own institution and in relationship to community members. From here, all team members can identify goals and apply iterative practices on the way to integrating newly established policies in regard to all issues of equity around hiring, professional development, and product and service development.

My approach to integration work involves building a foundation of cultural awareness and fluency that provides the source for all ongoing work and methodologies. This renders a complete understanding that this is a lifelong journey of learning and unlearning. We develop capacity to be resilient in our learning and continually open to building new structures, policies, and programs. For teams that want to do this work, empathy is core to working cross-culturally as well as the positive psychology of "building on what works." At the individual level, team members unpack their social roles and identities, where they are socially located and the biases attached to these social markers. Often this work is mistaken as work done in relation to the "other" and, instead, much of it is self-awareness, education, and probing for truth and understanding. Only then relationships built on trust and mutuality can emerge.

john a. powell [*sic*] and Stephen Menendian of *The Othering and Belonging Institute* use[d] Du Bois's phrase to expand on this idea, writing: "The problem of the 21st century is the problem of 'othering'" and "the only viable solution . . . is one involving inclusion and belongingness."[3] This approach goes beyond anti-bias training, which is insufficient, because we all have bias. We all have preferences that are a result of our cultural context. *That is bias.* More than this, we have *many* different types of biases. Our biases are implicit, conscious, unconscious, environmental, and so on. We cannot fight against the fact that bias exists or fight what we deem as negative outcomes from searching and naming our bias; we *can* take responsibility for acknowledging and navigating the outcomes of our biased behavior.

In order for organizations to be on the path toward integration, people also need to look at their own attachment to colorblindness. Colorblindness is a byproduct of the bias of generational liberalism—or what I call the "sleepiness" that folks are trying to "wake up" from now that the Civil Rights Movement has passed. Colorblindness has not served as a useful strategy to create cultural connections and in many cases has caused long-lasting harm in professional and personal interactions. In organizational work, we explore two important issues related to the bias intrinsic in colorblindness, which Mellody Hobson believes was an intentionally taught and therefore learned behavior.[4] First, we demonstrate (through the National Center for Cultural Competence continuum) that colorblindness gets us only halfway to being proficient in navigating across culture and difference in a meaningful, sustainable way. We acknowledge how treating each individual, student, or employee "the same" can actually result in negative outcomes of early departure, isolation, discrimination, and so on. We explore the strengths and shadows (or blind spots) of this worldview and discuss how we see these manifest in our lives professionally and in a broader cultural sense.

According to Dr. Mark Williams, people who live through the colorblind lens know how to build an inclusive team *from that lens*.[5] The problem is—and Williams shares this in his research—as soon as evidence of *systemic* bias or disparities show up, people who view the world through a colorblind lens fail to see nuances or acknowledge the impact of systemic inequities on individuals. Reverend Dr. Martin Luther King, Jr. implored us to make decisions about a person based on their character and not their skin color. His invitation was to judge a person on what you see that person do—their integrity, energy, and passion—rather than their birth circumstance that gave them a social identity and role they did not ask for or could control. This is true, but what Dr. King did not do is ask us to turn a blind eye on the privileges or barriers that social identities afford us.

The simplest step toward real equity in teams and organizations is the most important one and is often completely missed: establish and frame mutuality.

To practice cultural humility and build mutuality, most people need a framework to support them as "inviters" to see the power they hold by their mere capacity to "invite" people into their work in the first place. This work requires self-assessment, acknowledgment of others' work and contributions, and, at times, reconciliation and reparation. This must be done working alongside newcomer leaders and teammates, recognizing their power and influence as well. Trust cannot be built *without* mutuality. Mutuality is how teams move toward developing a systemic analysis on power, influence, and equity.

As organizations move into the work of deconstruction and reconstruction toward more equitable ways of working, teams practice what I call cultural reflexivity. This is where teams begin to respond to new learnings and insights with innovation and build new pathways and structures that could not have been imagined in old oppressive structures. This is where true transformation and liberation begins to seed itself.

MOVING TOWARD TRANSFORMATION AND INNOVATION

In 2020, anti-racism work moved closer toward the center of our collective consciousness. We saw the disparities of the COVID-19 pandemic, and we witnessed the modern-day lynching of George Floyd, televised within the context of a dictatorship of hate, fear, and ignorance. White supremacy was threatening to take hold for another four years. In our communities and in our organizations, people felt vulnerable and more interconnected. But well before this awakening, many organizations like my own organization (BRIDGE, a minority and women-run nonprofit) had been analyzing these constructs of gender, race, and class in our communities. We (have) examined and helped others examine what we do in our everyday lives and jobs to uphold oppressive constructs willingly and unwillingly.

Institutions and their structures should be designed to serve people and help people flourish, not the other way around. From tiny nonprofits to universities to large manufacturers, organizations need the ability to stay nimble and pivot, identify real community needs, and marshal the resources to address these needs. These things must all work together in tandem. *These* are the new measures of survival and the new definition of success. As we continue to respond to the challenges of a pandemic and its impact on all of us and as the Black Lives Matter Movement continues to garner long-overdue attention and momentum on the shoulders of the civil rights leaders of the past, we can embrace this unprecedented opportunity to change. It is up to leaders to cultivate a work environment that embraces these changes as something beyond "the right thing to do" and meets the seen and unseen needs of our workforce.

Still, some organizations want to delay equity and inclusion work (or do the work, in some instances, too quickly in ways that may be harmful to others). There is simply no time for heteropatriarchal, white supremacist structures that limit our views and paralyze us, forcing some of us to exit stage left or worse, disregarding or even going so far as to demonize new, hugely important and potentially hugely impactful work. Now is not the time to mute certain voices simply because they are different from your own. Reverend Dr. Martin Luther King, Jr. captured this necessary twenty-first century need for understanding of mutuality by writing, "In a real sense all life is inter-related. All men are caught in an inescapable network of mutuality, tied in a single garment of destiny. Whatever affects one directly, affects all indirectly. I can never be what I ought to be until you are what you ought to be, and you can never be what you ought to be until I am what I ought to be. . . . This is the inter-related structure of reality."[6]

Along these lines, when it comes to recruiting, creating an equitable workplace is not as simple as hiring for diversity. Organizations must learn to talk about race before hiring people just to fill a quota. The first step is to acknowledge the prevailing cultural beliefs, norms, and behaviors that limit or exclude other groups and address them. Organizations need careful preparation, investment of resources (time, funding, and staffing), and a commitment to ongoing work. Pacing for transformative long-lasting change versus reactivity is essential. Unfortunately, hiring for diversity without attention to workplace culture is all too common, and, consequently, there is a negative impact from these efforts. In place of investing diligent care, I have seen organizations and decision-makers extract both existing *and* newly arrived team members' time, expertise, ideas, and labor and, in the process, their hopes and aspirations.

What does hiring with care mean? Leaders must start by equipping *themselves* with tools to build awareness and trust. There are five areas of cultural competence: shared knowledge and language for how to talk about culture and diversity; examining diversity and representation; beginning bias-assessments; navigating cultural difference; and ultimately, applying these insights to strategy work like recruitment and retention. Then, it is about setting goals and being clear on what success looks like in this hiring process. What are our considerations? And once a hire is made—what are the conditions for success and how can I support those conditions? Embracing concepts like *adaptation* and *emergence*, holding the work of equity and justice, and modeling commitment to transformation are imperative. The conditions, or rather foundations, for equity and justice would be established with shared language and clear expectations aligned with the organization's mission, vision, and values.

Challenges are expected and embraced and when they arise, the leaders will and must pause to address them. Leaders will be able to respond effectively to issues as they arise in the workplace, the community, and the wider world. If they do not have the resources to do the work, they will know how to identify them. New programs will often emerge that reflect the energy, collective work, and wisdom of the entire team. Almost without fail, these organizations become the leaders in their sectors and advocates and allies for systemic change locally and nationally. As we rise to the occasion with this current set of challenges and build responsive, effective structures to support all of our communities, the time is now to create and fully embody a culturally responsive and responsible way of operating. When we lead with certainty, our flock will fall into formation in pursuit of this liberation.

I close with the recent words of Dr. Angela Davis during the BRIDGE Social Justice Conference in November 2020, "Abolition is not primarily about the negative act of elimination and revocation . . . but rather it is about a process of re-creation and building something new. . . . We do not get rid of the old and assume that the new will be constructed on the same foundation as the old. We create new foundations, new footprints, new institutions, new societies."[7]

NOTES

1. Laurence Overmire, *The One Idea That Saves the World: A Call to Conscience and A Call to Action* (Indelible Mark Publishing, 2012).

2. Barbara L. Frederickson, "The Broaden-And-Build Theory of Positive Emotions," *Philosophical Transactions of the Royal Society B: Biological Sciences*, 2004.

3. Othering & Belonging Institute, accessed January 23, 2021, https://belonging.berkeley.edu/vision.

4. Mellody Hobson, "Color Blind or Color Brave?," TED.com. March 2014, accessed January 23, 2012, https://www.ted.com/talks/mellody_hobson_color_blind_or_color_brave?language=en.

5. Mark Williams, *The 10 Lenses: Your Guide to Living and Working in a Multicultural World* (Capital Books, 2001).

6. Martin Luther King, Jr., "Letter from a Birmingham Jail," accessed January 23, 2021, Stanford University, The Martin Luther King, Jr. Research and Education Institute, https://kinginstitute.stanford.edu/king-papers/about-papers-project.

7. Angela Davis, keynote speaker, "New Pathways Social Justice Conference," accessed November 9, 2020, https://www.multiculturalbridge.org/new-pathways-social-justice-conference-2020.html.

Part III

CHALLENGING TWENTY-FIRST CENTURY NOTIONS OF DIVERSITY ON COLLEGE AND UNIVERSITY CAMPUSES

Chapter 9

Black Lives Matter on Campus

Choreographing Protest

Peter A. Campbell

As a participant in the 2017 Mellon School Program at Harvard University that focused on pedagogy, practice, and protest, I was fortunate to meet and work with *Black Lives Matter* activist and choreographer Dr. Shamell Bell. On the final day of our two-week seminar, she led more than thirty theater and performance studies faculty and graduate students in a workshop that emulated the kind of work she has done and continues to do as a part of *Black Lives Matter Los Angeles* and in other workshops and protests nationwide. Almost two years later, on April 4, 2019, as part of a semester-long exhibition at the Ramapo College of New Jersey campus art galleries entitled "!!!Public Art???: Inquiries, Encounters," we welcomed Bell to our campus for a similar workshop on what she calls "Street Dance Activism," which she aims to use "as a source of empowerment countering the disempowered energy often created by continuously witnessing Black death."[1]

Bell defines Street Dance Activism as "(a)n embodied experience to offer collective counter-narratives from systems of oppression by co-choreographing the struggle for personal and community liberation."[2] Street Dance Activism engages Black and allied bodies to form communities of moving bodies as a way to protest the precarity of Black bodies in public spaces. Through Bell's artistic and pedagogical processes, which center on the power of the radical imagination and the materiality of bodies in space as political engagement, the workshop both embodied and interrogated the relationship of art practice to political protest. Bell calls this "Corporeal Pedagogy" and defines it as "a peer driven, alternative way of knowing, thinking, and teaching through the body, specific to Black youth, that disseminates to popular culture and provides practical application for lived experiences."[3]

This chapter is about Bell's practice but also about the context of that practice within an institution of higher education whose students, faculty, staff, and administration are primarily white. My impulse in inviting her to Ramapo College of New Jersey in the first place comes in part from a need to bring more artists and scholars of color to our campus in order to offer more diverse voices, especially in the realms of the arts and political activism. As a middle-aged white male, I am aware of my racial and gender position and hopeful that I can be a strong ally to people of color as a part of the struggle for liberation and equality. As someone whose adult life has been spent in the privileged space of academia, I also recognize many of the obstacles and challenges of creating opportunities for artists of color, especially when their work is explicitly political, as Bell's manifests itself in public spaces.

It is important for me to relate the afterlife of that visit as a working space of description, analysis, and scholarship. The first iteration of this was in response to a *Call for Presentations* for a conference on diversity with a focus on race at the Massachusetts College of Liberal Arts in June 2019, and then as a part of this publication, an anthology commissioned from that conference. Throughout this process, I have felt the inherent privilege of taking on these observations about Bell's work and visit to Ramapo College of New Jersey in placing them into this scholarly context within the problematics of my white male voice being the one through which an audience may be discovering and considering that work. As a white man in this context, to use the powerful metaphor examined in Jeremy O. Harris's recent *Slave Play*, I fear infecting Bell's work with the virus of my white male position. And perhaps that is inevitable, yet I hope this might (*instead and also*) be a process of my erasure, as I present the chapter such that Bell's work will gain more audience and space to speak and perform with her own words and actions in whatever spaces she chooses.

So, let me begin, again, with the geographical and logistical context of Bell's visit. Ramapo College is situated in the suburban township of Mahwah, New Jersey, on the border of New York state, about twenty miles northwest of northern Manhattan. Mahwah is a majority white township (about 75%) and is at the northern point of Bergen County, one of the wealthiest counties in the United States with a median income of $95,000.[4] The College draws students from across the state but is still a majority white institution (about 65% white) and has a campus that has limited public access and transportation.[5] While the second goal of the current strategic plan of the College is to increase diversity and inclusion, the institution has struggled with the reality of successfully recruiting and retaining administrators, faculty, and students of color. To illustrate this point, just weeks before Bell's visit, there were some contentious discussions at the college among faculty and administrators about whether a recent faculty retirement in African American literature would be replaced with a tenure line position. There had also been recent concerns across several campus constituencies, including the Minority Faculty and Staff Association, that in the recent search for a new Provost, there were no finalist candidates of color. The college is located in a geographical area where even the mention of *Black Lives Matter* is seen by a certain segment of the population as a threat to the white supremacist structures of the social order. As an administrator in the School of Contemporary Arts, my faculty and I believed that we had to be aware of the intrinsic "white fragility" of our context in order to help present and produce a potentially paradigm-shifting experience for the spectators and participants in Bell's visit.

In her influential work *White Fragility: Why It's So Hard for White People to Talk about Racism*, Robin DiAngelo uses the term "white fragility" to describe the ways that white people preclude meaningful discussions of race and racism by shutting down conversations that even suggest that there is a racial hierarchy with whites at the top in contemporary American society. DiAngelo argues that because whites have been "socialized into a deeply internalized sense of superiority that we either are unaware of or can never admit to ourselves, we become highly fragile in conversations about race" and thus "any attempt to connect us to the system of racism" is "an unsettling and unfair moral offense."[6] For example, because our societal racial hierarchy refuses to recognize whiteness as a category but instead as a neutral template, the very recognition of someone as "white" is refused by many whites as a valid characterization, and, in fact, often leads to calls of racism against whites. White fragility also depends upon the identification of "racist" behavior as individual and morally reprehensible, and thus the term itself is so loaded as to shut down conversations because it triggers denials of individual racism. White fragility additionally demands that our definition of racism does not apply to the larger society, but only to bad individual actors. According to this logic, a racist is a morally bad person who does something terrible, like turn fire hoses on crowds of African Americans during the Civil Rights Movement to prevent them from registering to vote. Most whites are not like that, so they are, therefore, not racist. In this example, the binary of bad/good means that many well-meaning whites are simply unable to confront the ingrained and socialized racism of the society in which they live. As DiAngelo argues, "These responses work to reinstate white equilibrium as they repel the challenge, return our racial comfort, and maintain our dominance within the racial hierarchy." While white fragility seems to indicate weakness, it is actually "a powerful means of white racial control and the protection of white advantage."[7]

Given this context, and as a white male administrator at a primarily white public liberal arts college, how can I help create an atmosphere that will allow for productive dialogue to take place without provoking so much white fragility that the conversations never happen?

Beginning with the first considerations of Bell's visit, months before the actual workshops, the director of the Art Galleries and I had been planning and strategizing to make Bell's visit and workshops as well-attended and politically effective as possible. First, the exhibition itself was wide-ranging and included many different types of art, performances, and public discussions. Much of the visual art in the galleries focused on ideas about monuments; for example, one series of photographs depicted the results of the recent removal of monuments celebrating Confederate military heroes.

Bell's visit included a panel that took place in the main art gallery, "Disrupting Blackness: Public Art and Choreographies of Protest," with another scholar, Deshonay Dozier, curated by Dr. Kimberly Welch, at the time a visiting assistant professor of African American literature at Ramapo College. The panel was on the day before the workshop, to increase Bell's visibility on campus and to offer a framework for the workshop before it happened. We also made concerted efforts to reach out to several student and administrative groups on campus, including the Black Student Union, the College Democrats, and the Office of Equity, Diversity, Inclusion, and Compliance. At the same time, we did not do much outreach off-campus, as we did not want to garner too much interest from local police and government, who might see an outdoor public workshop led by a *Black Lives Matter* activist as a potential threat. As Bell states in her documentary, "Black bodies moving freely is an act of political resistance in a white supremacist society."[8] While we were not afraid of the event being canceled or censored, we were afraid it might be compromised or become a locus of negative energy if it were framed by the wrong people in a manner that made it seem threatening, which is the epitome of how white fragility functions and succeeds in breaking down meaningful discussions of race and racism.

Bell's work itself is also conducive to creating opportunities for productive engagement and bypassing some obstacles of white fragility because of the way she frames it in terms of a practice of art and mindfulness. This is one of the reasons we wanted to invite her in the first place as a part of the Public Art exhibition. Taking her cues from theorists like bell hooks, Bell focuses on issues of well-being and seeks to create what she calls "The Lighthouse Effect": "A shift from our tendency to jump into fraught waters trying to save others, toward the calmer waters of *ALL* of us being Lighthouses, taking inventory of our own skills and learning how to be most effective in healing ourselves, shining our light for others to see, and guiding others."[9]

Street Dance Activism is meant to create moments of individual empowerment and healing that then allow communities to form and be empowered as well. As Bell states, the goal of Street Dance Activism is ultimately creating a community that can move "from me-centeredness to we-centeredness as a way of living, as a way of knowing."[10] There is an apparent paradox here, in that activism is usually constructed as an active form of protest against something. The Hegelian dialectic of protest places it as the antithesis to whatever the status quo is; a successful protest would then lead to a new synthesis. Bell's Street Dance Activism, however, disrupts not by necessarily protesting against something but by celebrating something else entirely. The interruption of the norm is the protest. For Street Dance Activism this means interrupting the normal of a white supremacist culture that is violent and oppressive to people of color with celebratory and liberating movement and community-building by those people of color and their allies. The interruption through the "radical joy" created by Bell's Street Dance Activism is creating a new kind of community that may create change in the larger status quo but is more interested in transforming "space from trauma to radical joy; lifting frequencies, lifting vibrations, and healing."[11]

Bell begins each of her presentations by asking everyone who can to stand up and close their eyes. She then asks the participants to acknowledge the native peoples whose land they are on, including the many ancestors whose lives were lost on the land on which the workshop is taking place. At Ramapo College, she acknowledged specifically the members of the Ramapough Lenape Nation, whose land and native identity have been a site of contestation for centuries and who have a tradition of protest through embodied practice, including recent sit-ins in support of the pipeline protests across North America. Bell then points out that the acknowledgment is a part of both a political practice and an art practice by pointing out that as a political relationship, it is doing ideological work that, like an art practice, might make someone consider the world from a different or new perspective.

Bell engages her participants physically almost immediately with the acknowledgment of the native peoples. While she also introduces the workshops verbally, her primary mode of engagement is to have groups, which she calls "crews," create their own choreography. The participants first create a movement vocabulary of gestures or dance moves that each member suggests and demonstrates, based on a group intention or collective vision. The crews are then given about fifteen minutes to come up with a name for their crew and to create a dance from these movements. Each group then presents their work, with the entire group moving and clapping along in support.

At Ramapo College, with a large and diverse group of people in a large space outdoors in a paved courtyard near the iconic red stone arch at the center of the campus, Bell spoke through an amplified body mic that allowed her to move around and still be heard by both the dozens of participants and the many observers who stayed on the edges of the space throughout the hour-long event. The area of the arch is a significant space. It is used as the logo for the college and serves as a central gathering place for events for constituents across the college and the community. The arch is also a central symbol to the students, who "enter" the arch in a ritual when they begin their education at Ramapo College, and then "exit" the arch in the other direction as a part of graduation and commencement ceremonies. It is thus public and central, a necessary hub of activity and passage. It is a passageway to get from some places of the campus to other places. Even during the event, for example, students, faculty, and staff would walk through the space between their classes or to get their lunch from the cafeteria. In fact, since Bell's workshop took place during a shared common hour, at 1:00 pm, many were walking through with their lunches in hand, with some putting down their food to join the workshop.

Bell broke the group into four crews of about twelve and managed to quickly put together diverse crews of faculty, staff, and students in each group. This made for an interesting dynamic, and some faculty could not resist their pedantic impulses and became leaders of the groups trying to help some of the meeker students to produce gestures and speak up. Bell was effective in moving among the groups and helping them find a collaborative and consensual process to break through the challenges of disempowerment that the hierarchies of educational institutions reveal even in non-curricular settings like this one. I was regularly identified as the "dancing dean" both during and after the event, as an authority figure who had engaged, even in my business casual attire, in the street dance choreography that I co-choreographed with my crew. It was a source of delight, of course, but it also highlighted the structural dynamics of the institution, which does not expect someone in my position to participate in such events and perhaps, through some eyes, to endanger the authority of my position in the social, institutional, and even the racial hierarchy. While there was broad participation, most of the faculty and staff who participated were already active in diversity organizations and initiatives on campus, although a few came because of the "Public Art" exhibition. The students were less easily identifiable, as many professors had required students to participate from classes across campus. The students were not only of theater or dance or African American studies majors or members of the Black Student Union or the Diversity Action Committee, who might be inclined toward such an event because of its content, but also those taking courses in visual arts, communication arts, political science, history, and even some studying business, nursing, and biology. Thus, the event itself created a more diverse group than would usually be found at a common hour event around a particular theme or activity, which was a major part of the intent of our audience outreach.

The workshops create several critical points of political and embodied action. First, each participant is able to create their own piece of movement of embodied gesture to choreograph their own body. This is an empowering and sometimes frightening act for the many of us who are not always comfortable or self-aware about our bodies in spaces, especially in public spaces where we are seen. By breaking up into small groups, each individual is given space and a supportive environment to create their own small piece of choreography, to decide how they want their body to move in space. Only then do individuals share those gestures with the smaller group.

The next point of engagement is the bringing together of the individual gestures with the group to decide on an order and a larger structure to create the community of the crew. The crew also has to come up with a name for the group, so they quickly have to agree on an identity. Here Bell uses the language of gangs to instill a sense of belonging and shared purpose. Much of her writing and scholarship focuses on the dynamics of gangs in Los Angeles as important community formations that are necessary for the survival of those communities when the political structures of the larger society are not accessible or oppressive to them. Using this gang paradigm as a metaphor for the choreographic work reveals its political inspiration and also makes many of the participants begin to consider (or perhaps re-consider) their initial feelings about gangs, which for many of us have only been experienced through news media and entertainment. Finally, during the performance, the newly formed community works together and shares their dance with the other groups involved.

Flashing back to my initial encounter with Bell at the Mellon School, our cohort broke into two groups of about fifteen and moved to opposite sides of the theater space in which we were working. It was an energized space, filled with the relief of getting out of our seats after almost two weeks of intense study and discussion. While I was initially hesitant about participating, it quickly became clear that Bell's energy was infectious, and even those of us least comfortable in our bodies participated willingly. Beyond the sense of release was a clear sense of political possibility in a space where thirty theater and performance scholars and practitioners had worked and studied together using our minds and words, to be able to embody our energies in a corporeal practice, and to work together in that embodied way, felt like it had the potential for a different kind of communication and community. It was in those moments that some of the bonds that had been built tentatively over the course of the seminar were solidified, and new connections emerged with people we may have not engaged with much. It felt like possibility and progress and appropriate for a seminar that focused on performance practice, pedagogy, and activism.

Bell's work is in line with many radical Black theories of revolution and progress, but takes most clearly from radical Black feminists like Angela Davis, bell hooks, and Maxine Greene, whose idea of "aesthetic education" focused on being "freed as embodied beings, as thoughtful and wondering beings, as beings caught up in process, in the pursuit of possibility."[12] The process-oriented practice of Street Dance Activism reveals how central the making of the work is to the work itself, marking it as something constructed and made. This is the clearest affinity Bell's work has to Augusto Boal's *Theater of the Oppressed*, which insists that all theater is political theater because everything is political and that, therefore, the most vital theater is always already an engagement in political action and should be treated that way. For example, Boal rejects the distinction of audience and performer, instead insisting that "all must act, all must be protagonists in the necessary transformations of society."[13] Only through taking over the "means of theatrical production" can the oppressed change their society.[14] Bell refers to Boal's practice as using "co-choreography" as a means of production.

For Bell, co-choreography is central to the creation and performance of Street Dance Activism: "In co-choreography, interconnectedness is key, a co-choreographing that encourages participants to include their own choreography while co-creating not only dance movements, but also daily movements in their lived experiences with each other. Doing life with each other."[15] For Bell, Street Dance Activism is always already political, whether it is a protest in a public space or a workshop at a college because it comes from lived and shared experience. It is always already interrupting space and the structures in place, and its means of production are meant to produce the content, which is a process of transformation and change in the actors and onlookers. Put another way, the crews are not telling an abstract story about other lives or other people but are performing a version of themselves in a new and shared community made by the activity itself. The creation of the community is the process of the work, and the presentation is the epitome of the community.

Bell considers her work most closely informed by Robin D. G. Kelley's insistence in *Freedom Dreams: The Black Radical Imagination* that Black survival and liberation depend upon an embrace of the political and artistic methodologies of surrealism. Kelley's surrealism is "a movement that invites dreaming, urges us to improvise and invent, and recognizes the imagination as our most powerful weapon."[16] If the goal of surrealism is "to lessen and eventually completely resolve the contradiction between everyday life and our wildest dreams,"[17] we can see how that might be attractive as a revolutionary model. The challenge, of course, is that it is unclear how exactly that model becomes an effective political strategy with concrete outcomes. Nonetheless, this kind of surrealism is about the actualization of dreams into reality, a hopeful movement that is both individually empowering and potentially paradigm-changing, especially for people who have historically found themselves marginalized from the hegemonic societal hierarchies. For Bell, dance is a potentially surreal action: "Dance provides air bending qualities with the ability to allow dancers to spiritually detach from worldly problems:

bending air as the element of freedom. Dancing, the ability to transcend, to exist beyond the physical realm and exist beyond the normal."[18]

Only three days before her arrival at Ramapo College, one of Bell's neighborhood heroes, the hip hop artist, entrepreneur, and activist Nipsey Hussle, was killed in his Los Angeles neighborhood. Bell talked about her sadness over his death, but also used it as a reminder about the urgency of the work. For her, and for many, Hussle's story was all-too-common but also absolutely unique—great potential shot down—literally—meaninglessly. Bell included Hussle in the list of her ancestors, and then said: "I can't believe he is now an ancestor." This, of course, is the other way the surreal speaks to the Black experience in the United States especially. As Richard Wright wrote seventy-five years ago in *Twelve Million Black Voices:* "The noise of our living boxed in stone and steel, is so loud that even a pistol shot is smothered."[19] This kind of "surrealism" is more of the popular understanding of the term: an event or sequence of events that are so unlike what reality is perceived as that they are unbelievable, yet they have somehow become acceptable or at least common. The violence toward Black bodies in American culture certainly still fits into this idea of the surreal.

In her practice, Bell insists that all she is doing is interrupting the space of the everyday in order to disrupt the structures and expectations of the everyday. And, in this, I hope we can see the surrealist art practice at work and as political tactic. For Bell, bringing a group of non-dancing people together to dance in a space that is not for dancing is a political act *BECAUSE* it is an artistic act. It demands a reconsideration of space and bodies in those spaces. When those are Black bodies in public spaces, like a *Black Lives Matter* protest outside the Los Angeles Police Department headquarters, the political stakes are often quite clear, as is the disruption of joyful dancing in a place and time of great solemnity. However, when they are diverse bodies in less political spaces, like a group of college students, staff, faculty, and administrators at a majority white college in suburban New Jersey, the less intense political stakes do not necessarily affect the potential for artistic intervention and thus, Bell would argue, political efficacy.

Participating with the students during Bell's visit to Ramapo College was especially valuable, as it allowed for them not only to explore power dynamics more freely but also for students of color to feel confident about their own presence. Bell's presence and delivery encouraged all the students, but I noticed students of color taking leadership roles, helping peers and faculty members with gestures, and helping coordinate in ways that demonstrated their comfortability in the space and with the process. While some of it was comical—like a young woman of color productively critiquing two faculty members' twerking technique—it was also indicative of Bell's focus on embodied performance and its empowering ability for people of color. I saw students feeling empowered in the process and not judged but encouraged to use their bodies and show off their skills and experiences. Several students remarked afterward to me that they not only were surprised how fun it was but also that they understood some of the political implications. One student asked me if Public Safety had threatened to shut us down if we got too loud. While the answer to that was no, we did have to end at 2:00 pm exactly, because classes would be in session and would be disturbed by the loud music and noise. And while the workshop had to end, the process kept moving in the conversations and discussions that followed.

If change and revolution depend upon imagining something that has not existed before, perhaps this kind of practice in unexpected places with unexpected participants is the surrealist action, the action with the greatest potential for change. Take from this what you will—the chief diversity officer, a very new cabinet-level administrative position at our college, participated joyfully in Bell's workshop, while another administrator walked through it without stopping to look or participate on the way to lunch. While this series of events confirms a certain structural and institutional binary, the administrator who just walked through asked me later about the workshop, and the asking led to a productive conversation about diversity, hiring practices, and tenure lines. The interruption of space with bodies instigated discussion even among those who were not inclined to participate. This is evidence that the kind of "genuine dialogue" that Bell desires from her practice can come both by participating in the embodied practice and by observing it. Bell discusses the importance of this when she references bell hooks's insistence on this kind of dialogue among "individuals who actually occupy different locations within structures, sharing ideas with one another, mapping out terrains of commonality."[20] The shared language of space between hooks and Bell is striking, as is their common concern with healing and community-building as pathways to mitigate societal and cultural trauma. Both ultimately recognize that in order for true progress, communities must eventually be able to have productive discourse with other communities.

Choreographer Martha Graham has said that "the body says what words cannot."[21] Bell's work "privileges the body as a primary locus of experience while keeping social formations of race and gender, and their material effects, in focus."[22] Bodies, therefore, are both individual and a metaphor for society, holding within them individual and societal structures and traumas. Bodies of color are subjects and objects of resistance in a white supremacist society, whether they are acting in a form of resistance or not; their very existence is their resistance. Like Graham, Bell insists that bodies communicate and commune, and are responded to, just not in ways that we necessarily rationally understand or can explain in words. Bell's practice, based in Kelley's surrealism, is likewise ephemeral and resists being written, or written about, or described in the limited binaries of our language. What it offers instead is a way through the dialectics that define our political discourse, dialectics that continue to reach syntheses that oppress bodies of color. The beautiful potential of Bell's art practice is that it demands a re-thinking of those political dialectics that start with that which is most precarious and most difficult to talk about—the body.

Of course, we still need to go back to my initial anxiety about this whole project, and how I came to write all this down in the first place. Why am I, a white male college administrator, bringing a Black female artist and activist to the campus to do this kind of work? The dynamics of that remain problematic, and Bell's practice actually speaks to that problem—the efficacy of her practice is in bringing bodies of color to places of protest but creating communities of protest through dance and joy, not through violence and pain. In academic settings like the one at Ramapo College, bodies of color are still too often seen, as they are in American society at large, as threatening to the white template of community. There need to be more interventions like Bell's that create space for those bodies to do work in academic, institutional, and artistic settings. The work she is doing is what needs to be recognized, and the political function of it, regardless of the setting, is what makes it valid and vital to not just communities of color but to any community that looks to fight against racism and reach toward more equality and fairness in the expression of political power and the consequent distribution of resources.

From the evidence I have of what Bell brought to both the Mellon School and Ramapo College, the quality of community was improved by her presence and work in concrete ways. Through her achievement of corporeal pedagogy in the workshops, a group of diverse and disparate people were brought together in joy to create something ephemeral that was also representative of a larger accomplishment—a new way of considering community that, for many of us, especially in academia, resists the limitations of language and allows for a different kind of communication to transcend and transform individuals into members of a new kind of community, even if in small moments—a community that has experienced Street Dance Activism and is, as Bell desires "dancing toward freedom."[23]

NOTES

1. Shamell Bell, *Living is Resisting: Rize to Street Dance Activism as a Corporeal Pedagogy* (PhD Diss Prospectus, UCLA, 2018), 27.

2. Shamell Bell, *Living is Resisting: An Autoethnography and Oral History of Street Dance Activism in Los Angeles*, Documentary Film, 2018.

3. Bell, "Prospectus," 1.

4. "Census Reporter, Mahwah, NJ," accessed May 19, 2020, https://censusreport er.org/profiles/06000US3400342750-mahwah-township-bergen-county-nj/.

5. "Ramapo College of New Jersey," *College Factual*, accessed May 19, 2020, https://www.collegefactual.com/colleges/ramapo-college-of-new-jersey/student-life/ diversity/.

6. Robin DiAngelo, *White Fragility: Why It's So Hard for White People to Talk about Racism* (Boston: Beacon Press, 2018), 2.

7. *Ibid.*

8. Bell, "Documentary."

9. Bell, "Prospectus," 14.

10. *Ibid.*, 27.

11. *Ibid.*, 14.

12. Maxine Greene, "Foreword," *Researching Drama and Arts Education: Paradigms and Possibilities*, ed. Philip Taylor (London: Falmer Press, 1996), xv–xvi.

13. Augusto Boal, *Theater of the Oppressed* (New York: Theatre Communications Guild, 1979), x.

14. *Ibid.*

15. Bell, "Prospectus," 27.

16. Robin D. G. Kelley, *Freedom Dreams: The Black Radical Imagination* (Boston: Beacon Press, 2002), 159.

17. *Ibid.*, 158.

18. Bell, "Prospectus," 28.

19. https://archive.org/details/in.ernet.dli.2015.175481.

20. bell hooks, *Teaching to Transgress: Education as the Practice of Freedom* (New York: Routledge, 1994), 30.

21. Martha Graham, "Martha Graham Reflects on Her Art and a Life in Dance," *New York Times*, March 31, 1985, 2:1.

22. Bell, "Prospectus," 18.

23. Ibid., 28.

Chapter 10

Black Maleness at a Public Regional University

Mark Wagner and Katherine L. Cleary

Begun in 2015, the Worcester State University (WSU) Civic Corps is modeled in part on a 2011 program developed at Georgia State University in which the university gave small grants to approximately 200 students identifying as African, Latino, Asian, or Native American (ALANA) and who had been dropped from classes for nonpayment. The grants—each less than $1,000 on average[1]—kept most of the students from dropping out, resulting in higher graduation rates in the long term. Following this example, the partners in the WSU Civic Corps—the Office of Multicultural Affairs, International Programs, the Sociology Department, and the Binienda Center for Civic Engagement—received an internal Strategic Planning Incentive Fund grant of $5,000, which has been renewed by WSU's leadership for the next five years. This article examines how this financial assistance in combination with the educational tools of civic engagement and service-learning aided three Black male students at WSU.

The WSU Civic Corps has begun each year by working with the Office of Informational Technology to identify ALANA students who have accumulated between eighteen and thirty credits and whose expected family contribution or Pell Grant eligibility indicates financial need. Respondents accepted into the program are given $500 for local service and $1,000 to participate in faculty-led study away. To date, fifty-four students have received Civic Corps scholarships: eleven are active this year and forty-three have completed a project; of these forty-three, six identified as Asian, eleven as Black, fourteen as Latino, two as white, and ten as mixed race. Of this cohort, twelve have graduated, and twenty-eight remain active.

Institution-wide programs and policies to improve the graduation rates of ALANA students include pre-college preparation, admission policies, affirmative action, and financial aid—all of which WSU employs. The following case studies, however, specifically explore how civic engagement and service-learning, which are nontraditional educational tools that are underrepresented in current research, remediated traditional obstacles and challenges faced by Black male students at WSU.

At four-year institutions in the United States, Black men complete their degrees at the lowest rate compared to all other demographics.[2] To redress this inequity, the case studies in this article explored how civic engagement and service-learning create linkages between classroom learning and real-world experiences to help three students develop a sense of belonging and to support them in overcoming the "battle fatigue" brought on by the negative perceptions of Black males as "threatening, unfriendly, and less intelligent than any other distinguishable segment of the American population"[3]. Highlighting civic engagement and service-learning organized by mentors who understood the financial, legal, and social challenges of their students, these case studies also allowed us to make specific recommendations aimed at improving the retention and success of Black male students.

BACKSTORY

Boyer[4] coined the phrase *New American College* to describe how civic engagement and service-learning in higher education could contribute to national renewal—a notion supported by Eyler and Giles,[5] Kuh, Kinzie, Cruce, Shoup, and Gonyea,[6] Furco,[7] and Saltmarsh and Hartley,[8] among others. As these scholars have maintained, through service-learning and civic engagement, the academy might effectively present solutions to pressing social, economic, and civic problems.

While ALANA students have historically had the lowest retention and graduation rates in higher education, those rates are lowest for Black males.[9] In the past, the experiences and needs of this identity group may have been lost or gone undetected because they made up a small percentage of students, but higher education in the United States has become significantly less white. From 1999 to 2012, college attendance rose 58 percent among Hispanics/Latinos, 30 percent among African Americans, and 16 percent among whites.[10] The success of ALANA students, and Black male students in particular, is important to the integrity of higher education.

As Travers wrote: "In the field of higher education, there have been more peer-reviewed journal articles, books, and national reports published on Black college men than any other group. Yet still only about one-third of Black men who enroll in college end up graduating."[11] While some litera-ture has anticipated civic engagement and service-learning fostering a more inclusive campus climate,[12] research on how (or whether) civic engagement and service-learning contributes to the success of **ALANA** students has been lacking. According to Hickmon:[13] "Race, class, gender and all the other 'isms' should be contextualized both in and out of the SL [service-learning] classroom. . . . Critical reflection about all participants' subject positions and how they interact with their work and with society at large is necessary if SL is to become a space that moves all who are engaged closer to becoming democratic citizens who operate with values that bend toward justice, equality, and freedom."[14] For this reason, the aforementioned authors considered both the literature in civic engagement and service-learning the literature of the Black male experience.

Ehrlich located civic engagement and service-learning as areas of student development in higher education that "make a difference in the civic life of our communities and develop the combination of knowledge, skills, values and motivation to make that difference."[15] This collaboration between institutions of higher education and larger communities represents an opportunity for a mutually beneficial exchange of knowledge and resources in a context of partnership and reciprocity.[16]

As the Lumina Foundation maintained: Like other forms of application, civic inquiry requires the integration of knowledge and skills acquired in both the broad curriculum and in the student's specialized field. But because civic preparation also requires engagement—that is, practice in applying those skills to representative questions and problems in the wider society—it should be considered a discrete category of learning. Higher education is experimenting with new ways to prepare students for effective democratic and global citizenship. Virtually all of these efforts use experiential or field-based learning as a means to develop civic insight, competence in public affairs and the ability to contribute to the common good.[17]

If one accepts civic engagement and service-learning as discrete categories of higher learning and as means to a common good, employing these tools to improve the retention and success of **ALANA** students, and Black male students in particular, will require an understanding of the social and economic milieus in which students develop. Brooms and Garibaldi held that examining Black males' collegiate experiences opens a broad canvas for investigating the intersections of race, gender, history, and political climate. In *Being Black, Being Male on Campus*, Brooms noted the "delicate nature of one's sense of self and how normative masculine constructs might limit one's development, social interactions, and engagement."[18]

Critical race theory (CRT) is one way to connect the disciplinary failures of higher education to students' social and economic situations. Growing out of the work of W. E. B. DuBois, CRT has been used to understand how race is situated within an overwhelmingly oppressive structure.[19] In Dubois's classic framework, Blacks were born into an internal struggle as a result of being both American and Negro. According to Delgado, CRT evolved further out of legal studies during the 1980s as a movement that sought to account for the persistent role of race and racism in the United States.[20] The phrase *driving while Black*—reinforced by Ellison,[21] Baldwin,[22] Coates[23]—illustrated this social tension. Black men "drove" in a white space and faced the conundrum of being both being present and unseen. They were seen by the police as problems while driving but unseen as individuals with rights when confronted by the criminal justice system. They existed as problems or, in extreme cases, targets: "Between me and the other world there is ever an unasked question: unasked by some by feelings of delicacy; by others through the difficulty of rightly framing it. All nevertheless flutter around it. . . . How does it feel to be a problem?"[24]

Multicultural education has developed strategies for responding to the many issues created by the rapidly changing demographics of students in the United States. ALANA student support networks, which took the form of Black student unions, third world alliances and offices of multicultural education, grew out of the Civil Rights Movement of the 1960s as a way to eliminate discrimination in public accommodations, housing, employment, and education. Arguably, higher education's multicultural focus grew in large part from the efforts of the Student Nonviolent Coordinating Committee, which emerged from the first wave of student sit-ins and employed a totalistic approach, combining anti-war movements with a wide variety of programs and practices related to educational equity, women, ethnic groups, language minorities, low-income groups, LGBT (lesbian, gay, bisexual, and transgender) people, and people with disabilities.[25]

As a compliment to CRT and multicultural education, Black maleness is also a useful framework for highlighting some of the forces working against Black men in academic life. Brooms noted that "Black men [continue] to be viewed as 'troubled' which has social, personal, and academic consequences."[26] These racial and gender stereotypes have come from media portrayals of Black men as criminal, oversexed, lazy, violent, and unintelligent, and from experiences and social learning over lifetimes in segregated or inhospitable schools and institutions. Educators, however, have not been immune to picking up and acting on such stereotypes. Brooms wrote: "In theorizing Black masculinities, Mutua argues that Black men routinely faced suspicion, which narrowed their life possibilities . . . being Black and male on campus leaves them open to an array of challenges and their activities, locations and forms of expression are insignificant in how they are often imagined and projected."[27] To explore the dynamics of civic engagement and service-learning as it relates to race, Hickmon recommended "questioning what SL experiences look like across identity groups and working to ensure the pedagogy truly becomes a space dedicated to social justice, community, and equality—values it has always championed."[28]

THREE YOUNG MEN

Three Black male students from WSU's Civic Corps were identified for this exploratory study. (Pseudonyms have been used in the following cases to respect the students' confidentiality.) While the Civic Corps' initial goals were to foster engaged citizenship by promoting civic engagement and service-learning and to support ALANA students at a critical moment in their college experiences, the exploratory case-study method also allowed the authors to better understand complex social, cultural, and economic forces that obstruct academic success for Black male collegians. Such insights served "as powerful rejoinders to the current post-racial discourse."[29] Moreover, the case studies offered a "narrative pleasure," allowing the authors to focus more intensely on individuals whose experiences identified broader sociological trends from which the authors could make specific recommendations.

Due to the lack of general knowledge about how civic engagement and service-learning contribute to the retention and success of ALANA students, the exploratory case-study approach provided a phenomenological method for considering the lived experiences of the study participants. Creswell wrote, "Phenomenology is an approach to qualitative research that focuses on the commonality of a lived experience within a particular group. Through this process the researcher may construct the universal meaning of the event, situation or experience and arrive at a more profound understanding of the phenomenon."[30]

The authors gained access to this lived experience each year by inviting (via email) ALANA students who had accumulated between eighteen and thirty credits to apply for a Civic Corps scholarship. In the application, the Civic Corps project asked students to identify a faculty member with whom they wished to work or a project on which wanted to focus. If they did not identify a faculty mentor or project, the Civic Corps offered to mentor them in taking on a project, such as Jumpstart, an AmeriCorps preschool literacy program, or another ongoing service project that WSU's civic engagement center supported, such as the Neighbor Helping Neighbor program. In the application, the Civic Corps asked students to explicate the ways in which they had been introduced to civic or community engagement, and what those experiences had meant to their development as students, family members, and agents in their communities.

After evaluating applications, our team of faculty, residential life, and student affairs administrators invited each applicant for an interview during which we explained the expectations of the Civic Corps. Expectations included participating in an afternoon workshop at the start of the semester, attending a retreat at the end of the year, committing to completing a project, and delivering a presentation on the student's project at either WSU's annual

Celebration of Civic Engagement or the annual Celebration of Scholarship and Creativity, both of which take place annually in April.

Finally, the Civic Corps project addressed issues of the historical fatigue of ALANA students by offering nontraditional forms of mentoring. That is, because WSU has a full-time Center for Civic Engagement, the Civic Corps project was able to provide mentoring that included more than test preparation or tutoring. For example, in one case study, our Center for Civic Engagement provided logistical support in setting up interviews for a study on men in recovery; in two cases, offered transportation to and from service sites; in one, offered legal aid; and in another, helped a student transition from a menial job to employment at a university hospital emergency room. The Civic Corps' methodology included supportive mechanisms around aspects of student life that went beyond traditional approaches to the retention of ALANA students. Distinct from the Academic Success Center and the Office of Multicultural Affairs, WSU's Center for Civic Engagement provided a place to go—a place of belonging—and intervened with respect to students' projects. These interventions ranged from phone calls to probation officers to setting up presentations with city managers to locating jobs in students' chosen fields to welcoming friends to apply to the Civic Corps.

EPHEMERA OF GRADES, REALITY OF BOOKS

The [Civic Corps] assisted me where I constantly lack and that is paying for books. My freshman year, I was not able to get my grades to where it needed to be because I was missing books. This semester the aid helped me out and took some weight off my shoulders. (Derek, Civic Corps member)

Derek was a business major, a track athlete, and had a fairly severe speech impediment, which lessened as the authors got to know him. His GPA was lower than 2.0 after his first year, which had put his athletic participation at risk. Derek worked on the Neighbor Helping Neighbor civic project, in which students assist elderly neighbors with snow shoveling and yard work. While his $500 Civic Corps scholarship helped Derek to purchase books, he also developed an ongoing relationship with an elderly resident helping her with her pellet stove, snow removal, and yard cleanup. The resident reported "when [her husband] died, he left me tools to keep the house, but I am now getting too old to use them." Though this human quality to the Neighbor Helping Neighbor project is critical, when Derek reported that the Civic Corps helped him pay for books, his comment illustrated a central concern of our study—that there are no university structures in place to "listen" to this participant's particular situation. His "failure" in his first year was not a cognitive, academic occurrence, but an economic hardship. The fact that the university recorded his first year as an academic failure is a matter for discussion.

The modern disciplinary structure of higher education has its roots in the late nineteenth century when the primary goals of colleges and universities were to meet societal demand for "marketable" and business-relevant skills.[31] The structure of academic disciplines has remained largely unchanged since that time. Indeed, the "silo" structure of the disciplines, professional identities, and loyalties—and the resulting "turf language"—have hardened in the twentieth century, with the "tribes and territories" of the academy laying claim to discipline-centric knowledge: "These monolithic structures are blocking the next phase in the evolution of universities. . . . Students lose out too: poorly managed course development across disciplines can lead to a joint degree that is two mealy halves joined together rather than a seamless matrix of ideas and challenges."[32]

In Derek's case, his oppression took the form of economic need, compounded by his inability to ask for help and the university's inability to create pathways to that help. Derek's grades in his first year should not be seen as valid assessments, but as codes that misrepresent Derek's intellectual ability. With access to books, Derek is capable of succeeding in the academic climate (at this writing, after his second year, Derek is again above a 2.0.), but that same climate largely ignores the long-term economic challenges created by academia's racial myopia.

By its third year, the Civic Corps project began to gain participants by word of mouth. In spring 2018, Sorcy came to the Center for Civic Engagement, asking where to find work that did not require unwieldy interviews and transportation arrangements. "I am a friend of Derek's," Sorcy introduced himself. This appeared to be a moment when the identity and character of one Black man was not threatened by the confines of economic needs and stereotype management. Derek and Sorcy were exhibiting cooperative masculinity; because Sorcy felt he could ask for assistance, the economic sphere became, at least for our little network, less racialized. Such referrals are welcome and point to some element of progress in combating the "pressures, profiling, and insults that all work to diminish the values that Black men bring to institutions."[33]

When these Black men reached out for help to academics (some of whom were white) through word-of-mouth referrals and to the Neighbor Helping Neighbor project, it felt indicative of some minor transformation of campus-social and campus-public spaces. In addition, while Derek's speech impediment may prevent verbal elegance, Derek has become a notable figure on campus in the years we have known him. He set a school record in track. He has also referred some of his peers to the center to secure work or support. The

Civic Corps project allowed our community to "listen" to a Black man about economic hardship, to celebrate cooperative masculinity among Black men, and to argue for creating and redirecting campus resources to and for them.

BLACK MALE INVISIBILITY AND THE POLICE

Chris—a tall Black gentleman sporting a 1960s-style afro—came to the Center for Civic Engagement one day. He needed community service hours. In September 2016, while driving he had swerved to avoid an accident, and in doing so hit a light pole with his car. The police told Chris they needed to impound his car, claiming that he had damaged city property. Chris explained that his car was drivable, that he lived nearby and would drive home. The police refused to let him do so, and the situation escalated. As the police refused to hear this young man's interpretation of events and prevented him from keeping his car, Chris repeatedly verbally insulted the officers. The officers arrested Chris, eventually charging him with seven counts, including resisting arrest. They impounded his car and phone, and temporarily jailed him until he could be released on his own personal recognizance.

The Civic Corps accepted Chris as a member and began a two-year journey in which the Center for Civic Engagement provided mentoring and legal aid to support Chris in clearing this event from his record. The authors met with Chris frequently, sometimes more than twice a week, and secured him a job at the local YMCA. The head trainer, Brenda, was a local activist, on a first-name basis with the police chief and congressional representatives. Through Brenda, who added to this narrative, we not only advocated that Chris's case be dropped, but also questioned the actions of the police.

Historical circumstances might have played a role in both Chris's frustration and the police officers' overreaction. In the month in which Chris was arrested, *Black Lives Matter* (*BLM*) was active in protesting police brutality. In Baltimore, *BLM* activists marched as hearings began in the Freddy Gray police brutality case. Chris informed us that he had been stopped eighteen times, in what were clearly *driving while Black* incidents.[34] Brenda informed Chris that, in Massachusetts' courts, the claim that a person developed anxiety around police officers serves as a valid defense. At the same time Brenda and the university's Center for Civic Engagement began to advocate for Chris in the legal system, Chris designed and delivered a chess program at Valley View School, teaching fifth graders the intricacies of the game. He also began to work with the YMCA's Super Saturdays program for teens. As he told us, "I was always one of the kids who ended up going to school early. . . . One day, someone grabbed the chess set sitting idly in a corner of the classroom.

Then we started learning, teaching ourselves every single morning for pretty much the whole year of school."

About his involvement with the program at Valley View, Chris's mentor wrote, "Chris was a tremendous asset to [the] . . . Chess Club. The students looked forward to his Thursday visits to ask him chess questions and challenge him to a game. He developed a friendly competitive relationship with the students where he would challenge and teach at the same time." Chris "found us" as a result of his community service requirement (as a result of his incident with the police), but this pointed to the question: How is it that most public higher education institutions do not have dedicated resources for students facing legal issues?

Heilman wrote, "The devastating effect that even a 'minor' legal issue can have on an individual's academic progress makes it essential for both law professionals and academic leaders to recognize the absolute need for students to have access to low-cost/no-cost legal aid: providing assistance, advice, referrals, and representation. A single instance of this need going unattended can completely derail an individual's academic and career progress—in some cases, irreversibly."[35] Many Student Legal Services (SLS) programs that developed in the 1960s and 1970s at colleges and universities did not survive education reform in the ensuing decades. Yet, the rise of *BLM* (e.g.,) highlighted the need for legal assistance for students. Some larger universities did maintain SLS programs.

From its inception through June 2013, Rutgers referred 746 cases through its SLS program—but Rutgers is an exception. The totalistic approach to social justice issues that began in the 1960s has broken up into Pride Movements, Women's Studies Departments, Disability Service Offices, and the creation of "Black spaces." As social commentator David Brooks opined, "There is a misplaced idolization of diversity. The great achievement of the meritocracy is that it has widened opportunities to those who were formerly oppressed. But diversity is a midpoint, not an endpoint. Just as a mind has to be opened so that it can close on something, an organization has to be diverse so that different perspectives can serve some end. Diversity for its own sake, without a common telos, is infinitely centrifugal, and leads to social fragmentation."[36]

This social fragmentation has left behind elements of the original purposes of multicultural education, one of which was student legal assistance; however, colleges and universities may serve as resources for rethinking the surging corrections cases and populations in the nation's prisons. To this point, on February 28, 2018, Chris came into our office and showed off his signed "continued without finding" paperwork, stating that his arrest record and the charges filed against would be scheduled to terminate. Chris graduated that spring with a degree in both business and sociology.

At our end-of-year retreat, Chris reported:

The Civic Corps gave me quality time outside my own personal bubble of selfishness, focus of school life, work life and the other stresses we face each day as individuals. To help give back to the community and humble myself, while ensuing more drive within me because of the faces of the children I would help, I met different individuals striving for their own path as well. The pursuits we have are to better our future networks, and being in school generates a better education for more than ourselves. Technically if you cannot be selfish for yourself, who will be? A part of being selfish is doing things you enjoy, a major one for me is working with kids. From Chandler Magnet, to Valley View and YMCA, the Civic Corps helped me out a lot. Even with the ever-changing landscape of our minds in the future we wish to have blowing in the wind, it made me really think about getting into the subject field [of working] with kids.

BLACK MALE INTELLIGENCE

When I began this academic year with an invitation from the [Civic Corps] I was both surprised and pleased. I'd honestly not known of the Center, but I was happy to learn about what they did. Throughout my life, service has always been a big part of who I am. Whether I served as a Boy Scout or through activities organized by my church, I learned to appreciate how pleasing it was to serve another person. . . . The support of the Center strengthened my resolve to serve others and afforded me the opportunity to take a step back from my own concerns and help someone else with theirs. In doing so I've felt reinvigorated as I've continued to pursue my path through academia and as I prepare to become a professional. The Center also gave me the chance to meet inspiring students who share a desire to serve and contribute to their communities. This chance to meet like-minded individuals has likewise helped me to understand how central service is to who I am. (Andre, Civic Corps member)

Andre came to the Center for Civic Engagement hurried, since he was on his way to work, but he had been invited (and wanted) to apply to the Civic Corps. Our team asked about his job, and he told us he worked as a cashier at a local discount store. He was also a biology student with a 3.7 GPA who wanted to go to medical school.

In 1978, 1,410 Black males applied to medical school; by 2014, that number had dropped to 1,337. Likewise, the number of Black male matriculants to medical school showed virtually no change in that thirty-five-year period: in 1978, 542 Black males matriculated, and in 2014, the number had fallen slightly to 515. No other minority group experienced declines. The inability to find, engage, and develop candidates for careers in medicine from all members of society limits the ability to improve health care for all.[37]

As an honors student with a 3.7 GPA in a pre-medical track, Andre had found support, and his intelligence was engaged. His struggles were not related to academic structure but to building a network that would support his goal to attend medical school. To that end, the university's civic engagement center had been involved for five years with an opioid recovery program, run by the state's Department of Public Health. Our work there had focused on financial literacy, access to health care, and "Back on the Books," a program for reestablishing active tax status for men who had been incarcerated. At the Hector Reyes House, a recovery program run by the Massachusetts Department of Public Health, in collaboration with the Latin American Health Alliance, the WSU Center for Civic Engagement had been active with Dr. Matilda Castiel, Commissioner of Health and Human Services for our city.

The authors introduced Andre to Dr. Castiel and developed an internship with the city in which Andre (and two other corps members) surveyed men in recovery and made recommendations to the city manager as to how to support successful recovery. (Andre's report that grew out of that survey was published as part of Celebration of Scholarship and Creativity, Worcester State University, March, 2018.) With Dr. Castiel's direct intervention, Andre transitioned from his job as a cashier to a job as a "scrub" at the emergency room of a university hospital.

Though Black men may find support in the disciplines in exercising and developing their cognitive skills, the ability to advance in a career in the medical field requires access to influential people. The American Association of American Colleges and Universities found that practices involving direct application of skills are more critical to career success than acquisition of discrete bodies of knowledge. For Black men, this skill application is confounded by racial and social factors.[38] For example, Brooms noted that African American males might act in ways that do not fit teachers' or professionals' preferences for proper etiquette.[39] If they grew up in fragile families and neighborhoods marked by violence, drugs, or economic blight, Black boys and male teens may behave frenetically and respond to frustrations by acting tough and engaging in bravado posturing. These social factors become compounded as teachers and professionals bring stereotyped attitudes into the classroom or workspace, especially if they have had limited experience relating to Black males. Intelligent Black men with the goal of becoming doctors often face challenges different from those faced by Derek and Chris, challenges more deeply rooted in media stereotypes that distort Black male intelligence, challenges involving access to quality higher education, and challenges accessing influential people. As noted by Nivet, this has resulted in declining enrollments of Black males in medical establishments.[40]

The WSU Civic Corps project allowed Andre access to a social network and to a key figure in his chosen field. Andre also had an opportunity to present to city officials and to publish his work. In short, civic engagement allowed Andre to overcome some social and racial factors that have historically limited Black men in medicine and to advance his goals by publishing, by becoming more comfortable with people in power, and by landing a job in his field.

CONCLUSIONS AND RECOMMENDATIONS

WSU's Civic Corps project seeks to remediate the challenges and obstacles that can institutionalize persistent failure among ALANA students by implementing the educational tools of civic engagement and service-learning. To build upon the WSU Civic Corps' minor success, institutions need to provide resources and infrastructure for programs employing civic engagement and service-learning while educating mentors about the complex financial, legal, and social forces that obstruct academic success for young Black men. The authors offer further recommendations in the closing paragraphs.

REDIRECT EXISTING RESOURCES

WSU spends tens of thousands of dollars each year bringing speakers and promoting programs aimed at educating individuals about issues of social injustice and inequity. Each year, a campaign such as Latin American History Month might compete with the Diversity Lecture Series that might compete with the Provosts' programs. These programs are often built in accordance with traditional disciplinary hegemony and in some cases compete—and not always in a collegial manner—with other programming. The authors recommend establishing racial equity planning committees that assess how university monies are spent, particularly programs that advance "diversity," and to redirect some of these funds to scholarships for ALANA students that increase access to the high-impact work of civic engagement and service-learning.

REINSTITUTE STUDENT LEGAL SERVICES

The legal troubles facing young Black men are complex and endanger the academic success of many students. Colleges and universities, particularly in urban settings, need to develop access to legal services through which Black male students can receive guidance and support in negotiating what are oftentimes trivial legal matters that can nevertheless derail students' lives. University networks and local elected officials need to be made aware of and develop means to alleviate tensions between young Black men and the police, and to advocate for these young men in criminal justice systems when these matters process.

PROVIDE ACCESS TO SOCIAL NETWORKS

Becoming a physician or pursuing a particular specialty may be less attractive to young Black men when they do not see people similar to them in academic classrooms or medical professions. Civic engagement and service-learning are tools for colleges and universities to employ in creating programs that allow Black males to have meaningful interactions and to establish connections with people in positions of power who look like them. This will be aided by hiring practices aimed at increasing diversity among faculty and staff. As stakeholders build out these hiring practices, it will be important to resource civic projects that interface with governmental and community structures, and that gave ALANA student access to people in influential positions.

The authors look forward to continuing our work with Civic Corps students, both during their enrollment and after they have graduated. We encourage more research that explores how civic engagement and service-learning can transform campus climates such that ALANA students can feel a greater sense of belonging and flourishing, and can become critical agents in the transformation of the negative consequences of the nation's racist history.

NOTES

1. T. Dovey, A. Ludgate, and J. Tutak, "Success by Design: Improving Outcomes in American Higher Education," *Deloitte Insights* (2011), accessed from https://www2.deloitte.com/insights/us/en/industry/public-sector/improving-student-success-in-higher-education.html.

2. L. DeAngelo, R. Franke, S. Hurtado, J. H. Pryor, and S. Tran, *Completing College: Assessing Graduation Rates at Four-Year Institutions* (Los Angeles: Higher Education Research Institute, UCLA, 2011).

3. M. J. Cuyjet, "African American Men on College Campuses: Their Needs and Their Perceptions," *New Directions for Student Services* 80 (Winter 1997), 5–16.

4. E. Boyer, "Creating the New American College," *Higher Education* 58 (1994), accessed from https://digitalcommons.unomaha.edu/slcehighered/58.

5. J. Eyler and D. Giles, *Where's the Learning in Service-Learning?* (San Francisco: Jossey-Bass, 1999).

6. G. D. Kuh, J. Kinzie, T. Cruce, R. Shoup, and R. M. Gonyea, *Connecting the Dots: Multi-faceted Analyses of the Relationships between Student Engagement Results from the NSSE, and The Institutional Practices and Conditions that Foster Student Success* (Indiana University Center for Postsecondary Research, 2007), accessed from http://nsse.indiana.edu/pdf/Connecting_the_Dots_Report.pdf

7. A. Furco, "The Engaged Campus," *British Journal of Educational Studies* 58, no. 4 (2010), 375–390, doi:10.1080/00071005.2010.527656.

8. J. Saltmarsh and M. Hartley, eds., *To Serve a Larger Purpose: Engagement for Democracy and the Transformation of Higher Education* (Temple University Press, 2011).

9. E. Tate, "Graduation Rates and Race," Inside Higher Education (2017), accessed from https://www.insidehighered.com/news/2017/04/26/college-completion-rates-vary-race-and-ethnicity-report-finds.

10. D. Leiberman, "Rethinking How We Perceive and Approach Service Learning," (2015), accessed from https://www.aacu.org/leap/liberal-education-nation-blog/rethinking-how-we-perceive-and-approach-service-learning.

11. C. Travers, "When Do You Feel Smart?" *Inside Higher Education* (2017), accessed from https://www.insidehighered.com/views/2017/11/03/rethinking-how-teach-black-male-students-essay.

12. J. Plaut and J. Campbell, "Promoting Inclusive Access and Success through Community Engagement" (2008), accessed from https://www.aacu.org/diversity democracy/2008/spring/plaut-campbell.

13. G. Hickmon, "Double Consciousness and the Future of Service-Learning," *Michigan Journal of Community Service Learning* (Fall 2015), 86–88.

14. G. Hickmon, "Double Consciousness and the Future of Service-Learning," *Michigan Journal of Community Service Learning* (Fall 2015), 86–88.

15. T. Ehrlich, *Civic Responsibility and Higher Education* (Oryx Press, 2000), 6.

16. J. Saltmarsh and M. Hartley, eds., *"To Serve a Larger Purpose": Engagement for Democracy and the Transformation of Higher Education* (Temple University Press, 2011).

17. Lumina Foundation, *The Degree Qualifications Profile* (2011), accessed from https://www.luminafoundation.org/publications/The_Degree_QualificationsPProfile.pdf.

18. D. R. Brooms, *Being Black, Being Male on Campus* (State University of New York Press, 2017), 186.

19. W. E. B. DuBois, *The Souls of Black Folk* (New York: Dover, 2005; originally published in 1903).

20. R. Delgado, ed., Critical Race Theory: The Cutting Edge (Temple University Press, 1995).

21. R. Ellison, *Invisible Man* (New York: Vintage, 1995; originally published in 1952).

22. J. Baldwin, *Nobody Knows My Name* (New York: Dial Press, 1961).

23. T. Coates, *Between the World and Me* (New York: Spiegel & Grau, 2015).

24. W. E. B. DuBois, *The Souls of Black Folk* (New York: Dover, 2005; originally published in 1903), 1.

25. N. Maclean, *The Civil Rights Movement: 1968–2008: Freedom's Story* (2009), accessed from http://nationalhumanitiescenter.org/tserve/freedom/1917beyond/essay s/crm2008.htm.

26. D. R. Brooms, *Being Black, Being Male on Campus* (State University of New York Press, 2017), 15.

27. D. R. Brooms, *Being Black, Being Male on Campus* (State University of New York Press, 2017), 15.

28. G. Hickmon, "Double Consciousness and the Future of Service-Learning," *Michigan Journal of Community Service Learning* (Fall 2015), 86–88.

29. B. J. Baldridge, M. L. Hill, and J. E. Davis, "New Possibilities: (Re)engaging Black Male Youth Within Community-based Educational Spaces," *Race, Ethnicity and Education* 14, no. 1 (2011), 121–136.

30. J. W. Creswell, *Qualitative Inquiry and Research Design: Choosing Among the Five Approaches* (SAGE Publications, 2013), 77.

31. R. L. Wallace and S. G. Clark, "Barriers to Interdisciplinarity," *Issues in Interdisciplinary Studies* 35 (2017): 221–247.

32. Z. Irani, "The University of the Future Will Be Interdisciplinary," *The Guardian* (2018), accessed from https://www.theguardian.com/higher-education-network/2018/jan/24/the-university-of-the-future-will-be-interdisciplinary.

33. D. R. Brooms, *Being Black, Being Male on Campus* (State University of New York Press, 2017).

34. D. Kocieniewski, and R. Hanley, "An Inside Story of Racial Bias and Denial," *The New York Times* (2000), accessed from https://www.nytimes.com/2000/12/03/nyregion/inside-story-racial-bias-denial-new-jersey-files-reveal-drama-behind-profili ng.html.

35. D. C. Heilman, *Student Legal Services: An Emerging Provider of Legal Aid on Campus* (2014), accessed from http://apps.americanbar.org/litigation/committees/access/.articles/summer2014-0714-student-legal-services-emerging-provider-legal-aid-campus.html, p.5.

36. D. Brooks, "The Strange Failure of the Educated Elite," *The New York Times* (2018), accessed from https://www.nytimes.com/2018/05/28/opinion/failure-educat ed-elite.html, para. 4.

37. M. Nivet, *Altering the Course: Black Males in Medicine* (2015), accessed from https://members.aamc.org/eweb/upload/Altering%20the%20Course%20-%20Black %20Males%20in%20Medicine%20AAMC.pdf.

38. Association of American Colleges and Universities, *Employer Priorities for College Learning and Student Success* (2013), accessed from https://www.aacu.org/sites/default/files/files/LEAP/2013_EmployerSurvey.pdf.

39. D. R. Brooms, *Being Black, Being Male on Campus* (State University of New York Press, 2017).

40. M. Nivet, *Altering the Course: Black Males in Medicine* (2015), accessed from https://members.aamc.org/eweb/upload/Altering%20the%20Course%20-%20Black %20Males%20in%20Medicine%20AAMC.pdf.

Chapter 11

Meta-Reflections

Teaching Black Psychology at a Predominantly White Undergraduate Institution

Sandra Virginia Gonsalves-Domond

Bookstores and libraries are replete with autobiographical and biographical accounts of lived epistemologies. Among academics, there is a seemingly conspicuous reluctance to author their personal stories, and only a handful of published accounts on psychologists' autobiographical memories exist. This work focuses on a tiny aperture of my academic life, teaching Black psychology but, in essence, it is a catalog of landmarks in the self-portraiture of my embraced pedagogic philosophy. In researching book-sized autobiographies authored by psychologists, only seven names emerged. The most sonorous, with a riveting title, was authored by a psychologist from Jamaica. Ira Lanan Ferguson wrote, *I Dug Graves at Night to Attend College by Day: The Story of a West Indian Negro-American's First 30 Years in the United States: An Autobiography: Volume I.*[1] He would go on to chronicle the remainder of his life in other volumes, dying at the age of ninety-one. Since 2005, the *Teaching of Psychology in Autobiography: Perspectives in Exemplary Psychology Teachers* now chronicles the autobiographies of teachers employed in high schools and colleges.[2]

In this meta-reflection with a succinct archiving and centering of memories in my professional identity, I hope to share some cursory personal narratives, articulated course goals, pedagogic methodologies, (a few) course-related topics, and (some) students' comments about the Black psychology course's positive impacts. I also interrogate the plethora of roles for Black women in academia, situating the dynamic intersectionality of our struggles to position ourselves and solidify owned spaces in the academy. Shelia T. Gregory's ethnographic work with forty-four Afro-Caribbean women faculty at the three campuses at University of the West Indies amply illustrates that finding space is renegotiated through intersecting oppressions of race, class, and color.[3] An explicit subtext is toward the orchestration of more dialogue on optimizing pedagogy around sensitive or controversial topics in predominantly white academic institutions. In fact, I was delighted to see included in the 2017 APA Convention a symposium entitled, *Teaching Multicultural Psychology-Perspectives of Faculty of Color* in which issues surrounding social injustice fatigue and proactive strategies to address resistance among the student community were explored by presenters.[4]

Autobiographical memory serves as a narrative arc, a reflective and meta-reflective guide in the quest or search for authenticity. This search for meaning, mining our "glimpsed truths," is certainly within the purview of the humanist-existential perspective, which I am theoretically aligned.[5] It permits rearview perspective-taking, recounting the past, remembering self, while simultaneously permitting wider frontal perspectives in experiencing selfhood, what the renowned sociologist Dr. Patricia Hills Collins refers to as the "lived epistemological space."[6]

In this work, attempts are made to examine conscious experiences—lived, remembered, and by teleological definitions, discovered ways to grow and be transformed—as I shepherd this course and its evolution over organic reshapings. Reinforcing the foregoing assertion on the utility to narrate one's academic sojourn, Gregory in her article *Black Faculty Women in the Academy: History, Status, and Future* calcified, "the need for Black scholars to write about their experiences"[7] and especially so in light of the statistics from the 2019 U.S. Department of Education where only 2 percent of full professors are Black men with Black women also accounting for 2 percent.[8]

Franz Fanon, a Martiniquais psychiatrist of the twentieth century, in elucidating his iconic work, *Black Skin, White Masks*, said, "The architecture of this work is rooted in the temporal. . . . Ideally, the present will always contribute to the building of the future."[9] I may just add parenthetically that the present is the fulcrum on which the future, the teleology, can be crafted and especially so when that distillation is rooted on clarion moral assertions or on affirming social justice imperatives. These concepts are the roots of my pedagogy.

Dowoti Désir, president of *Durban Declaration & Programme of Action Watch Group*, and a curator of contemporary art with a focus on art in public spaces impacting the global African community, in her eloquently written article on the *Memorial to the Abolition of Slavery Nantes, France*, makes the full-throated assertion that "memory requires consensus."[10] From her perspective of ancestral memorialization, she is absolutely correct; however, from the point of view of autobiography, external corroboration may be helpful but not always required as individuals reflect on the subjectivity and interiority of their lives. This kind of nonfiction, especially if one can be reflective, yet critical, can distill truisms about the nature of one's life space, ethos, and human existence. In my view, the unspooling of meaning and self-realization rejects Cartesian dualism, which polarizes and dichotomizes experiences within binaries. My reflection, therefore, embraces the nuanced complexities of Afrocentrism, and at its core, values the importance of that lived space within Afro-diasporic lens.

In fact, Dan P. McAdams in an article on the role of meta-narrative in Personality Psychology states that the life story can "be an internalized and evolving cognitive structure or script that provides an individual's life with some degree of meaning and purpose while often mirroring the dominant and/or the subversive cultural narratives within which the person's life is completely situated."[11] In my case, my public life as an academician has been shaped through the prism of my immigrant, diasporic Afro-Caribbean experience simultaneously coupled with ferreting out meaning within overlapping and nested transcultural lens. As a scholar-activist, I have served as an independent contractor/mental health consultant with Head Start Programs in under-resourced, New Jersey communities. Pondering on the search for self, the feminist psychoanalyst, Karen Horney searingly notes, the search of the self is "most agonizing."[12] Further, Jung privileges the subjective spaces over any statistically or scientifically based assessments, and asserts the worthiness of this endeavor in spectrums of excavations and self-interrogations.[13] This perspective of self-reflection is manifest in other disciplines as well beyond the traditional, nonfictional accounts in literature. Daniel Fox ponders the inherent challenges in the politics of making public health policy.[14] He published his personal narrative in a recent article in the October 2017 publication of the American Public Health Association, while concurrently offering "best practices" recommendations for practitioners based on his self-analysis.[15]

HISTORICAL FRAMEWORK IN TEACHING BLACK PSYCHOLOGY

Permit a preamble to my introductory remarks through my painting a thumbnail sketch of initial experiences teaching a *Black Psychology* course. It occurred nearly four decades ago, bookmarking a forty-year history of college teaching. Having achieved that milestone, I can afford the luxury of such rearview reflection. At twenty-four years old, completing my doctoral dissertation in a social/personality psychology graduate program, I was offered a consequential, one-year teaching position at a prestigious New England College triggered by a sabbatical leave of a full-time, male faculty.

Proposing a *Black Psychology* course was "acte provocateur" as it was the first such course offered in the psychology program in what was then well over a century and three decades of providing liberal arts education in Maine. The singular faculty member tasked with the curriculum review process illuminated the first layer of jaundiced, microaggressive/racist resistance, and arrogance. He asked whether "Black" should be in lower or upper case "B." His interrogation represented an assaultive semantic and linguistic tool of oppression, a staggering lack of understanding of the Civil Rights struggle.[16] His question, I interpreted, was an overt denigration of Blackness. What was particularly jarring was that this individual was a cultural anthropologist by training. He was in a discipline that ironically touts its non-ethnocentrism, privileges cultural relativism, or at the minimum chides against such explicit biases. His vexing inquiry left me incensed and flummoxed; this backhanded assault and blatant lack of racial and cultural respect, along with his expressed racism, ignorance, flagrant disrespect for the geopolitical and ethno-racial significance of the Civil Rights struggle and for the struggle waged in owning an upper case "B," was pathogenic. The uppercase "B" in Black speaks to agency and self-identity that were hard-won on the backs and shoulders of our foremothers and forefathers. I recoiled at the offense, the effrontery, and bristled with rage. I felt the compelling need for a primal scream. I asserted, "upper case B, of course." In the case of expediency and the explicit understanding of this individual's absolute absence of racial sensitivities and consciousness, my public rage, tirade, diatribe, or overtly irritated pronouncements would have decimated the opportunity for the course being approved by this unenlightened "committee" of one. In the most alliterative pronouncement, the course carried, and by the conclusion of the course opened a spirited, well-needed discourse in a racially homogeneous, privileged, and upper-class liberal arts college in the 1980s.

Fast-forwarding to the past two-and-a-half decades, having pioneered this course at my current academic institution and served as co-convener in Africana studies, there are a number of salient variables that require a modicum of professional disclosure. The micro-historical narrative under which I began to teach this course shifted at Ramapo College. I experienced no open or expressed resistance in terms of the curricular offering. My *Advanced Topics in Black Psychology* course is a capstone course offered to undergraduates at least twice a year. The course has evolved over the years, and throughout its iterations may serve as a blueprint for curricular offerings elsewhere.

It is important to note that although enrolled in their senior year, a number of students still arrive into the classroom with generally limited information on the Black experience except in the arena of the lived epistemological spaces of our few Black students who are psychology majors.

Lisa Whitten in her article *Infusing Black Psychology into the Introductory Psychology Course* argues for the defensible points of inflection in introductory course topics in which multilayered intersectionalities of race, class, gender, orientation, and culture widen the analytic matrix for assessments of human behaviors and dynamics.[17] I fully concur with her views that Black Psychology should have an early weave or threading in this survey course. Rao, Andrasik, and Lipira state that "an intersectional approach . . . views race, class, and gender as categories that interact with systems of social and power relations in society. Intersectionality conceptualizes these categories as mutually constructed and fluid, continually shaping and shaped by dynamics of power."[18] This approach is fully embraced in the power of plural ideas disseminated in the course.

Given that most students enroll in my course in their junior or senior year following their completion of *Research Methods and Data Analysis*, they dive into the course having completed major undergraduate requirements and a school core course in social issues. Our student body is disproportionately female and white. Many of my students enrolled in the capstone course have some familiarity with me, my pedagogic style, and philosophy in other courses I teach such as *Cross-Cultural Psychology*, *Theories of Personality*, *Child Psychology*, *Developmental Psychology*, and, most recently, *Psychology of Aging*. I conjecture that the social psychological concepts of "exposure effect" or the "mere familiarity effect" may serve to attenuate the kinds of resistance that would be typical when students are enrolled in a course where the instructor and course contents are entirely new or unfamiliar with overtly controversial contours. My *Cross-Cultural Psychology* course, in essence, introduces concepts of cultural humility, relativism, and prepares those who have completed the course for a more respectful and fulsome examination of Afrocentrism, openness to engage social change, and social justice imperatives. Stanley Milgram, a former graduate school professor (in his infamous experiments of acquiescence to authority) asserts that people "can become agents in a terrible destructive process."[19] My goal is the obverse. Transparently then, I yearn for my students to become agents in a co-constructive process. I aspire for my students to pursue well-being, gain personological insights, and raise critical consciousness about becoming agents of social change on micro or macro levels as they pursue an anti-racist agenda. This is what I wish to bequeath to them—these and other uplifts reflected in thematic and content coherence.

My explicit goals center on making clear the erasures and distortions embedded in Eurocentricity in profiling African Americans and others in Afro-diasporic history. Patricia Hills Collins makes critical points about epistemological issues in knowledge production on Black women, when she advocates using terms such as "our" and privileging the more qualitative approaches.[20] This approach that she advocates is a radical approach, which is in opposition to traditional research that "objectifies the subject" with a sometimes contemptuous and disdainful stance to any methodology that is not quantitative.

Additionally, I voice with the spirit of great humility that I value pedagogic excellence as the first and only untenured faculty at Ramapo College to receive *The Henry Bischoff Award for Excellence in Teaching* in 2001. I remarked in a public address to the campus community after receiving the award that students can be intellectually ignited, superseding intellectual engagement that smacks of banality. These outcomes are achievable within a synergistic interplay of variables and skillful deployment of pedagogic tools. On the platform of cultivating student-focused relationships, I know my students' names. This introduces a centrifugal force, a personalization of learning, sine qua non, and shifts the relationship from "gesellschaft" to "gemeinschaft."[21] Ultimately, the goal is to make students critical partners in the consumption and deconstruction of information.

THUMBNAIL DESCRIPTION OF THE
BLACK PSYCHOLOGY COURSE

Let me now transition to my course description. I assign a text entitled *The Psychology of Blacks: Centering our Perspectives in the African Consciousness*, authored by Thomas Parham, Adisa Ajamu, and Joseph White now in its fourth edition, published by Psychology Press. The leitmotif of this text privileges an Afrocentric perspective.[22] As a capstone course, the upper limit in enrollment is twenty students. Since its college designation is a writing intensive class, students are required to complete a fifteen- to twenty-page APA documented paper. The class generally meets for 3.3 hours in one large teaching block, with a course break of about 15 minutes. One topic usually dominates each weekly session, which combines readings from an assigned text and multiple, peer-reviewed readings. A midterm and final exam are administered; in-class exams are writing intensive.

Students are also required to do a PowerPoint presentation on any range of self-selected topics, broadening the conversations on the plural Black experience. They own the topic and become "novice-experts," the hybrid word being an oxymoron. Students are empowered with providing a lecture and critical deconstructions on the topical area. The oral presentations and subsequent papers are linked to the writing intensive nature of the course. Students experience full autonomy of the material, moored in a decidedly learner-centered space. To help scaffold their final work product, a rubric included in the syllabus furnishes them with guidelines to ensure quality.

They are required to include peer-reviewed articles and to deconstruct them all. This presentation precedes the APA-style paper that is due on the day of the final exam.

One of the first centering videos I have students watch is an eighteen-minute TED Talk by Chimamanda Adichie entitled "The Danger of a Single Story." In an engaging and disproportionately extemporaneous and nonjudgmental style, this Nigerian writer unpacks, jolts, and warns us about the inherent dangers of short-cutting cultural narratives without the benefit of reading.[23] She encourages that we explore and not buy into a singular or unidirectional narrative construction of any group or community. She makes the following important points: single stories can seriously derail a storied description of a people and engender stereotypes, which Adichie notes: "flattens the experience of a people," erroneously validating the power of the person enforcing this single narrative.[24] To put a finer point on the issues relative to my course, the Black experience is by no means monolithic, and my students are exposed to multiple and intersecting narratives.

One of the topics I choose to perennially discuss is the Tuskegee Syphilis Study. I devote an entire class period to the details of this U.S. Public Health debacle, and we view a talk delivered by Dr. James Jones entitled, "The Tuskegee Syphilis Experiment: A Tragedy of Race and Medicine," which chronicles the back story and weaves in contemporaneous narratives about the forty-year, nontherapeutic, morally bankrupt study conducted on African American men in Macon County, Alabama.[25] Cover-ups, conspiracies, co-options, and concealments are at the epicenter of this genocidal atrocity committed by doctors employed in the U.S. Public Health Service.[26] To get into the granular, we also analyze President Clinton's 1997 White House apology speech and explicate the biomedical and ethical breaches.[27] There is so much to unpack here. Institutional racism, not serendipity, in the selection of isolated, rural, unlettered Black men to serve as guinea pigs, the denial of treatment for over four decades, refusal of access to treatment from penicillin when it became available in 1946, and the ultimate cover-up and exposé documented in 1972 are a lot to psychologically absorb.[28] For most of my students, this is their first exposure to this maleficent study. On the other hand, they are usually familiar with either or both the Milgram and Zimbardo social psychological studies in the course of their academic journey. To their credit, my students are able to identify violations from one or more of the APA-generated principles. They are engrossed in the processes of deconstruction, critical analyses, and level-scorching indictments of the U.S. public health doctors. The reverberatory impacts of this collateral damage that assaulted the Black community are still being felt decades later as clinical trials demonstrate a fact pattern of noninvolvement, dissolution of trust, as they wrestle with a paucity of African Americans participants.[29]

The early introduction of the syphilis topic is to support the ubiquitous, affective domain of student engagement. Additionally, the *Bad Blood* video is powerfully evocative and catalyzes empathy. Citizens were ethically violated, used, abused, and exploited with grave personal, familial, community, and societal consequences. This study denied pharmacological interventions to American-born men in the tertiary stages of their syphilitic infection. Hearing the public heath doctors and officials employ rhetorical styles of dehumanization, objectifying ailing humans as "those men" is beyond disheartening and psychically shattering.[30] My students get the full import of the doctors' amoral pseudo-inquiry. I ask them to viscerally connect by conjuring up images of their own fathers, grandfathers, and uncles.

It is also noteworthy that we interrogate the social psychology of prejudice and racism. This discussion is non-sanitized and intellectually honest. Although inevitably integrating an historical perspective on the social constructions of race, racial differences, and structural racism, we chronicle the inequities up to our contemporary realities examining police brutality, white privilege, power, *Black Lives Matter*, and mass incarceration. Although familiar with Dr. John H. Bracey's arguments about the penalties of how racism affects white Americans, the onus is placed on its toxicity on the Black psyche as racism confounds metastatic manifestations in a sleuth of physical, mental health issues, and public health disparities.[31] My goal is to animate the discussion by centering it within threaded contexts of race, class, power, and engage in conjunctural analyses to trigger self-reflections and social agency. I share my stories as well.

Additionally, students are asked to engage in two enrichment activities to further scaffold their experiential-engaged learning. Some of these activities may include the following: volunteering in a Head Start program, attending a Black cultural activity on or off campus, attending a Black church, or interviewing a Black person for a case study analysis. I will expound on this later.

ARTICULATED GOALS OF THE BLACK PSYCHOLOGY COURSE

What, then, are the articulated goals of my Black psychology course? Frankly, the ambitious, overarching goal is to build social legitimacy for a structure of change in our civil society starting with a greater consciousness about racial, cultural, and patriarchal privileges. The transparent intentionality is to revolutionize depictions of Blackness and to learn about the nuanced and cascading impacts of structural inequalities and health disparities. Moving past mere rhetoric, students will gain insights into privilege and social injustice. Buoyed with intellectual and moral courage, students have the capacity to become refractive in the marketplace of ideas. Other goals include academic and personal goals to highlight our common humanity, engage the question and illuminate the conceptual dissimilarities in Afrocentrism and Eurocentrism, privilege more inclusive philosophies, gain insights into the unifying themes in multiple oppressions such as gendered racism, develop expanding empathy for others and reduce ethnocentric judgments, and enhance and support a spotlighted discourse of the structural constraints that thwart growth outcomes. Further, ambitious goals include broadening the lens on the matrix of oppression, developing a critical consciousness that transcends or internalizes into personal or collectivist actions, building multicultural competencies on micro and macro levels, and garnering insights into the disparate public health outcomes causally linked with racism and micro-aggressions. Further implicit and explicit goals include gaining clarity on the complexity of the Black experience and not conceptualizing it as monolithic; understanding the mistrust and underutilization of mental health services, garnering sensitivities about the survival and sufferings of others, offering and evaluating strength-based approaches in interventions, identifying the multiplicity of conditions impacting life narratives, and integrating new scholarship as nascent voices and perspectives become increasingly relevant at inflection points in our contemporary realities. These goals are not singularly occurring but co-occurring for my students; in the end, they provide an axis from which paradigm shifts can internally evolve and externally manifest.

INITIAL STUDENTS' RESPONSES, PEDAGOGIC PHILOSOPHY, AND TOOLS

In prefacing students' initial responses, some students arrive with some normative anxiety as they are exploring an area of knowledge that is terra incognita. My principal and omnipresent pedagogic style is to ensure non-threatening and safe spaces for students to grow and thrive as I am cognizant that they are in varying stages of metamorphic consciousness. This framework speaks to the affective domains and ensures that students can exercise intellectual risks and, for some, not fossilize into a default resistance mode. Some of the general but not rigidly based assumptions made are that some students are not always paying attention to a number of larger issues involving race as white privilege may be normatively operating in their lives. With the COVID-19 pandemic and protests over the past couple of months, this may be less so now. Peggy McIntosh understood this social ecology and ignited this construct referring to it as an invisible knapsack of white privilege abrogating the myth of meritocracy.[32] Justin Ford's TED video on the *Pedagogy of Privilege* extends the concept of privilege from a single group target to a more holistic, multidimensional construct entailing multiple identities we possess along that continuum.[33] Tatum metaphorically refers to this privilege as the "smog in the air."[34]

Second, since a number of our students live in segregated, racialized communities, they may not have any or limited-lived epistemological understanding of other people's realities.[35] Their distortions may emerge through any of the combinations in this listing: the media, family, social media platforms, disinformation, misinformation, other modes of cultural transmissions, unexamined ideas, and historical distortions.[36] Or, students may operate on the social-psychological principle of the "just world hypothesis" where only bad things happen to bad people.[37] Putting a finer point to the foregoing statement, I can state that as students read, engage, interrogate, learn critical tools of understanding, do the spade work, and some heavy lifting in the case of eradicating entrenched, flawed worldviews, they can internally pivot or galvanize for action, and as Tatum declares, "make conscious acts of reflection."[38]

Before we achieve this outcome, however, it is also noteworthy that some may enter my class with derogatory perceptions, stereotypes, implicit biases, uninformed, or misunderstandings about African American history. Additionally, some students in our community of learners entertain the illusory concept of a color-blind society and efforts directed at whittling down and dispelling those myths along with other misperceptions require me to examine the parallelisms to sexism, which in a predominantly female class is an invaluable portal. Change for some of these students may not be linear as they toggle back-and-forth in cognitive dissonance with their lived experiences while learning about the authentic epistemologies of other people. Moreover, the explicit recognition that Black psychology is intersected with multiple cognate disciplines, such as history, anthropology, diasporic studies, public health, and epidemiology accentuate the finer points of explicating the complex nature of human experiences. *It is never unidimensional; it is multilayered.* Additional challenges include having students name and acknowledge intellectual luminaries, the Black psychologists who are forerunners and among those who have and continue to make formidable contributions to the field. By the time students conclude the course, they are imbued with awe, knowledge of an acclaimed set of eminent psychologists who created, polished, and published scholarly work under the wrenching and vexing toxicities of racism, sexism, and paucity of institutional support.[39]

What, then, are some of the core priorities articulated to my students? Put quite bluntly, these objectives entail paradigmatic shifts and deconstructive connections with traditionally taught theories. In African-centered psychology, deconstruction is defined as an approach to psychological inquiry carried out by an African-centered psychologist who "refutes, falsifies, or otherwise renders void anti-African theses and research findings that prevail in Eurocentric psychology."[40] Further, students are required to strengthen the following skill sets: reevaluate Cartesian dualism, dismantle perspectives that devalue the Black and diasporic experience, create new epistemological connections with Black and multicultural knowledge productions, embrace intersectionality, and value qualitatively rich areas of information in what Dr. Patricia Hill Collins, a womanist sociologist, refers to as "subjugated knowledge of the Black woman's experience."[41] Also, students learn to elevate the importance of the oral tradition and the etched role of spirituality in the space of Black lives in formulating concepts of mental well-being. An extension of this affirmative, positive, humanistic experience is to demonstrate some other narratives about the survivorship and resilience of African peoples in the diaspora.[42]

Guided by the vagaries of the external situation, white students situated at different points along the continuum of their race consciousness may not consciously view themselves as harboring or nursing racist beliefs or implicit biases. With critical self-analysis, they may arrive at some extractive truths. In support of the foregoing, my colleague, clinical psychologist Dr. Heinze in a critical discussion—published in the *White Papers* in his article entitled, "Why White People Love White Supremacists: A Psychanalytic Group Relations Perspective of White Antiracism"—states an inconvenient truth that "being born white in US society makes it virtually impossible to be immune from both mythical images of white superiority and the concurrent stereotypes of people of color."[43] He makes the point that two elements may coexist; even though individuals may not identify with extremist white nationalist views, they also may not resent advantages such as white privilege. Given this nonlinearity in racial awareness, it behooves me to be more empathic given the reality of these de facto, intrapsychic dynamics. My implicit and explicit goals are to have students become life-long learners, and as an epiphenomenal outcome, social change agents toward developing the skills to deconstruct, think critically, and examine the contradictions in the social ecology of their lives and that of others. These exercises are grist for the mill; yes, indeed, these are ambitious goals.

What, then, are the pedagogic tools to help implement these august course goals? First, I have students bond with each other through a brief interactive interview. Gathering data and information, they report out to the entire class. I share information about myself and work deliberatively to recall all their names, achieving a number of important outcomes in fueling and individualizing the learning experience. I educate within decidedly interdisciplinary perspectives as the "gemeinschaft" of our lives revolve within the context of enmeshed systems as Urie Bronfenbrenner's socioecological model explicates.[44] Enabling students to understand the nexus of experiences that are co-occurring on personal, familial, and institutional levels is critical gateway into the course. Other tools include carefully prepared lectures, discussions, videos, documentaries, rhetorical questions, and outside speakers, and preparing myself for the anticipatory thorns on the horizons, that is, learning to script and choreograph answers to perennial push-backs. Other tools are my constancy in retooling, reading materials from the most culturally pedestrian or banal to academic journals, as well as other peer-reviewed articles. Being ready to educate our community of learners emanates from multiple ties into the universe.

Additionally, students are encouraged to take deep dives into culturally enriching, experiential activities. These events ensure visceral and cognitive plugs in the course. Students can visit a Black church. They can also volunteer in a Head Start classroom, day care center, early childhood developmental center, Boys' and Girls' Club, afterschool programs, food pantries, shelters, homeless programs, as well as attend an on-campus or off-campus event. Our learners can view two films—a comprehensive list of recommendations is folded into the syllabus. Students write a report to describe the experience and respond critically. This constitutes 5 percent of their grade, and part of the more than 100 percent of experiential learning. In particular, those who have visited the Black church learn about the reciprocity of the *call-response* mode in that psycholinguistic space, the dynamism and energy of the spiritual experience, the communal interconnections, liturgical dance, and the chorus of voices in the uplifting sounds of gospel music. Post attendance, students report being transformed, deepened in their understanding of the role of spirituality in promoting mental health and community in African American lives.

Further, Elizabeth Barkley in chapter 4 "Promoting Synergy between Motivation and Active Learning" of her book *Student Engagement Techniques: A Handbook for College Faculty* states that "engaged classroom environments are those in which the teacher and students perceive themselves as members of a learning community."[45] She further argues that this community of learners should value respect and build on cooperative activities where "knowledge is socially constructed rather than discovered."[46] I would argue against such a binary in favor of both the social construction of knowledge production and the shared discovery of knowledge. These are not mutually exclusive activities.

A large part of the subtext of pedagogic excellence is a personal, professional demeanor where excellence is normalized and actively models cultural competence. With all candor, and as mentioned before, I am in a constant state of retooling and thoughtfully considering the ways of weighing (for prioritization) materials for inclusion in a one-semester experience. In tandem, I simultaneously allow students to develop ownership in a chosen, relevant topic. In unlocking this door, students engage and practice explanations that advance discourse and crosscutting intersectionalities as they traverse the academic space as independent learners.

CONCLUDING COMMENTS ON
MY META-REFLECTION

Conclusively, I remain committed to knowledge production where learning continues to be an important vehicle for evolution along with the hegemony and command of shaping my ongoing personal and professional narratives. I remain committed to providing instruction in this capstone course as part of continuity and change. My wish list is to provide a year-long experience in *Black Psychology*. We are eyewitnesses to so many changes in our present epistemological realities, experiencing inflection points in our "new normal" cycle of the sociopolitical landscapes. These topics represent new arenas for course inclusion weighted for prioritization. These include but are not limited to the emergence of *Black Lives Matter* as a sociopolitical, advocacy movement, Afro-futurism, and Afro-pessimism. The issues of police brutality as discussed in Paul Butler's book entitled *Chokehold: Policing Black Men* and the foregrounding of historical data on white rage as a regurgitated backlash to Black progress argued by the sociologist Dr. Carol Anderson, and Michelle Alexander's book on mass incarceration are major entry points of contemporary import. Further, there are urgent issues of climate change and environmental justice, population and global health with the new paradigm of humanitarian tied to the developmental nexus, and more on the intersection of racism, discrimination, and health disparities even more evident in the COVID-19 pandemic.[47]

My passion of translating scholarship into best practices social policy is reignited. In fact, to celebrate survivorship and positive psychology leads me down the pathway to craft creative spaces, a mini-think tank, to lob dialectical analyses, and fashion micro- and macro-level changes for impacting communities of color. Another wish list item is to highlight the role of spirituality, pastoral psychology, traditional healing, and ethno-medicines as mechanisms for the active promotion of mental health. The interconnections with public health both on our domestic shores and globally must be embraced in full partnerships as well to promote global health equity.

My continuing goals are to leave my students with affirmational anchors into the vibrant and resilient humanity of Blacks in the diaspora. Braided through the foregoing is an explicit understanding of the interconnected complexity and variability of our plural life spaces shaped by the intersectionalities of social class, gender, region, country, and sexual orientations, to name a few. I long to have my students internalize and develop a calcified insight into the structural inequities and the cascading ill-health, wealth gap, and socio-psychological byproducts of disparities. Cornel West in his book *Race Matters* shows that in a race-conscious society, the putative myth of color-blindness is false.[48] I remain committed to pedagogy in my discipline of psychology, my wheelhouse, and redoubling my efforts to ensure that this capstone course remains an institutionalized part of the curriculum. Part-and-parcel of this course is to assist our community of learners to deepen their command of how structural systems, fossilized over centuries of unequal power inform the politics of space, geography, and location. By extension, I consistently place under interrogation the dislocations in communities of color that within a transformative pedagogically space argues for the creation of allies and the collective movement to eradicate social oppression.

In engaging the question of the roles of Black women in the academy across disciplinary lines, and regardless of our institutional affiliations or characterizations in Historically Black Colleges and Universities (HBCUs) or Predominantly White Institutions (PWIs), our presence and voices must remain transformative, as we aid communities of learners in self-agency, self-determination, and aspirational achievements. As scholar-activists, we live in uniquely situated spaces. I am wedded to fostering intellectual growth among all of my students, engaging in multidisciplinary analyses, advocating for the moral high ground, promoting holism in our conceptual (re)thinking of flawed pseudoscientific theories while privileging the tenets of Afrocentrism. I keep a shrewd eye on fulfilling quadfurcated responsibilities: skillful teaching, mentorship, research, and service to community and college.

Further, if one perceives teaching as a disciplinary tool in sculpting the future and shaping the next generation, I certainly hope in the spirit of humility that I have been a co-participant in building solidarity and in laying down tracks of consciousness into the vast universe. Our stories are under-archived; therefore, taking ownership of one's own story is a fruitful knowledge production strategy of Black womanist epistemologies in the academy. It serves a vital space to invite plural voices into relevant and timely conversations about the dynamic interplay of personhood and professionalism. I suspect that we will locate common discourses and denominators in our extraordinary sojourns, unlatching yet reinforcing the empowered potentiality of our high-value as Black womanist educators and role models in the professoriate.

My sojourn continues.

NOTES

1. Ira Lunan Ferguson, *I Dug Graves at Night to Attend College by Day: The Story of a West Indian Negro-Americans First 30 Years in the United States: An Autobiography* (New York: Gaus, 1968).

2. Robert Bubb, *The Teaching of Psychology in Autobiography: Perspectives from Exemplary Psychology Teachers* (2014).

3. Sheila T. Gregory, "The Cultural Constructs of Race, Gender and Class: A Study of How Afro-Caribbean Women Academics Negotiate Their Careers," *International Journal of Qualitative Studies in Education* 19, no. 3 (2006): 347–66.

4. "Teaching Multicultural Psychology-Perspectives of Faculty of Color," *APA Convention*, Washington, DC (2017).

5. "Teaching Multicultural Psychology-Perspectives of Faculty of Color," *APA Convention*, Washington, DC (2017).

6. Patricia Hill Collins, *Toward an Afrocentric Feminist Epistemology* (New York: Routledge, 1990).

7. Shelia T. Gregory, "Black Faculty Women in the Academy: History, Status, and Future," *The Journal of Negro Education* 70, no. 3 (2001): 124.

8. "Characteristics of Postsecondary Faculty," *National Center for Education Statistics*, accessed January 2, 2020, https://nces.ed.gov/programs/coe/indicator_cs c.asp.

9. Frantz Fanon, *Black Skin, White Masks* (London: Penguin Classics, 2020), 13.

10. Dowoti Désir, "The Memorial to the Abolition of Slavery in Nantes, France," *The International Review of African American Art Plus, Extending the Coverage of the Print Journal*, accessed February 1, 2020, http://iraaa.museum.hamptonu.edu/pa ge/The-Memorial-to-theAbolition-of-Slavery-in-Nantes,-France.

11. Dan P. McAdams, "The Role of Narrative in Personality Psychology Today," *Benjamins Current Topics Narrative—State of the Art* 16, no. 1 (2007): 17–26.

12. Karen Horney, *The Adolescent Diaries of Karen Horney* (New York, 1980).

13. Carl G. Jung, *The Undiscovered Self* (London: Routledge, 2014).

14. Daniel M. Fox, "Toward a Public Health Politics of Consequence: An Autobiographical Reflection," *American Journal of Public Health* 107, no. 10 (2017): 1604–5, https://doi.org/10.2105/ajph.2017.303929.

15. Daniel M. Fox, "Toward a Public Health Politics of Consequence: An Autobiographical Reflection," *American Journal of Public Health* 107, no. 10 (2017): 1604–5, https://doi.org/10.2105/ajph.2017.303929.

16. Geneva Smitherman, "Language and Liberation," *The Journal of Negro Education* 52, no. 1 (n.d.): 15–23.

17. Lisa A. Whitten, "Infusing Black Psychology into the Introductory Psychology Course," *Teaching of Psychology* 20, no. 1 (1993): 13–21. https://doi.org/10.1207/s 15328023top2001_3.

18. Deepa Rao, Michele P. Andrasik, and Lauren Lipira, "HIV Stigma among Black Women in the United States: Intersectionality, Support, Resilience," *American Journal of Public Health* 108, no. 4 (2018): 446–8, https://doi.org/10.2105/ajph.2018.304310.

19. Thomas Blass, *The Man Who Shocked the World: The Life and Legacy of Stanley Milgram* (New York: Basic Books, 2009).

20. Patricia Hill Collins, *Toward an Afrocentric Feminist Epistemology* (New York: Routledge, 1990).

21. Ashley Crossman, "The Meaning of Gemeinschaft and Gesellschaft in Sociology," *Thought Co*, August 7, 2019, https://www.thoughtco.com/gemeinschaft -3026337.

22. Thomas A. Parham, *The Psychology of Blacks: Centering Our Perspectives in the African Consciousness* (New York: Psychology Press, 2017).

23. "Chimamanda Adichie—The Danger of a Single Story," TED Talk, n.d.

24. "Chimamanda Adichie—The Danger of a Single Story," TED Talk, n.d.

25. James H. Jones, *Bad Blood: The Tuskegee Syphilis Experiment* (New York: Free Press, 1993).

26. James H. Jones, *Bad Blood: The Tuskegee Syphilis Experiment* (New York: Free Press, 1993).

27. "Bill Clinton Apologizes for the Tuskegee Experiment," *Teaching Tolerance*, accessed February 1, 2020, https://www.tolerance.org/classroom-resources/texts/bill -clinton-apologizes-for-tuskegee-experiment.

28. James H. Jones, *Bad Blood: The Tuskegee Syphilis Experiment* (New York: Free Press, 1993).

29. Sandra Virginia Gonsalves-Domond, Henry Vance Davis, and Tilahun Sineshaw, "Conspiracies, Racism, and Paranoia in the African-American Experience," *Clio* 7, no. 3 (2000): 129–31.

30. James H. Jones, *Bad Blood: The Tuskegee Syphilis Experiment* (New York: Free Press, 1993).

31. John H. Bracey, Sonia Sanchez, and James Smethurst. *SOS Calling All Black People: A Black Arts Movement Reader* (University of Massachusetts Press, 2014).

32. Peggy McIntosh, "Unpacking the Invisible Backpack of White Privilege," *Peace and Freedom Magazine* (1989).

33. "Pedagogy of Privilege," Jason Ford, TED Talk, n.d.

34. Beverly Daniel Tatum, *Why Are All the Black Kids Sitting Together in the Cafeteria? and Other Conversations about the Development of Racial Identity* (New York: Basic Books, 1997).

35. Beverly Daniel Tatum, *Why Are All the Black Kids Sitting Together in the Cafeteria? and Other Conversations about the Development of Racial Identity* (New York: Basic Books, 1997).

36. "Pedagogy of Privilege," Jason Ford, TED Talk, n.d.

37. Beverly Daniel Tatum, *Why Are All the Black Kids Sitting Together in the Cafeteria? and Other Conversations about the Development of Racial Identity* (New York: Basic Books, 1997).

38. Beverly Daniel Tatum, *Why Are All the Black Kids Sitting Together in the Cafeteria? and Other Conversations about the Development of Racial Identity* (New York: Basic Books, 1997).

39. Aaronette M. White, Robert L. Williams, and Robert D. Majzler, "What Makes a Distinguished Black Psychologist? An Empirical Analysis of Eminence," *Journal of Black Psychology* 37, no. 2 (2010): 131–63, https://doi.org/10.1177/0 095798410373762.

40. Curtis B. Banks, "Deconstructive Falsification: Foundations of a Critical Method in Black Psychology," *Minority Mental Health* n.d.: 59–74.

41. Patricia Hill Collins, *Toward an Afrocentric Feminist Epistemology* (New York: Routledge, 1990).

42. Patricia Hill Collins, *Toward an Afrocentric Feminist Epistemology* (New York: Routledge, 1990).

43. Peter D. Heinze, "Why White People Love White Supremacists: A Psychoanalytic Group Relations Perspective of White Anti-Racism," *The Whiteness Papers* 5 (2006): 2.

44. Ashley Crossman, "The Meaning of Gemeinschaft and Gesellschaft in Sociology," *ThoughtCo*, August 7, 2019. https://www.thoughtco.com/gemeinschaft -3026337.

45. Elizabeth F. Barkley and Claire Howell Major, *Student Engagement Techniques: A Handbook for College Faculty* (Hoboken, NJ: Jossey-Bass, 2020), 25.

46. Elizabeth F. Barkley and Claire Howell Major, *Student Engagement Techniques: A Handbook for College Faculty* (Hoboken, NJ: Jossey-Bass, 2020), 25.

47. Carol Anderson, *White Rage: The Unspoken Truth of Our Racial Divide* (New York: Bloomsbury, 2017).

48. Cornel West, *Race Matters* (Boston: Beacon Press, 2018).

Chapter 12

The Case for Inclusive Instructional Design

Samantha Calamari

FOREWORD

The following is a collection of design practices and approaches based on my research and experience as a learning designer and educator over the past twenty years. Throughout my career, I have taken an iterative ("experiment and fail and try again") instead of a perfectionist ("get it right the first time") approach. During this journey, I have had to be nimble and very humble. I have made mistakes, some small and others big, but I learned from each one. Then, based on what I learned, I reiterated. Iteration is the core of instructional design. It is what allows us to create engaging, transformative learning experiences that hopefully are never perfect.

Inclusive Instructional Design (IID) is both a new and old concept. It is old because some have been inclusive in education for as long as education has existed but new in that we are just starting to articulate approaches and create systems to support efforts of inclusion. Because the formal practice is so new, we are still figuring it all out: experimenting, failing, trying again, and sharing what we learned.

I invite you to do the same.

INTRODUCTION: ADAPTING EDUCATIONAL SYSTEMS FOR DIVERSE LEARNERS

Educational systems were founded on the premise that students assimilate to a norm. Specifically, the premise suggests that there is only one way to learn and learners must adapt and mold themselves to be successful in those environments. But what happens to those who are not able to adapt as well

197

as others? Race, ethnicity, socioeconomics, gender, learning preferences, and a variety of disabilities have impacted the academic standing of various populations for generations. Students have been left out and not included in teaching modalities. Whether students in the United States are only being taught about Euro-American history instead of including African American or Native American history, students do not have access to transportation to school, or the physical ability to sit in a classroom, the chasms that these divides create not only impact the individual but also are detrimental to the learning spaces and the communities students live within.

In her book *White Fragility*, Robin DiAngelo notes that recent research shows that in the United States, 82 percent of teachers and 84 percent of college professors are white.[1] What impact does this percentage have on communities of color when the people who stand in the front of a classroom are not a reflection of those they are teaching? And what message does this instill in white students if the only people they are learning from are white?

Let's picture something different. What if teachers were reflections of the race and ethnicities of the students they teach? And what if white communities had access to teachers from different races and ethnicities from themselves? What if there were a possibility of empowering rather than disenfranchising people through education systems, a possibility of students being seen and heard? What if educators designed learning as a way for students to commune, collaborate, and feel that they are being welcomed and celebrated?

In an opinion piece (*New York Times*, February 13, 2020), David Brooks writes about the philosophy behind the Scandinavian education system explaining, "The German word they used to describe their approach, *bildung*, doesn't even have an English equivalent. It means the complete moral, emotional, intellectual, and civic transformation of the person. It was based on the idea that if people were going to be able to handle and contribute to an emerging industrial society, they would need more complex inner lives."[2] What if our learning systems aimed to reach the complete moral, emotional, intellectual, and civic transformation of the person? What impact would that have on not only individuals but also the greater society? What would the design to support those systems look like?

WHY INCLUSIVE INSTRUCTIONAL DESIGN?

People of different backgrounds are beginning to emerge more and more into learning spaces. In classrooms, we are adapting physical spaces to be accessible as well as accommodating of those who are neurodiverse and from different cultures. In the online space, learners from all over the world come together and connect with others in ways they never have before. Think about the types of connections that are happening. For the first time in history, a student in a remote part of Colombia could be working on a trigonometry problem with another student in Iceland. Such a small example is illustrative of a collaboration of unique perspectives and ideas in transforming the way people learn. This kind of learning in the online environment happens not only from having access to content but also from sharing the content among learners while creating connections among them. By creating and supporting spaces that include all voices, we are shaping the future of education to reflect the global population by granting pathways to education that have not existed before.

So how can a person who creates and delivers online learning experiences include an expansively diverse and ever-growing global population? The answer is simple. *You design for a diverse and growing global population.*

IID applies methods to designing learning content and experiences for people with a range of perspectives and learning needs. These needs and perspectives not only guide design decisions but also shape and enhance the overall learning experience. This concept may seem similar to Universal Design for Learning (UDL). UDL is a framework that aims to give all students an equal learning opportunity. The difference between UDL and IID is that Universal Design attempts to design for *everyone* and IID attempts to adapt the learning experience to reach the full *range* of a potential audience. An inclusive approach to learning design takes the learner's full self into consideration and then designs content and systems that will adapt and accommodate that full self. The result? Learners and teachers have richer interactions, a deeper understanding of subjects, and connectivity to those around them. This is where learning methodologies can become transformative for all who seek to learn and specifically those of diverse populations.

WHY IDENTITY MATTERS IN LEARNING DESIGN

Can we agree that who we are and how we show up pretty much impacts everything that happens in our lives? This is a basic life concept. And, can we also agree that each person on the planet has their own set of unique characteristics that make up who they are? So, then, why do we have so many systems in education that are designed to mesh unique people into similarities instead of celebrating differences? The obvious answer is that we have held onto a belief in educational realms to streamline learning systems to make them work. Another school of thought is that the "one size fits all" is a simpler and perhaps (perceived) better approach to learning. This approach has allowed us to standardize what we expect from both educators and students. With the advancement of technology and the evolution of human intellect, we have the ability to step away from these limited systems and create more customized ones that allow people to be more successful and honor, as Brooks states, "the complete moral, emotional, intellectual and civic transformation of the person."[3] Society is beginning to see this happen in education, particularly the way in which educators design learning experiences for children and adults.

Capitalization learning is the idea that we get good at something by building on our natural strengths while *compensation learning* requires us to adapt and overcome to get good.[4] Many of us have relied on a combination of these two approaches to learning throughout our educational journeys. For example, we might have the natural talents and strengths to be a master gardener, painter, or long-distance runner, but in most parts of the world, we have to learn enough algebra to graduate from school. It is important that as learning designers there is a conscious and deliberate practice that considers learners who are participating in both capitalization learning and compensation learning. Essentially, we need to find design solutions at all times for learners who are coming from both angles.

PROFESSIONAL IDENTITIES

We spend our adult lives creating, molding, and growing our professional selves. There are some people who might be in one profession such as a tattoo artist or pediatric nurse and that is who they are throughout their professional life. Yet, in the twenty-first century, it is common for a person to change roles, careers, and industries multiple times in their lives. A 2019 study conducted by the Bureau of Labor Statistics followed Baby Boomers throughout their careers until the present and found people held 12.3 jobs between age eighteen and fifty-two.[5] Given the ever-shifting job market, one can imagine this number will continue to grow for younger generations. It is safe to say that most of us, no matter where we are in our career journey, have a multilayered professional identity and most likely will have to continue learning to support our professional journeys.

So, what is your professional identity or identities? Are you a CPA *and* a dog groomer? Are you a life coach with a side-job as a forest ranger? Take a few minutes to think about your multilayers and feel free to write a few down in the space below:

_____

_____

_____

OUR WHOLE SELF-IDENTITIES

Outside of our professional lives, we continue to have layers of identity. And, of course, these layers impact how we come into a learning experience. For example, if you are a single parent, this not only affects the time and energy you might have but also the nature of your personality and the insight you bring into a learning space. So, think outside of your work life. Who are you? Are you a man, woman, or nonbinary? Do you check a specific box on those ethnicity questionnaires or check "prefer not to answer"? Think of all the identities that resonate with you. Which stand out as primary ones and which are more covert? Use the space below to jot down some of your identities.

_____

_____

_____

Once you have your list compiled, go a little deeper. Think about an area of your identity that might impact the way you take in information and learn. What is something that might be "invisible" or at least hard for others to know about you (e.g., dyslexia or a hearing impairment)? Take some time to think and jot down those invisible identities.

_____

_____

_____

Now let's think together about the role of a learning designer and how they are/should be designing not only for multiple people with different entry points to learning but also for the identities for unique individuals. Again, the "complete moral, emotional, intellectual and civic transformation of the person" comes to the fore (here) and diversity and inclusion speak loudly. To move toward inclusion, all these learners need to feel that the learning reflects who they are and that there is space for them in the learning environment.

An area that is core for inclusive instructional designers to think about is intersectionality, which addresses the multiple identities people embody. The concept particularly refers to race, class, gender, ethnicities, and so on that are marginalized and the points where those identities intersect.[6] In the case of education, I would add the social categorization of *differently abled learners* since these are identities that impact one's learning experience. So, for example, if you are a Hispanic gay woman with ADHD, you would have four points of intersectionality: person of color, woman, LGBTQ, and differently abled. Intersectionality gets at the heart of the whole person that comes into a learning experience: the multiple layers of self, and past discriminations persons may have experienced. Now imagine, as an educator, having information about these layers and intersectionality points before and during the design of a course, training, or learning platform. How might the design of the learning be approached differently?

ONLINE LEARNING AND INCLUSION

When considering how to design learning experiences for an individual's whole self, educators should shift considerations to the *who* is being taught along with *what* is being taught. Online learning expands the ability to design for the *who* because it offers the ability to reach a growing and diverse population. Most online learning systems by nature are flexible and have the functionality to be personalized, which demonstrably supports whole self-learners and communities. Further, online learning systems allow for connection and relationship building within the virtual space.

Best College's 2019 Online Education Trends Report found that populations in the online learning environments are diversifying in the following categories:

- Age: The number of older students is increasing while younger student representation continues to rise as well.
- Location: Students are enrolling not only outside of the local area but also internationally.
- Race/class, languages, and disabilities: There is also an increase in students with disabilities, learners for whom English is a second language, underrepresented minorities, and economically disadvantaged students.

These findings tell us that diverse communities have already arrived in the online learning space. So, how can we transform and fully embrace the interaction, content, and features in the space to be inclusive of all these populations with unique identities? And, importantly, how can we take what we are able to do in an online space and adapt it to our in-person learning practices?

ASSESSING YOUR CURRENT STATE

The first stage of designing an inclusive learning experience (whether online or in-person) is to assess *what* you are already doing and *who* is a part of your learning audience. By evaluating your *current* state, you will begin to form a vision of the range of students you can bring into the space and how you can support each and every one of them. Here are three questions to ask in your assessment of your current state:

1. *Who are you reaching at this stage?* Define your learner and what you know about their identities.
2. *Who are you not reaching?* Identify the populations you are not reaching. Go broad and go global with this because, ultimately, if you are attempting to be more inclusive, you want to consider anyone and everyone that is currently missing from your learning community.
3. *How can you reach those you are not reaching?* I suggest segmenting these learning populations into three time-related categories such as immediate, soon, and projected. Make sure what is listed under these categories are both actionable and reasonable.

Once you have answered these questions, take some time to speak with colleagues and other designers to gather additional input and perspectives. Perhaps they have additional ideas of who is missing from your learning communities and how to bring them into the fold.

IDENTIFYING YOUR LEARNERS

Let's look back at our first exercise in whole self-identification and apply it to current and potential learners. What is known about your learners' demographics such as race, age, gender, and ethnicity? Who are they outside of the known demographics? Are they working parents, single, or married? What do they do for work? Do they live in urban or rural areas? Where do they want to be in five to ten years, professionally and personally?

Many educators may ask the question: How am I supposed to know any of that information or why should I know personal information about my students? It can seem overwhelming at first; however, in effectively providing learning experiences in the twenty-first century and designing learning experiences for the whole learner, the answer shifts from "supposed to know" to "a responsibility to know."

In both designing and teaching online courses, I conduct a survey before a course begins to get a sense of the skills, proficiency, and general intentions learners have coming into the educational space. Beyond that, I want to get to know my learners. What are their favorite foods, what keeps them up at night, what number are they in their family order? This rich information helps me to not only design and direct a learning experience but also to connect with the learner as their whole self. And, in the case of online learning, this is more important than ever because you are not sitting in the same room as your learners, so making connections beyond what can happen in the physical classroom is essential to their success (and yours too). If this sounds like a lot of work, it is. You must be dedicated to this work to evolve your students' experience.

Another question you can ask your current learners at the end of the learning experience is who they thought was missing from their learning community. This will help answer your third current state assessment question: *How can you reach those you are not reaching?* Your community of learners may add populations that you have not considered and ones that might make for a more well-rounded group for an enhanced learning experience for all involved—learners and educators.

As for trying to design for populations you are not currently reaching, it is truly difficult to imagine getting to know a population when you do not have access to them. If you do want to include the populations that you have not reached, you have to devise investigative methodologies to find out who they are. Start by surveying an external group to gather this type of information and look for support from your professional network. Are there people in your greater network that might have access to or even are the people you are not reaching? Once you gather a group of five to ten people, send them a survey, and ask them to share it with one other person in their network. Chances are this person will be someone you might not have contact with and who can offer a new perspective.

I must warn you that this type of discovery can feel never ending, so consider this a journey and one where you must take a first step on the path to better understanding your current and potential learners. Doing so can be daunting, but, ultimately, this action can create synergy and empower you as a designer and an educator. As you continue to gather this information, you will be better equipped to provide a meaningful learning experience for everyone that comes into your space.

APPLYING THE FOUR PILLARS OF IID

Now that you have determined your learners whole self-identities and to whom you want to expand your reach, let's design a learning environment that is inclusive. Through my experience and research, I have identified four design pillars that ensure individuals and groups feel included in a learning experience. I offer these pillars to experiment with and apply where they work but in no way will they be applicable in all cases. Just like learners, each learning asset is unique. These pillars can be used in both online and in-person learning environments; however, there are some elements that might work better in the online space and others in-person. Consider which of these

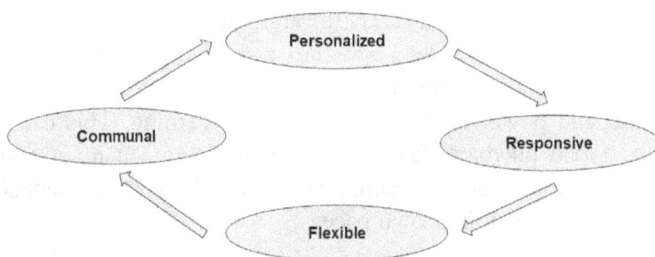

Figure 12.1   Four Pillars of IID. *Source*: Samantha Calamari, 2020.

pillars seem like a good fit before you invest too much time and effort into any one design approach (figure 12.1).

Pillar 1: Personalized

The first pillar of IID is to make the learning personal. Personalized learning occurs when a learner can choose the learning experience that best meets their needs. This not only makes them feel like the experience is their own but also they are more committed to and reflected in the learning process.

I like to offer pre-assessments before a training or course starts. This will not only help gauge where your learners are when coming into the learning but also they can assess their own proficiency in a subject. This, in turn, can empower learners to determine what they want to focus on in the learning stream and what they can bypass.

Doing this sets you and your learners up for the next design element, which is to allow learners to create their own learning paths based on what they want to learn and what they already know. For example, perhaps there is a module that a learner is already competent in and instead wants to focus double the amount of time in another area. Integrating answer-specific feedback into your assessments can lead your learners to which content to review or move on to the next level. This not only gives your learners an opportunity to review content but also gives them a sense that their learning path is unique and customized to them. Putting the power of how and what they want to learn into their hands makes learners understand the control they have over their learning experience and gives them ownership over it.

I also suggest providing various assignment options for learners to choose from such as tests, essays, and practical projects. This way, learners can pick the most successful way to execute these assignments based on their learning preference. Delivering the learning content in multiple formats such as video, audio, written, and even a practice method also provides learners with options toward choosing the best ways for them to absorb content information. Doing so supports differently abled learners through the learning process as well as other learners who simply have a way they most successfully learn.

Creating flexible pacing options throughout the learning experience is an additional and powerful way to personalize learning. This can come in the form of video playback features, untimed testing, or a set assignment cadence. Regardless of the approach, make sure to let your learners choose to absorb the instruction at their own pace.

Pillar 2: Responsive

A shift is happening in teaching and learning all over the world whether in classrooms of seven-year-old children, single parents taking online courses at night, and even in traditional university settings. Learners are becoming more represented in their own ways of learning. Instead of squeezing and adapting, educators have begun adapting to their students, even "co-creating" learning in some cases. Here's the key: to do so, educators and designers must be responsive to their learners.

As previously discussed, conducting a pre-course survey provides an opportunity to gather a great deal of information about who will participate in your classroom—online/virtual or face-to-face. Allow the space for students to share what they choose to share. As educators, once you have the results, be sure to act on the information. Are there tweaks you can make to help learners who have full-time jobs? Long commutes? Those who felt isolated in previous learning experiences? How can you adapt your design to support them?

Another effective way to build rapport and be responsive is to provide timely feedback. If a participant reaches out to you and you don't respond for weeks, they are likely to feel that they are not important and, moreover, (especially online) that you might not exist. In all cases, make sure that you reply to emails and discussion board posts within the week they are posted. In addition to providing feedback and communicating directly with learners, create one-to-one connections for your participants. Find ways for the learners to interact with each other. By encouraging them to talk to each other, either online or in the classroom, an entirely new learning dynamic is established, one that can and will encourage new learning. Once you have created the opportunity to interact, do not just sit back and be passive. Stay involved in the conversation. If needed, facilitate, and (even) monitor the dialogue so all learners feel safe and heard in the new learning spaces you are forming together.

Pillar 3: Flexible

By incorporating flexible design practices into the learning experience, you will, in turn, allow for learners to personalize and for you to be responsive to your learners. If you are incorporating multimedia into your design, be sure your video and audio media players have pause, speed setting, and rewind features. These empower learners to be able to move through multimedia content at their own pace. Also, offering closed captioning is imperative for learners who speak a different language than you offer in your course or for those with hearing or cognitive impairments. For the same reasons and to support your learners who prefer written information or would like to translate the content, always provide a transcript in a downloadable format.

When considering assignments, timed testing can be a huge disservice to learners who are differently able. By eliminating timed testing, you avoid alienating these learners. If you are worried about people having time to search for answers on the internet, establish a strict policy about this and make sure you enforce it. Additionally, when scheduling assignments, offer an extended deadline and be consistent. For example, in the online courses that I teach, I make assignments due each week on Sunday midnight at 12 (time zone flexible) in and outside of a classroom. This way it is consistent and learners know the expectations, so they have the entire week to work on assignments and plan their time accordingly.

Pillar 4: Communal

If there is one fundamental design element to apply to make a learning experience more inclusive, it is to create community in the space you provide for learners. The beauty of this effort is that once you start to create connections among the learners, the process will take on a life of its own. To begin building this community, start with yourself. Post a welcome and introduction to the course. This can be in-person or online in the form of video. By sharing your goals and vision for the learning experience while also telling personal stories and anecdotes, you are letting your learners get to know you and modeling how they can share. This can immediately set the tone for openness and safety in the learning space.

Whether in-person or online, discussion boards can turn a static online experience into a dynamic learning playground. Discussion boards allow participation without the pressure of being in the spotlight and provide learners with the time to consider what to say before they say it. They also reveal peers' thoughts and opinions and encourage conversations among people from different cultures who may be connecting and learning about each other for the first time.

Another great interactive yet anonymous and more immediate tool is polling. There are many free apps that students can download on their cell phones and that can be integrated into a learning management system. By asking questions and getting answers in real time, you have an opportunity to create participation and guide where you might want to take the assignments. Learners also get a sense of other responses which can deepen connections.

Creating group projects or study groups is another effective way to form bonds between your learners. Again, think about how meaningful it is to have people from different cultures bring in their perspectives and learn from each other. Make sure to offer learners guidance around expectations and form small groups to keep them focused. Encourage the groups to use video conferencing or voice chat when they are first getting to know each other. It is also very important to be sensitive to learners who might want to be more private. Offer the option to post an icon of themselves instead of a picture in their account settings with alternatives to communicating with their groups through email or direct messaging.

Another idea for creating inclusion in diverse groups of learners is to experiment with peer-to-peer grading or evaluations. This fosters relationships and offers the learner, as a grader, a different point of view in understanding the material. It also gives learners a deeper sense of ownership in their learning and that of their peers. Creating a rubric will further ensure that learners, who are grading their peers, are clear on the assignment's expectations.

Finally, forming a group on a social media outlet like Facebook or LinkedIn is a way your learners can stay in touch with one another after the course is done. Creating fun, personal prompts that relate to the course topic can launch the page. You can then promote continued connectivity by asking for a student to lead as the social media administrator.

One note about interaction among peers whether on a discussion board, group project, or otherwise is to make sure you set clear guidelines about what constitutes acceptable behavior. As the authors in the book *Culturally Inclusive Instructional Design* so keenly note, discourse is perceived differently across cultures.[7] This goes for general interaction as well. What might seem like a lively discussion could be alienating or offensive to others. Be sure to consider all the cultures you have engaging with one another when you develop these guidelines. Always keep your (figurative) door open for learners to come to you with concerns.

THE FUTURE OF INCLUSIVE INSTRUCTIONAL DESIGN

As online learning systems have created novel ways to reach new learning communities, artificial intelligence (AI) may continue to open doors (and portals) into how we connect with learners. Possibilities around directly interacting with students or being able to translate languages seamlessly create new ways of interacting and engaging learning communities. Simply put, it offers empowerment to students. Imagine being able to choose the demographic persona of the teacher! This could create an entirely different experience in feeling reflected in who is teaching you.

Similarly, augmented and virtual reality (AR and VR) are expanding learning opportunities. By providing truly immersive experiences, learners can personalize and adapt learning to their own needs. Furthermore, AR and VR have proven to be effective for learners with sensory or attention disorders such as autism and could support these populations in new ways.[8]

While these new and innovative technologies will pave new pathways to how we learn, it is important that cost and access barriers do not keep learners away who can benefit from these developments. As with the internet, there could be a new form of digital divide and, therefore, being cautious that these technologies are inclusive instead of exclusive in the form of access will be imperative to integrating these as tools for IID.

CONCLUSION

Here's the thing about inclusion. *It is never ending.* There is no quick fix or checklist to create an inclusive learning experience. We must explore and expand our reach. Remember—just as we reach a milestone, the next one opens for us.

So, how do you jump in? I suggest doing so by being focused. Design for a targeted group in your first run of a course or training or platform build. For example, maybe you want to design specifically considering sight-impaired learners and focus on building content and tools for this group. Then in your next iteration of your course design, you design for those with lower-bandwidth connectivity. The good news as you cater to one group in one version of the course, you have the existing foundation to build on. Soon, your reach will really grow!

Also, be realistic about your availability and support for your learners. If you are facilitating the training, make sure you set aside time to communicate with your participants, individually or as a group. Having an opportunity to build relationships with your learners and make connections will build community and a sense of belonging. Above all, the most important step is to be entirely learner-centric and commit to each learner's success while setting an intention of expanding your reach.

Once you really take this pledge, you will naturally design and cater to your richly diverse audience.

NOTES

1. Robin DiAngelo, *White Fragility* (Boston: Beacon Press, 2018), 31.

2. David Brooks, "How Scandinavia Got Great," *The New York Times*, February 13, 2020, https://www.nytimes.com/2020/02/13/opinion/scandinavia-education.html.

3. David Brooks, "How Scandinavia Got Great," *The New York Times*, February 13, 2020, https://www.nytimes.com/2020/02/13/opinion/scandinavia-education.html.

4. Malcolm Gladwell, *David and Goliath* (Boston: Little, Brown, and Company, 2013), 112–13.

5. U.S. Bureau of Labor Statistics, Economic News Release, accessed November 8, 2019, https://www.bls.gov/news.release/nlsoy.nr0.htm.

6. Dolly Chung, *The Person You Mean to Be* (New York: Harper Collins, 2018), 105.

7. C. Gunawardena, C. Frechette, and L. Layne, *Culturally Inclusive Instructional Design: A Framework and Guide to Building Online Wisdom Communities* (London: Routledge, 2019), 78.

8. A. Whitfield-Madrano, "2020 Ed Tech Trends Focus on Equity," accessed January 20, 2020, https://edtechmagazine.com/k12/article/2020/02/2020-ed-tech-trends-focus-equity.

Index

About the Contributors

Catherine L. Adams is associate professor of African and African American studies at Claflin University in Orangeburg, South Carolina. She has held full-time teaching positions at three Historically Black Colleges and Universities (HBCUs): Allen University, University of the Virgin Islands, and Paine College. She completed graduate degrees at Temple University and the University of Massachusetts-Amherst in African American studies. Her research interests include Africana literary history, Africana-based pedagogy and curriculum development, Africana science fiction, speculative fiction and Afrofuturism, digital humanities, and freedom and maroonage narratives. Her work has appeared in the *Killens Review of Arts & Letters*, *The Compass*, and the Newberry Library Web Exhibit. In 2020, her work with undergraduate students as co-researchers appeared in *Rediscovering Frank Yerby: Critical Essays* edited by Matthew Teutsch (University of Mississippi Press).

Nancy Wellington Bookhart is an artist-philosopher who models the aesthetic framework, which argues art and philosophy as equals in the evolution of humankind. Her research focuses on the intersection of race, history, and art as a social experiment in Western schools of thought. Bookhart is a professor of art at Paine College in Augusta, Georgia, and is presently a doctorate candidate, ABD, at IDSVA (Institute for Doctoral Studies in the Visual Arts). Professor Bookhart interrogates the invention of race and stereotypes in her dissertation, *The Black Veil of Freedom: On Kara Walker and the Aesthetic Education of the Black Man*. She is presently involved in the examination and philosophical excavation central to the debate on the Confederate Monuments' place in American history. Bookhart recently presented talks on the monuments at Bridge: New Pathways Social Justice Conference,

Montserrat College of Art, and SECAC (formerly the Southeastern College Arts Conference).

Samantha Calamari is an expert in inclusion and learning design with years of experience working at Microsoft, LinkedIn, and Brown University as well as a number of nonprofits and tech startups. Samantha has the added distinction of work as a Fulbright Specialist. Her work spans global online platforms with the goal of creating equitable educational experiences for adults and children. She creates human-centered learning programs and develops design strategies and practice points of view for instructional application. Ms. Calamari also leads teams to shape and implement customized Inclusive Instructional Design frameworks.

Peter A. Campbell is a theater director, installation artist, writer, teacher, and scholar. Professional productions include *Can't Get There from Here*, which was developed in residency at MASS MoCA, and *medea & medea/for medea, iph.then,* and *Yellow Electras* at the Incubator Arts Project in New York City. He is currently working on a series of installations based on public documents such as the CIA Torture Report and Mark Zuckerberg's testimony about Facebook for the U.S. Congress. He has published essays and reviews in venues such as *Theatre Topics, Modern Drama, Theatre History Studies, Contemporary Theatre Journal,* and *The Journal of Dramatic Theory and Criticism.* He recently served as president of the Mid America Theatre Conference, and is dean of the School of Contemporary Arts and Professor of Theater History and Criticism at Ramapo College.

Katherine L. Cleary received her bachelor's degree in political science from Kent State University and her master's in student affairs in higher education from Slippery Rock University. During her career in residence life, Katie always had an interest in how community engagement connects students' classroom lessons with real-world applications. She enjoys helping students learn to become strong advocates for themselves and others. When not working, Katie loves to read and binge-watch Netflix. She currently lives in Worcester, Massachusetts, with her dog.

Sandra Virginia Gonsalves-Domond is a full professor of social/personality psychology and former convener of the Africana Studies Program at Ramapo College. She previously taught at Bates College and Sarah Lawrence College. She has been an academician for many years, having taught over thirty-one different undergraduate psychology courses, including a capstone course on *Black Psychology* and *African Spirituality*. Gonsalves-Domond is a published author, book reviewer, Head Start Trainer/Facilitator/Workshop Leader, and poet. She enjoys reading, singing, museum-visiting, traveling, and theater. Her most recent publication threads Obeah practices in the Anglophone Caribbean to Yemonja.

Eden-Reneé Hayes is the director of the Davis Center at Williams College in Williamstown, Massachusetts. She has been involved in cultural competency, retention efforts, and inclusion in organizations for over fifteen years. An expert in the social psychological factors related to bias, and the intersecting identities of race, class, and gender identity and expression, she has presented papers on her research at a number of conferences including the American Psychological Association, the International Convention of Psychological Science, and the Society for the Psychological Study of Social Issues. She has published her research in various outlets including *The Handbook for Feminist Diversity* and serves on the editorial boards for journals including *Cultural Diversity and Ethnic Minority Psychology.* Hayes's passion for being involved in the community includes mentoring with the Rights of Passage and Empowerment Program and serving on the Board of Directors for several organizations focused on diversity and inclusion. Hayes also enjoys being a mom of two human energy balls.

Sharon Albert Honore is the former chairperson and current associate professor in the Department of Communication, Art, Theatre, and Music at the University of the Virgin Islands on the St. Thomas (STT) and St. Croix (STX) campuses. She is the mass communication internship faculty advisor to Black News Channel HBCU Show, the *UVI Voice 2.0.* online student newspaper, state monitor for the Dow Jones Newspaper Fund, and peer evaluator for Middle States Commission on Higher Education (MSCHE). Honore also is the founder/coordinator for the only film festival in the USVI territories, *Caribbean Film & Artistic Cinematic Festival (CFACF),* which was first held on STX in 2019. Honore is the first African American to earn a doctor of philosophy in mass communications from the University of Iowa.

Karl Ellis Johnson is associate professor of African American studies and chair and co-convener of the African Studies Group and major in the School of Humanities and Global Studies at Ramapo College of New Jersey. He is an expert on the African American history of popular culture and political treatment of people of color in America; sub-Saharan African Medieval civilizations, kingdoms, and culture; rap/hip-hop cultural transfer from Black Americans to Africa and its Diaspora; and the history of African Americans in film. Johnson has a BA in history and economics from Rutgers College, MA in history from Rutgers University, Newark, and a PhD in history from Temple University.

Saisha Manan graduated summa cum laude from Bard College at Simon's Rock in psychology. In addition to her work on gender representation in children's literature, her senior thesis explored and evaluated community-based trauma interventions as an accessible form of mental health care. She continues her work in a mental health advocacy and funding organization in India with a commitment to promoting a rights-based approach to mental health care. Saisha grew up in India, Thailand, and Nepal.

Anthony Sean Neal is an associate professor of philosophy in the Department of Philosophy and Religion and a Faculty Fellow in the Shackouls Honors College of Mississippi State University. He is a 2019 inductee into the Morehouse College Collegium of Scholars. Neal received his doctorate in humanities from Clark Atlanta University. He received his master's degree from Mercer University and a bachelor's degree from Morehouse College. Neal is the author of two books, *Common Ground: A Comparison of the Idea of Consciousness in the Writings of Howard Thurman and Huey Newton* (Africa World Press, 2015) and *Howard Thurman's Philosophical Mysticism: Love against Fragmentation* (Lexington, 2019).

Willette Neal is an independent scholar in the Atlanta, Georgia, area. Her doctorate is in education with a focus on global training and development. Her research areas are cultural intelligence, cultural awareness, and intercultural interactions. She applies these focus areas to the fields of diversity, equity, and inclusion. She is a manager in the federal government in the field of aviation and works extensively with public, private, and nonprofit organizations to address issues that are directly related to inequality in underrepresented communities. Neal chairs an adult cultural exchange program that focuses on intercultural interactions between U.S. citizens and citizens of Africa and Asia.

Gwendolyn VanSant is a trainer and facilitator in diversity leadership, cultural competence, and coalition building for justice and equity. She is the chief executive officer and co-founding director of Multicultural BRIDGE. She contributes to several teams across the region to promote safety, equity, and trust in communities and workplaces. Gwendolyn has worked with corporations, schools, colleges and universities, law enforcement, hospitals, teaching, leadership institutes, and more. In addition to designing cultural competence trainings, Gwendolyn is a frequent speaker and long-time activist deeply rooted in racial justice, gender equity, and positive psychology. In 2018, she was recognized as an Unsung Heroine by the Massachusetts Commission on the Status of Women. In 2019, she was recognized as the Woman of the Year in Achievement by Berkshire Business and Professional

Women. In 2020, Gwendolyn received an award on behalf of BRIDGE from MCLA, the President's Medallion.

Mark Wagner is a writer and researcher whose recent scholarship includes Care Theory, ALANA student success, non-cognitive skills, and classroom communication. He is the founding director of the Binienda Center for Civic Engagement at Worcester State University in Worcester, Massachusetts. Mark is also the author of two books of poems: *A Cabin in a Field* and *Building Home*. In 2001, he released a collection of photos and writings about living with Alopecia Universalis. In 2020, Mark and his band Pope Markus and Co. released a collection of songs *Waking Up in a Dream*.

www.ingramcontent.com/pod-product-compliance
Lightning Source LLC
Chambersburg PA
CBHW050643280326
41932CB00015B/2764